LOST AND FOUNDER

LOST AND FOUNDER

A PAINFULLY HONEST FIELD GUIDE
TO THE STARTUP WORLD

Rand Fishkin

PORTFOLIO/PENGUIN

Portfolio/Penguin
An imprint of Penguin Random House LLC
375 Hudson Street
New York, New York 10014

Most Portfolio books are available at a discount when purchased in quantity for sales promotions or corporate use. Special editions, which include personalized covers, excerpts, and corporate imprints, can be created when purchased in large quantities. For more information, please call (212) 572-2232 or email specialmarkets@penguinrandomhouse.com. Your local bookstore can also assist with discounted bulk purchases using the Penguin Random House corporate Business-to-Business program. For assistance in locating a participating retailer, email B2B@penguinrandomhouse.com.

Image on page 24 courtesy of Kim Scott.
All other images courtesy of the author.

Library of Congress Cataloging-in-Publication Data

Names: Fishkin, Rand, author.
Title: Lost and founder : a painfully honest field guide to the startup world / Rand Fishkin.
Description: New York : Portfolio/Penguin, [2018]
Identifiers: LCCN 2017050230| ISBN 9780735213326 (hardcover) | ISBN 9780735213340 (ebook)
Subjects: LCSH: Internet industry—United States. | New business enterprises—United States. | Entrepreneurship—United States. | Success in business—United States.
Classification: LCC HD9696.8.U62 F56 2018 | DDC 658.1/1—dc23 LC record available at https://lccn.loc.gov/2017050230

Printed in the United States of America
10   9   8   7   6   5   4   3   2   1

Book design by Daniel Lagin

To my grandparents Pauline & Seymour,
my mom, Gillian, and my wife, Geraldine.
Your love and support were my first investors.

CONTENTS

CONTENTS

INTRODUCTION
THE STARTUP CHEAT CODE

U niversal truths we learn by age twelve:

1. Never feed a mogwai after midnight.
2. Breakfast cereal DOES taste better if you substitute chocolate milk.
3. (And most relevant to our story . . .) The first time you play a new video game, you'll suck.

The controls are foreign. The game mechanics are inscrutable. Make it through level one, and level two will undoubtedly get you. But that second time around, you'll do better. And if you play for a few hours or a few days, you'll start to feel the flow—eventually, you're unstoppable. In the zone. A juggernaut of win. THE RULER OF YOUR CASTLE (though in this case, the castle is probably your parents' basement). But even if it's your first time playing, there's a way to jump ahead of the learning curve: cheat codes.

Starting a business works this same way. The first time you build a company, it's scary as hell. Accounting? Payroll? Customer acquisition? Recruiting? Hiring? Fundraising? People management? No wonder first-time founders, like first-time gamers, die on the first level. Customers won't pay. Employees quit. Your investors make your COO your boss, then fire you. You will very much want to retreat into a basement and play video games for several long hours, possibly years.

The good news: there's a cheat code here, too.

In my third year as a first-time, what-the-hell-am-I-doing CEO, I got an email from a Seattle entrepreneur I deeply respected, inviting me to join a local group of startup movers and shakers at a local bar. When I arrived, I was introduced to a handful of people whose names I knew from the startup news websites and blogs I followed. These were founders and technologists I'd read about but never thought I'd meet—basically the coolest nerds in my universe. I played it cool. We drank. We talked. Well, they mostly talked; I mostly listened.

What I heard shattered my long-held illusions about startup life.

These men and women were scared, just like me. They were uncertain. They struggled, they felt fear. They needed help. Those who'd been through an experience gave advice and offered assistance to the first-timers. The longer we stayed and the more we drank, the more vulnerability emerged. No one pretended to have all the answers, but when someone had insight, they opened up.

When I got home, I tipsily typed an email to myself with some of what we'd talked about. I stared at it, trying to figure out if it was possible to avoid the pitfalls, a way to not suck the first time around.

Here are some of the more tactical takeaways I learned that night (apart from four Tom Collinses are one too many):

- Raising prices for your product every year or two and grandfathering in existing customers is a great way to increase loyalty and grow your profit margins. (We did this several times over the next few years; it worked like a charm.)

- If you want to raise money from an investor, ask for help with your business. If you want an investor to help with your business, ask for money. (From later experiences I can verify that, yes, this totally works.)

- Many voting rights for funded companies have some provision that gives special consideration to "preferred shareholders." Usually, these are the investors, but smart entrepreneurs know this and thus will buy a small amount of preferred shares in their own companies during a funding round so they will also share these rights.

- The Hacker News website (https://news.ycombinator.com) has an algorithm that filters out high quantities of votes from a single geography. So if you want to ask your friends to help up-vote something to page 1, make sure they're not all in the same city. (Also, make friends in other cities.)

- Recruiting for software engineers is best done directly by founders. Find people who look interesting, uncover a connection you have to them in your network, get an intro, meet for coffee, get them excited about your company, and if they're not interested, ask who they know who might be. Not one of the group's members had success with external recruiters (at least, not in the early stages). Oh, and Craigslist still works way better than most of the other job sites, at least in Seattle.

How did these entrepreneurs acquire this knowledge? How did they have answers to questions I didn't even know I should be asking?

The answer: they had startup cheat codes. (Sadly, it's not as easy as the Konami code.)

The hard way to earn those codes is experience. You struggle through a problem, follow conventional wisdom until you prove it's not working, make all sorts of mistakes, and then, eventually, stumble onto a solution that succeeds. It's agonizing, but sometimes it's the only path available.

The cheat is to have connections to people—mentors, advisers, friends, family, partners, employees—who've been through the problems you're facing before and can give you a map out of the woods and onto a path that works. You need to be willing to listen. You need a network whose problems and solutions match. But when you can short-circuit the painful quagmire of stumbling through an issue alone, it's gold.

That's one of the biggest things I've learned about startups: *it's dangerous to go alone.* You want people around you who've been through this before and are willing to openly share their experiences.

That's why second- and third-time entrepreneurs have such better track records than their first-time peers. And why investors are so much more likely to back a founder who's been through the game at least once before.

This book is one really long cheat code. I wrote it so that you don't have to repeat the mistakes I've made. So you can leapfrog the wasted months, the wasted cash, and the heartache too many of us endure. So that if you don't live in a geography with lots of other startup founders, you can still get the inside scoop. To unlock these cheat codes, you'll need context, stories, data, and thorough explanations. And I won't share just the tactical tips and tricks; I have to include the ugly, heartbreaking realities, too. If I held back out of fear or a desire to make myself or my company look better than it is, I'd be failing you. That's why this book is so transparent about the things founders don't normally discuss. Money. Depression. Layoffs. Failure.

I'll tell you how I turned down a life-changing acquisition and how I regret it to this day (hell, I'll even show you the email). I'll walk through how we raised money and explore why it's so rarely the right move (and why it may even have been wrong for us). And I'll show why so much of classic, Silicon Valley–startup advice is flat-out wrong, mangled by survivorship bias, and only applicable to a tiny subset of companies and founders (even though it's dispensed to everyone with one-size-fits-all uniformity).

The next seventeen chapters are here to dismantle the shady logic born from the oversimplified, opaque stories of what startup success looks like. Instead, I'll share real stories, show real numbers, and offer real solutions.

How the Valley Fooled Us All

The aggrandized archetype of the "startup founder" is powerful and pervasive. These entrepreneurs pull themselves up from nothing and create jobs, wealth, and world-changing tech despite their meager beginnings.

It's also total bullshit.

Univerity of California–Berkeley economists analyzed shared traits of entrepreneurs and found that, in reality, most come from backgrounds of wealth and privilege. (I complain about having no friends as a kid, but let's be clear: I had a friggin' Nintendo game console. In 1989. That's basically the child equivalent of a free coke hookup in the '80s!)

But anyone can succeed in the gold rush of tech startups, right? That's the whole point, isn't it?

Nope. Sorry. More BS. More than 75 percent of early-stage technology companies fail to return their investors' capital (nevermind make a profit), according to a Harvard Business School cohort analysis. If we

5

look at only tech-centric, venture-backed startups, it's more than 90 percent! Even surviving the first few years was no guarantee of success—a full 50 percent of the companies still alive in year 4 went under.

Founders are usually young, just out of school, yeah? Nope. The Kaufman Foundation found that most founders are between thirty-five and forty-four years old, not the twentysomething college drop-outs epitomized by popular culture.

If this data has you questioning the way you think about startups . . . good. It should.

I hate these mythological stories for a personal reason: I spent a decade pursuing this precise, vaunted myth of startup success and went off the rails.

As a white, Jew(ish)* American dude, I've enjoyed a life of relative wealth and privilege compared to 99 percent of the world. But I wasn't fated to or groomed to become a tech entrepreneur. I'm not a programmer. I didn't go to an Ivy League school or a Computer Science program. My company wasn't founded in Silicon Valley. When I started, I didn't know a single venture capitalist or any entrepreneurs who'd raised money. I was never recruited into the startup or technology world.

Maybe the only correlation I've got with the vaunted startup-founder myth is that I dropped out of college . . . mostly because I had a fight with my dad, and he stopped paying my tuition. Does that count?

Suffice it to say, I'm a pretty unlikely tech founder/CEO. Yet somehow, remarkably, accidentally, that's exactly what I became.

In 2001, I started working with my mom, Gillian, designing web-

---

*I'm ethnically Jewish (97 percent Ashkenazi, according to 23andMe), but not religious. Bring on the bacon.

sites for small businesses in the shadow of Microsoft's suburban Seattle-area campus. Side note: "Mom & Son Consultancy" is probably the least likely startup combination in this field; it raised plenty of eyebrows along the way (after a while, I took to calling her by her first name in work contexts—that helped). The dot-com bust and my sorely lacking business acumen meant we struggled for years, but eventually, after trial and error, missteps and heartache, tragedy and triumph, I found myself CEO of a burgeoning software company, complete with investors, employees, customers, and write-ups in *TechCrunch*.

By 2017, my company, Moz, was a $45 million/year venture-backed B2B software provider, creating products for professionals who help their clients or teams with search engine optimization (SEO). In layman's terms, we make software for marketers. They use our tools to help websites rank well in Google's search engine, and as Google became one of the world's richest, most influential companies, our software rose to high demand.

Moz is neither an overnight, billion-dollar success story nor a tragic tale of failure. The technology and business press tend to cover companies on one side or the other of this pendulum, but it's my belief that, for the majority of entrepreneurs and teams, there's a great deal to be learned from the highs and lows of a more middle-of-the-road startup life cycle. Outliers like Facebook (on the wildly successful end of the spectrum) or Secret* (on the opposite end) make for terrifically interesting shock pieces, but neither is willing to disclose enough or, perhaps, be self-reflective enough to provide great insight into the

---

*The social networking website Secret infamously raised $100 million in funding after six months of stealth operations, of which the founders pocketed $25 million privately. A year later, the company shut down after achieving zero traction with a nonexistent business model.

subjects that bring value to those who'd follow in their footsteps (or who try to avoid doing so).

This book intends to do exactly that by tackling tough subjects through anecdotes, stats, and harsh self-inquiry. Admittedly, my perspective is biased by my experiences, my background, and my unique view of the startup world as an employee, a CEO, and a board member. I try to be as up front as possible about all of that. I believe that to get the most from any singular experience, you need to know the author's journey and position. Given that perspective (via this introduction), you can take my biases into account as we embark on this examination of startups and entrepreneurship.

Moz is different from many of the most written-about tech startups in a few ways I should mention:

- As a B2B company, our product is almost always marketed to and purchased by companies and consultants rather than directly by consumers. This is worth noting because the most visible and written-about tech companies are usually consumer-facing, either in software (like Facebook or Google) or physical products or services (like Tesla or Airbnb).
- Our products are self-service, rather than sales driven. This means anyone can, at any time, visit our website, enter their credit card, and get full access to our software without ever talking to or interacting with a person on our team (because, let's be real: phone calls are terrifying). This approach has been historically uncommon in B2B, primarily because sales were viewed as critical to forming relationships between businesses and a way to push through large, expensive, ongoing contracts. Today, with the rise of web-enabled delivery and a generation of business owners/professionals more comfortable with a hands-off, low-pressure sales approach, self-

service B2B sales funnels are slowly on the rise (as evidenced by companies like Slack, SurveyMonkey, Dropbox, or MailChimp).

- Moz is creating and serving a new market, rather than disrupting an existing one. SEO software has been around since only the mid-2000s. We were one of the first providers (starting in 2007) to offer it via a web subscription (versus downloadable, desktop software), and one of the largest in our field (both by revenue and by customers). As of this writing, we aren't aware of any direct competitors who are many multiples of our size, any whose stock is publicly traded, or any who has massively more customers or revenue.

But though we have some outlying attributes, Moz does have many of the other features stereotypical to tech startups:

- We've raised funding from traditional venture capital firms (as of 2017, $29.1 million across three rounds).
- Nearly all of our revenue comes from software.
- We operate with relatively high gross margins (75 percent and above).
- We employ very expensive, talented, highly-in-demand engineers, product designers, marketers, and customer service folks. The average Moz salary is more than $100,000/year, and with benefits and taxes, a new employee costs us about $145,000/year. More than 70 percent of our costs come from the salaries and expenses of people on the team.
- We've fluctuated over the years from burning cash in attempts to grow faster versus staying profitable in order to limit risk (e.g., from 2014 to 2016 we consumed almost $20 million; as of 2017 we were profitable again with more than $7 million in the bank).

Since our founding in 2004, we've had some wild ups and downs. We've survived boom and bust cycles, raising and spending venture capital, making successful acquisitions and not-so-successful ones, hiring sprees and layoffs, new product launches and product retirements, and big changes in strategy.

In 2014, after a particularly brutal period, I stepped aside as CEO and took a role as an individual contributor. As of this writing, I'm chairman of Moz's board of directors and an adviser to several of our product and marketing teams. I speak at more than thirty conferences a year and spend about 25 percent of my days on the road, helping folks around the world gain a better understanding of how search engines and web-marketing channels work. I still walk to the office from the apartment I share with my wife, Geraldine, run tests that Google wishes I wouldn't, try to be a force for transparency both internally and externally at Moz, and do my best not to beat myself up for the mistakes of the past. (That last endeavor is the hardest.)

When I entered the startup world, I was predisposed to certain ideas about what it meant to be CEO of a company like ours—early stage, technology focused, rapid-growth seeking, and successful only if we earned big returns for our shareholders and investors. We all read the coverage of other startups and watch the TV shows and news that purport to have windows into this reality. But years into my own journey, I had a head-shaking, wait-a-minute-this-can't-be-right awakening. The media, the hype, the legends of how Silicon Valley startups work are just a carefully crafted model home. They're set pieces, painted by interested parties for their own benefits, built to hide embarrassing flaws. None of it is real.

You don't have to live, work, or start a company blinded, the way I was, to reality.

That's why this book exists, and that's why it's organized into tactical chapters, each unearthing the sometimes strange, hard-to-comprehend, or rarely-talked-about truths of the startup world. These chapters start with the common mythos epitomized by a famous quote from a notable name in the technology world. You'll see the words of famous investors, wildly successful entrepreneurs, and esteemed authors and, piece by piece, see their falsehoods and false impressions dismantled, first with stories of my own, and later through data, research, and analysis. Each chapter ends with ideas or tactics that have helped me (and sometimes others, too) overcome the problems within. I don't pretend to have all the answers. Not for a second. But I often have tactics that helped me out of a bind, and if they can help you, I'd kick myself for holding back.

So, get your controller. Insert your cartridge. It's ⬆ ⬆ ⬇ ⬇ ◀ ▶ ◀ ▶ B A SELECT and . . . let's get started.

CHAPTER 1

THE TRUTH SHALL SET YOU FREE (FROM A LOT OF $#*% STORMS)

You've got an interesting business, but we don't believe it will ever
get past a few million dollars in revenue.

—Anonymous Investor I Pitched in 2009

In 2005, my coworker Matt and I were working in a run-down, shared
office space above a noisy movie theater in Seattle when *he* walked
in. A hairy, barrel-chested, fortysomething guy with gold chains, a
mean grimace, and a stack of papers in a folder stared down at me.

He asked, "Are you Rand Fishkin?"

I was twenty-five years old, disoriented by his arrival, intimidated
by his appearance and tone, and utterly panicked. I'm usually a terrible liar, so was taken aback by how quickly a response left my mouth:

"Sorry, I don't think he's here."

We exchanged a few more words, but I remember none of them.
My heart was pounding. I hated lying, but I also had no idea what
might happen if I identified myself. Matt just put on his headphones

and pretended to be engrossed in whatever website he was working on. When the extra from *The Sopranos* left, I called Gillian, president of our three-person firm (who also happens to be *my mom*). I told her about the unexpected visitor. She guessed he was a debt collector, sent by one of the firms to whom a bank had sold our debt.

Oh, right. The debt. The $500,000 we owed, in my name, to finance our struggling consulting business.

Ten minutes after I returned to my apartment (actually, Geraldine's apartment—I was unable to pay my half of rent with my sometimes tiny, sometimes nonexistent paychecks, and couldn't pass a credit check, either), I heard a knock on the door. Assuming it was Geraldine carrying something she didn't want to put down to turn the key, I opened up without looking through the peephole.

It was the debt collector.

"Ha! Gotcha," he said.

I was mute.

"You're pretty good, kid. I totally bought that act today. . . ."

Scared senseless, I just stared at him.

He handed me the folder of papers I'd seen in his hands earlier and said, "Rand Fishkin, you've been served."

I couldn't even reach out to take them. He dropped them on the ground and walked away.

"Oops, I Accidentally a Startup"

In the summer of 2000, I was twenty-one with a year of college to go at the University of Washington in Seattle. I'm one of those lucky kids whose parents paid his tuition so he could "focus on his studies, not on work."

That is, until I got into a fight with my dad and he threatened to cut me off. I was too prideful and stubborn to back down, apologize, or reconcile, so, for the next two quarters, I had to pay my own way.

I worked part-time at the Wizards of the Coast Game Center, a giant arcade, gaming events center, and retail shop around the corner from campus. My $4.75/hour salary was supplemented by buying Pokémon cards with my employee discount and reselling them on eBay and Craigslist for a tidy profit. I designed and built a few websites on the side for some extra cash. And, thankfully, in the early 2000s, college tuition hadn't yet skyrocketed past the point of absurdity. A full quarter, including books, only cost around $3,000—a sum I scraped together while still managing to have enough to go out to the movies, buy the occasional used video game, and pay the rent on my small, shared apartment.

But two classes away from graduating, I threw in the towel. Part of it was the cost, part of it was the lack of value I perceived from school, but a lot of it was because of a failed romantic relationship (long distance + breakup = broken heart). I wish I could say entrepreneurship was the catalyst for dropping out, but the truth is the other way around. I wallowed in a little self-misery, watched a lot of *X-Files* reruns, and only then realized I needed something to do besides work retail. Web design was my path of least resistance.

In 1981, my mom, Gillian, started a marketing consultancy in Seattle, helping small businesses with their logos, Yellow Page ads, brochures, and other print and advertising materials. In the late 1990s, her clients started asking for websites, and she recruited me to learn FrontPage, Dreamweaver, and HTML so I could help out. I liked the work, and the extra money, and when I told my mom I wanted to work with her full-time and not go back to college, she obliged.

Over the summer of 2001, we dreamed big. Seattle's tech scene was booming in Microsoft's backyard. Startups like Amazon, Kozmo, and HomeGrocer dominated the local news. Everyone was switching from slow, dial-up modems to high-speed broadband. We thought we had an amazing opportunity to design sites for local businesses that needed a presence on the soon-to-be-ubiquitous Internet. When the dot-com crash hit, I barely noticed. Our clients still needed websites, and I didn't pay much attention to the falling prices, the late payments, or the commoditization of web design.

For the next three years, we struggled against increasing competition, pervasive doubt about the web's future, the challenges of getting our clients to pay their bills on time, and, worst of all, our own foolish beliefs about what would help our company grow. We were trying to sell our services in a crowded marketplace without a competitive differentiator. We wasted money on advertising that didn't bring in business. We leased high-priced office space, convinced that an impressive building would help us close deals. We hired contractors and employees who didn't work out. We rented booth space at events that didn't even pay for themselves. And, worst of all, we went into debt to do it.

When I started working with my mom, she had a small amount of debt on the business—less than $20,000 in total. But three years later, we'd amassed an additional $100,000 of debt, much of it from the aforementioned missteps. The great thing about a consulting business is supposed to be the low-capital requirements—smart operators often make their consultancies profitable from day one. We went the other direction, and in 2004, after we'd failed to secure yet another client project we thought could put us on the path to success, we defaulted.

It's hard today to imagine the pre-2008-financial-crisis world of personal debt, where banks would extend loans of $50–$100,000 to a college dropout with a tiny salary. At the time, credit card offers arrived almost weekly, promising $10,000 limits that would quickly rise to $15,000 or $20,000. Lending institutions were happy to offer us lines of credit and equipment loans despite our meager track record and nonexistent collateral. Promotional interest rates in the < 2 percent range were available for the first two to three years of an account. Seduced by these offers and in desperate need of cash just to make payroll and rent for three people, we went whole hog, racking up a balance that eventually came back to bite us.

We took out loans and put them in my name because I had, at the time, nothing to lose. My mom had her and my dad's assets on the line. They owned not only their home in Seattle's suburbs but my grandmother's house in Connecticut as well, which could have also been on the chopping block as collateral. So it was my social security number and my signature on the loans—something that, at the time, didn't really scare me. Defaulting on these loans never really crossed my mind.

Two of the most memorable days in my early career came that fall, of 2004.

The first was on a Sunday. Gillian had told me and Matt, my friend and our programmer, that we'd no longer be able to afford the rent at our pricey high-rise office tower. Moving out was our only option. We found a tiny shared office space in a run-down part of Seattle above an old movie theater for only a few hundred dollars a month (versus the $2,000-plus we had been paying), but we'd need to break our lease. That meant the landlord could potentially hold our equipment—including our computers, desks, chairs, and furniture—as collateral. We had to get it out of the tower and over to the new space fast, without anyone from the building noticing. This part's straight out of a movie.

Matt and I recruited a pair of friends—Marshall and Todd, a couple with two sets of big arms, strong backs, and a spacious truck to whom we promised dinner—and quietly entered the building via the loading garage.

We were halfway through loading up when the tower's security guard arrived. Cue heart falling into stomach.

After a brief, tense discussion on either side of our locked office door, we had the guard make a phone call to Gillian. Somehow, she convinced him to let us finish moving some of the items, but we had to leave a good deal behind to make it seem that we weren't actually "moving out" but rather "moving some things around." With our pulses racing, we took Todd's half-full truck out of the loading dock and across Lake Washington to our new, tiny, bare-bones but safe-from-seizure office. We'd sacrificed a good dozen pieces of unwieldy office furniture and some cheap supplies but felt lucky just to make it out with our computers and essentials. The next week, the company my mom had run for twenty-three years officially closed, and we started a new business under a new name.

But though we'd moved and changed our name, we were far from starting fresh. A couple of months later, that gold-chained debt collector showed up, and I called my mom in a panic.

Even though the debt was being used for business purposes, the creditors would be coming after me personally because it was my signature and my social security number on the applications. Gillian told me she'd try to take care of it. That was the first day I truly understood that most of the money our company owed was actually money *I* owed personally.

It made sense. If Gillian had used her name and her credit to take out even more of those equipment loans and low-interest credit cards, she and my dad could be held liable for repayment, and she already had some debt of her own. They could lose their assets and be forced into bankruptcy. My grandmother could lose her house.

That evening, walking home from work, I started processing our nerve-racking situation and my role in creating it. I'd willfully chosen to ignore and not ask questions about the financial problems we were in, ostensibly so I could concentrate on my part of the work but, in honesty, because I didn't want to deal with it. My mom could handle it. That was her job, right? I was just the web design guy. . . . That's what I'd told myself. But slowly I came around to the idea that sticking my head in the sand about our debt in the hopes it would go away was an untenable path.

When You're in Debt to the Truth, the Interest Rate Sucks

Considering the onslaught of "final notice" letters, threatening phone calls, and the visit from gold-chains-and-chest-hair guy (let's go with "Rocco," as he already fit every other debt-collector stereotype), the logical move would have been to declare bankruptcy. Most of the debt was in my name, a little was in Gillian's, and, because we had defaulted on the bigger chunks in my name, the black marks I was racking up on my credit report were having a similar effect to a bankruptcy (as of this writing, my creditworthiness is still in the toilet). But we had another impediment.

During the four years we built up debt, we'd been lying.

We'd never told my dad, Scott (to whom my mom was, and remains, married), that we had any financial problems, any outstanding loans, or any debt collectors breathing down our necks. We both feared, rightly or wrongly, that if he found out, he'd divorce my mom and break up our family.

It sounds too dysfunctional to be real, but this lie of omission wasn't without precedent. Growing up, my parents lied to each other all the time—mostly about little stuff (or, at least, those are the only things I knew about). Dad would say, "Don't tell your mom we did this" or, "If anyone asks, tell them you are only seven years old/were promised a discount/were told by the staff it was okay." Mom would say, "If your father asks, tell him we used a coupon/had to because of your school/went here on behalf of a client."

These were mostly innocent lies, crafted in order to prevent an altercation and keep relationships smooth. As an adult, reflecting on these memories makes me realize how profoundly unhealthy the dynamic between my parents was, but as a child and teenager, it made reasonable sense. The goal was to limit anyone getting angry or feeling hurt or left out or ignored. We were lying to keep the peace and maintain the veneer of a happy family unit.

That debt, however, was a much bigger lie than anything I'd ever been part of. I remember Geraldine and I talking about it at the time and for years after. We wondered how my mom could stand to be around my dad, day after day, holding in this giant secret, rushing to get home before him so she could shred any potentially incriminating mail, pretending that the debt-collection calls were wrong numbers, keeping up the appearance that things were fine at work—even bringing home an occasional paycheck to make him think things were okay when we probably should have used that money to stave off the next bank that might sell our debt to collections.

Gillian, ostensibly to keep us from worrying and to help us focus on our tasks, kept some of the details and progress of our struggle against debt hidden from me at the time. It wasn't until years later that I learned how she managed to dodge some of the worst debt collectors by proactively calling the issuers of the debt (Washington Mutual, Bank of America, Chase, Wells Fargo), sharing the details of our situation, and offering a smaller sum than what was owed in exchange for the creditor writing off the debt rather than selling to collections. Because a collections agency would typically pay the debt holder 5–10 percent of the actual amount owed, then try to collect the full amount and profit from the delta, my mom's tactic was often successful.

While my credit report took the brunt of our debt problems, Gillian bore the lion's share of the stress. She'd always taken care of our finances and transactions. Despite having more than half a dozen credit accounts with various companies, I never even looked at the invoices—I passed them to my mom and went back to designing websites. I knew things were bad, but I rarely asked for updates. I just went about my work, hoping beyond hope that we could somehow land enough contracts and make enough money to pay back what we owed.

Later, I'd hear stories of other small businesses and startups that faced similar situations. Although I wish it were true that cofounders and family business owners and small teams were always honest with one another, that's often not the case. Tinder grew to dominate the world of online dating apps, but behind the scenes, cofounder strife, political struggles, and outright sexism led to lawsuits, stunted growth, and power struggles. Zipcar, one of the fastest-growing players in alternative transportation, lost both its cofounders over years of politicking, infighting, and fundraising struggles. Twitter famously lost nearly all of its founding team. Facebook's cofounder, Eduardo Saverin, helped write a movie (*The Social Network*, released 2010) about his ouster. Despite these all-too-common conflicts, many businesses don't collapse; they find ways of coping, carrying on, and working through or around poor communication, dishonesty, and dozens of other challenging problems people in high-stakes relationships face. And that's what we did.

Transparency Is Hard, but It Works

There will never be a shortage of justifications for why you believe hiding the truth is the right path. You're worried about hurting someone's feelings. You're afraid if your customers find out about a problem, they'll leave your service forever. You're convinced that you're actually protecting your executive team from stress by redacting details of your investor meetings. You believe the competition probably has engineers idly waiting for some sign of how you've built your amazing technology so they can instantly replicate it and launch before you have the chance.

So you keep secrets. You distort the truth. You tell a few lies. And worst, you think you can get away with it.

Later, when reality comes crashing down (as it always does), you lose the faith of your team or your audience, your investors or your customers. But you justify it by telling yourself: "If things had only gone another way, no one would have even found out, and everything would have been fine."

I have to assume that's what Travis Kalanick thought about his visits to Korean escort parlors with the Uber executive team. And what Facebook thought about testing whether showing particular posts could influence people's moods. It's surely what Steve Ballmer believed about his infamous abusive tantrums at Microsoft leadership meetings. And it's undoubtedly why Tinder's CEO thought he could sexually harass and bully cofounder Whitney Wolfe. When people believe they can hide the truth, many of the incentives inhibiting bad behavior fall apart.

Every founder, every investor, and certainly every employee I've ever talked to in the startup world has stories about the secrets that eventually got out, costing trust, harming relationships, and often affecting revenue and growth, too. But there's another way—transparency. Transparency is making the choice to reveal even the most uncomfortable truths with relentless candor.

Transparency isn't the same as honesty. Honesty is saying only things that are true. Many founders and startup teams are honest (in that they don't directly lie). But transparency requires digging deep to find and expose what others would normally leave unsaid and refusing to take the easy, quiet road. It's tackling the conversations that make your stomach turn and your voice get caught in your throat. And like nearly everything in the world of startups, swallowing the bitter pill now is vastly superior to letting the disease of opacity fester.

If there's an underperforming person on your team, it's easy to ignore him for a while and hope his manager either helps him improve or fires him. It's much harder and more uncomfortable to thoughtfully process why you're unhappy with him, document instances of unwanted behavior, have a direct conversation with the team member, and, if necessary, coach him or work to find mentorship/coaching/classes (whatever it takes to give him the tools to get better if he has the desire). It could still end up that you (or his manager) may have to ultimately fire him. That's the thing with transparency: sometimes, the outcome is the same, but how you got there, and the downside risk, is remarkably different.

Say you're six months away from layoffs given your current revenue, expenses, and projections. You can be honest by simply remaining silent and imploring your team to improve the growth rate. Or you can be transparent by sharing your financials and your projections and explaining exactly what you need to do between now and month 6 to avoid cutting the team. Nine out of ten leadership teams won't share that information. They'll fear, perhaps rightly, that team members might start looking for new jobs or leak numbers to the press. But what happens when those layoffs hit? Yeah . . . your team will stop trusting you. They'll no longer believe that things are going "fine" when you say so. They'll always be looking for signs that the next crisis is around the corner. Those team members you hoped wouldn't look for new jobs—trust me, they're far less likely to stay than if you'd been up front.

Transparency's harder at first, and it feels especially painful when it reveals your mistakes or challenges the image you've crafted for your team or customers. Yet, it's immensely powerful, and it has an almost unbelievably positive impact on everyone around you.

Kim Scott, in her book *Radical Candor*, frames this concept in terms of a matrix:

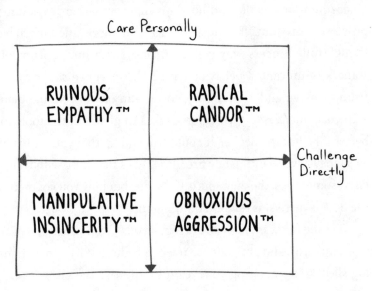

Courtesy of Kim Scott, author of *Radical Candor*

She outlines one of the most important things to remember when it comes to transparency: you need to balance it with empathy. If I tell you I hate your haircut, I'm being transparent. I'm also being an asshole.

If your funding discussions are not going well, it's easy to hold out hope, tell your team you're still "in the process," and only if/when the last investor backs out or the money in the bank runs dry do you let everyone know that cost cutting and layoffs are happening. Far more uncomfortable, but vastly more transparent, is to give regular status updates on the fundraising process internally so employees and executives know precisely what investors are saying, why the pitch isn't working, and where the business metrics are perceived to be weak and can then anticipate a realistic future and potentially contribute to a better result. It may feel like telling your team is admitting weakness and defeat, but in fact, you'll build camaraderie, support, and a powerful incentive to do remarkable work. I've been blown away, time and again, by the ability that "bad news" has to catalyze great effort and remarkable results.

But I can't do that! My team will freak out!

You'd be surprised at how people rise to a challenge once they know that there *is* a challenge. And don't kid yourself—you may think you're keeping them safe by keeping them in the dark, but some distorted version of the truth always leaks. Misinformation stokes fear and resentment in your team. That's never good for business—or for anyone's well-being. You need your team's trust, not just in that one moment when fundraising's going poorly or growth has stalled, but in the long term. Even after people leave, what they say about you and your trustworthiness will affect basic business functions like recruiting, sales, branding, and bizdev for decades to come.

The most meaningful benefit transparency brings might be its forcing function for deliberately ethical, rational behavior. As CEO, I'd often tell my executives and board that every email should be written and every conversation conducted as though it will one day be leaked. We should be proud, not embarrassed, by what and how we communicate, even when the doors are closed. There are good reasons for privacy—to avoid shaming an employee for a mistake or to enable discussion about private, personal, or professional issues (among others). But people change their behavior for the better when they assume their peers, their reports, and their leadership will get to see/hear the full story.

Transparency can't just be a tactic, though. It has to be a core value that's consistently followed. If you openly share some things, but hide others, credibility will suffer. Your team will always wonder what you're not sharing. Your customers, your investors, the press— whomever you interact with—will be trained to mistrust you. A reputation for caginess lasts a long time and follows you across companies and geographies.

When we adopted transparency as a core value at Moz, it wasn't always easy, and we didn't always live up to the ideal. But more than any other aspect of the company, transparency, and the trustworthiness it instilled in our team, our community, and our customers built the company's legacy. We shared our financials online (just as I have in this book). We wrote about our product struggles, our fundraising failures, our most difficult internal conversations, our strategy. We were called crazy and foolish for oversharing so much about the mechanics of the business. But we also became trusted, and, especially because the field of SEO and the broader world of tech startups are so often impenetrably secretive, it paid off.

Early in my career, I was deeply afraid of being transparent. I feared if our customers knew the truth about our tiny operation, or about my age and inexperience, they wouldn't want to work with us. Of course, when we signed a new client, inevitably we'd meet, or they'd search for me and find those things out anyway. I was scared like hell to admit I didn't know how some aspect of HTML worked, but by faking it, I outed my lack of knowledge even more blatantly. My mom and I covering up our debts and our missteps—hiding that risk from my dad? It only caused more stress and fear. Had we been honest from the start, he could have helped, could have saved us the hundreds of thousands in interest penalties we ended up owing. Instead, we created a nightmare of secrecy that nearly ended in professional and personal disaster.

Of course, years later, he did learn the truth. I heard about it from my younger brother, Evan, who told the story this way:

"Dad found out about the debt. Mom tried to play it off, but he found out. I went to my room and put on headphones, but he yelled so loud, the house was shaking."

My only consolation: my dad and I weren't speaking at the time. We've probably had three conversations in the last seven years. Secrets, lies, opacity—they tear families apart just as surely as they do startups.

My credit still sucks. My relationship with my parents remains rough. But I don't get any more unexpected visits from debt collectors who look like they could bench-press me. At least I can put that in the win column.

If we'd been transparent from the start, I believe we'd be in a different, better place today. The only solace is that this lesson, hard won through regret and carried forward in my personal and professional life, helped, over the next decade, to make Moz into something truly special. If you ask me why I'm so open, so bluntly honest about things that the startup ecosystem and business culture usually urge us to keep silent, this is why. I'm done with the pain of secrecy, happy to trade it for the challenges transparency brings.

CHAPTER 2

WHY THE STARTUP WORLD HATES ON SERVICES (AND WHY YOU SHOULDN'T)

(Consulting) is dancing with the devil as you pursue your dreams and try to pay the bills. I believe that it is near impossible to build a successful software product while maintaining a services business.

—**Giff Constable, 2010**

The Moz story should have ended with bankruptcy/failure/my dad shutting down the operation/me getting beaten up by Rocco the debt collector. How is it that thirteen years later, we're a 155-employee, $45-million-dollar-a-year software business?

Unbelievably enough, a side project that turned into a consulting business saved the day. The experts in the startup world will tell you that services and consulting are a waste of time. Fortunately, I hadn't yet heard that advice.

When I started working at my mom's company, our business model was exclusively service-based. Many small businesses start this way. We did projects as diverse as business card design, website usability consulting, e-commerce implementation, print media ad design (yup, like the ones in magazines and newspapers—my high school yearbook layout skills came in real handy), and, of course, search engine optimization.

The services model has some unique advantages and some frustrating drawbacks. On the plus side, costs are (supposed to be) low. You need to spend money only when you have client projects covering your outlays. Your work can be highly customized, which makes it easier to sell to disparate customers with little in common (versus the one-size-fits-all model of a product-focused company). The downside is that it's very hard to scale. The one hundredth client to whom you provide services needs just as much time, energy, and work as the fifth client (granted, you may gain some efficiencies, but it's nothing like the scale a product-based business can achieve).

We were never particularly strategic about changing our business model or thinking of ourselves as something bigger than a niche consulting firm. When, in 2002, Geraldine (yes, we dated a long, long time before getting married) asked me what I hoped Moz might become, I laid out a dream for a consulting firm with fifteen to twenty employees, a nice client list, a healthy profit margin of 20–30 percent, and some beautiful offices. I hoped that in five to ten years, we could become that company.

A couple of years later, I'd split my time between SEO work for our clients and hours chatting away on the SEO forums with like-minded practitioners around the world, trying to learn more about the practice. But I wasn't satisfied with the limited options for starting and replying to threads on other people's sites. I wanted my own platform and the freedom to publish my own way. So I spent a few nights coding up a blogging system in Dreamweaver (this was in the days before plug-and-play blog software like WordPress was popular) and, in October 2004, launched SEOmoz.org.

People ask about the name a lot. (The attempted pronunciations are usually delightful. For those of you wondering—*it's Ess-ee-oh-mawz*.) The name "Moz" was a reflection of my admiration for other "moz"-named projects on the web—the well-known-at-the-time open directory project DMOZ, the free restaurant and recipe website Chefmoz, and the open-source music discovery site Musicmoz.org. All of these names drew inspiration from the nonprofit Mozilla Foundation, itself a portmanteau for "Mosaic killer," Mosaic being the very first World Wide Web browser and Mozilla aiming to displace it with a free, open-source browser of its own. My hope was to build a similarly open-source, free, authoritative resource for the world of SEO and search engines. I'd registered it as a .org, redirecting the domain "seomoz.com" to "seomoz.org" to help communicate that a noncommercial focus was intended. A savvy adviser teased me about the .org domain extension.

"Are you in the business of being noble?" he asked. I laughed. I didn't know I was in the business of being anything.

The blog was a first step, built in my off-hours as a passion project with the goal of learning and sharing more about the weird world of ranking websites in the search engines. At the time, information about search engine operations and SEO practices was immensely hard to come by. So I enlisted help of the only kind I could afford: family.

My grandfather Seymour and I spent days poring over patent applications by Google and Yahoo!. We read technical papers from conferences on information retrieval (the science behind search engines). He taught me how PageRank, Google's famous, link-based algorithm, worked—the iterations required to get graph convergence, why a dampening factor existed, how new links on a page could siphon PageRank from the existing links, etc. His mathematics and engineering background was invaluable, and we turned a number of our technical-paper review sessions into blog posts and content pieces for the SEOmoz website.

He and my grandmother also get co-credit for helping potty train me and teaching me to ride a bike. Point is, I owe him a lot. (Thanks, Amma and Papa.)

As is true for many startups, the idea or business we eventually pursued came from a wholly unexpected place. That blog became a bootloader for the business, exposing the brand to a vast array of serendipitous experiences that led us to our eventual path. Today, it might be called "content marketing," but when I was writing, it was simply passion for sharing, a youthful craving for attention, and a hatred of the secrets Google kept that drove those nightly posts.

In the summer of 2005, I got an email from a reporter with *Newsweek* magazine, Brad Stone (who later went on to the *New York Times* and then *Bloomberg Businessweek*), who wanted to interview us for a potential story on the world of SEO.

I was thrilled and hopeful at the possibility of press coverage. Although we were gaining in popularity with search industry insiders, we were still hamstrung by debt. We had plenty of work from a handful of clients but needed to keep our expenses extremely low. Gillian had stopped taking a salary entirely. My coworker, Matt, and I were taking home a paltry $1,600/month each. The $1,000 I spent earlier that year on a Toronto speaking gig was a big drain.

That autumn, Brad flew to Seattle for a visit to our cramped office above the movie theater. I remember being deeply embarrassed about our dingy space (and the smell of popcorn that wafted up), but it didn't seem to matter to Brad. He was writing a story about the practice of SEO, something that almost no mainstream media outlet had previously covered, and wanted to feature SEOmoz in the piece. I don't think he cared one iota about the size or aesthetics of our office, with its flickering fluorescent lights, or that weird stain on the carpet where we were pretty sure a raccoon had given birth.

In December 2005, Brad emailed to let us know that the following week, *Newsweek* would be publishing a multipage article, including a large photo of me and my mom. I was thrilled. Then I panicked.

What if tens or hundreds of thousands of people visit and want to learn about SEO? The blog is too focused on insiders, and it won't be accessible to all these newcomers. They'll go search for SEO information somewhere else. I'd squandered an opportunity that didn't even exist yet!

That week I poured dozens of hours into a new project I called "The Beginner's Guide to SEO." It remains one of the most productive freak-outs I've ever had. The result was a giant document, almost a novella in length, detailing the many aspects of search engine optimization—how to do keyword research and discover what your customers are entering into the search engines, how to create content people and engines will both appreciate, how to identify problems or issues that could hinder search engines from effectively crawling and indexing your site, how to earn links and attention, the whole SEO shebang. Matt thought I was a madman. I barely made it into the office. I spent most days at home relentlessly trying to finish the guide. I even let some client work slip.

When my tome was at last completed, Matt used his design skills to polish it up and we posted the nearly forty-page guide on SEOmoz's website. We put a message on our home page welcoming visitors we hoped would see us in *Newsweek*, directing them to the Beginner's Guide if they wanted to learn more about SEO. Then, we waited.

The article came out online first, on December 11, 2015. Then it was in the print edition a week later, on December 18. Home delivery was somewhere in between. And the traffic bump we saw to SEOmoz across a two-week period surrounding it accounted for, based on our analytics, fewer than five thousand new visitors. Considering we normally received one thousand daily visitors, the article had been merely a small bump, a far cry from the hyper-growth accelerant we'd hoped for.

But that *Newsweek* piece helped us in an indirect way. The week prior, on December 6, we'd posted the Beginner's Guide to SEO in anticipation of the *Newsweek* article. Sometime on December 7, the popular technology news website Slashdot put the piece on its home page, sending more than thirty-five thousand visitors to SEOmoz in the first twenty-four hours. Dozens of other blogs and websites followed suit, sending huge amounts of traffic and attention our way. Taken together, the coverage of the Beginner's Guide dwarfed the traffic and press value from the *Newsweek* piece. My panic about how to teach *Newsweek* readers about SEO ended up as a far more effective catapult for SEOmoz's blog and brand than the audience for whom I'd written it.

That piece of content, built to help serve a handful of magazine readers, transformed us from a niche, industry-insider blog to one of the most recognized brands in the SEO space and brought us the clients we so desperately needed to survive. A few speaking engagements later, we were working with companies like eBay, Yelp, OpenTable, Zillow, and more.

As our revenue grew and the stress of just making it through the next week and dodging the debt collectors faded, I found myself frustrated by a cycle that many businesses get stuck in. We were getting . . . comfortable.

The bills got paid. The clients were usually happy. They referred us to their friends. Our salaries went up a few hundred dollars. These aren't bad things! But something was missing. I couldn't shake the feeling that our website was too popular for the consulting business to make sense. We had thousands of visitors every day, but could barely take on more than six or seven active clients in a month. Consulting is limited entirely by time and people. It took me two to three nearly full days to put together a basic site audit with recommendations. We hired a couple of recent college grads who, after a few months of training, could do the same work (with some oversight and review from me) in a week. Then there was communication overhead and keeping up with industry changes and writing on the blog and closing new deals and the surprisingly time-consuming process of turning away work that wasn't a good match. We were immensely busy, but adding to our capacity only drained us more (as every hire required closing more clients and training time and reviews). Many businesses get stuck in this cycle— not wanting to scale because it creates more work and less profit margin in the short run, thus limiting their upside in the long run.

Turning away business created this nagging sense in the back of my skull that we weren't executing on our opportunity, that SEOmoz could be more.

Luckily for us and mostly by accident, Moz transitioned from services to product. In late 2006, Matt and I hatched an idea to open up access to some of the proprietary tools we'd built to help with SEO tasks for our clients (things like tracking rankings in the search engines and checking for problems that could harm visibility). We were mostly seeking more traffic for the website but realized that having the tools available completely for free could overload our server bandwidth and cost way too much. Thus, we put the tools behind a $39/month PayPal subscription. We figured that this would help lessen the traffic overload risk and still get us more clients.

We had no idea it would, almost overnight, lead to a transformation of Moz's business model.

When the subscription to our tools opened in February 2007, it didn't feel like a momentous, overnight transformation. A few new subscribers joined every day, but by and large, business carried on as usual. Our primary focus remained centered on consulting. It was only a few months later, while analyzing our revenue, that we saw the potential of the subscription business. The run rate of our new product was growing like a weed. By the end of that year, we did about $400,000 in SEO consulting revenue (our fourth year in that business), and $450,000 in software revenue (even though we'd only had ten and a half months of it!). It was a wake-up call to the power of having a product that made money while we slept.

How to Escape the Services Hamster Wheel

Why is it that so few consulting businesses successfully launch a product? What made Moz's case unique? And why, given the success of our consulting efforts, did we decide to move to a software subscription model?

There are *two* traits fundamental to an effective product-focused business. The *first* is reach (i.e., the ability to influence a large audience). The *second* is scalability (i.e., an aptitude for growing revenue far more quickly than costs).

Traditionally, consulting businesses have little of either. Consultants don't need wide brand awareness or a large audience. They require only a small group of highly targeted individuals and organizations to be aware of their existence and services. Word of mouth is often enough to fill the pipeline for consulting businesses. In a product-based business, though, a much broader audience is typically required, and there's vastly greater need for brand awareness and market penetration. Word of mouth alone can power an exclusive list of enterprise-only product companies, but even then, the competitive landscape dictates a degree of coverage and scaled-up marketing that's almost never found in the consulting world.

Consulting businesses are rarely scalable, unless their firms are extremely well staffed (think Deloitte or McKinsey), and when they are, it's thanks to processes and people. In a product-based business, scalability comes from the adeptness of the product itself to serve a wide audience with a single offering (or a range of products that all benefit from the same design and development process). In a consultancy, hours and projects are what customers pay for rather than the goods or access (physical or virtual) that power a product-based firm.

As we looked at the differences between our nascent software subscription business and our years-old consulting business in 2007, it became immediately clear that our bias would be to the software side of things. That's not because it's right for everyone but because it was right for *us*. The things I loved to do most—helping people, writing, speaking, building community—were the marketing channels that enabled us to attract customers and serve them well. The background in consulting gave us empathy for our customers, because we'd done the same tasks they had and knew the products we (and thus, often, they) needed to better do our work. Unlike most consulting businesses, we could leverage a large community and a highly trafficked website we'd created on the side. We were committed to sharing knowledge openly with all of our competitors, and we happened to have a programmer on staff who could build software to scale our processes.

We'd unintentionally invested in many of the pillars needed to create a successful product business. Our strengths in content, community, and reach meant that even though our first product wasn't great, we had branded ourselves as trustworthy operators in a field where that had historically been rare.

But it wasn't just our strengths and passions that led us to software; the financial side had a big impact, too. The revenue we earned from subscriptions had superior gross margins, far less time investment per dollar earned, and required very little hiring or contracting compared to our consulting work. We discovered through trial and error what financial markets have known for years: the dollars earned from a recurring revenue model are vastly more valuable than dollars earned from services, thanks to scalability and margin.

Wait, So Some Money Is Worth More Than Other Money?

Financial models that value a company's revenue care a lot about gross margin (i.e., the percentage of a business's or product's income that can be serviced without additional cost). If you build software and provide it to customers, your costs are, basically, maintenance of that software, hosting of the servers, any data you have to buy to keep the software operational, and . . . not a lot else (maybe customer service and support). Conceivably, you could shut down all new development efforts and let go of most of your staff, and the subscription dollars would keep coming in. Hence, gross margins on software product businesses are often higher than 75–80 percent, while the margins on a consultancy are more likely in the 25–40 percent range.

These distinctions affect not just the business's revenue-generation process but how they're valued by potential buyers and investors, too. Every dollar you make from services will net you (on average) one to two times the amount in an acquisition or valuation scenario. This formula for a product-driven business, like our software subscription, is often in the three-to-eight-times range.

Say we have two entrepreneurs who've built similarly sized, strong businesses over the last few years and are both ready to sell and retire. Niki's firm is a software-subscription business, and Silvio's is a consulting firm. Both have fifty employees, $10 million in revenue over the past twelve months, and a growth rate of 30 percent in each of the last four years. My examples here are vastly oversimplified, but the raw, average outcomes are instructive.

Niki can reasonably expect that her company will yield, on the very low end, $30 million, and on the high end, $80 million in a sale. It could be even higher if her technology is especially in demand or if the skill sets of her engineers, the unique data she's collected, or the market she's tackling is massively interesting to multiple powerful companies.

Silvio can probably anticipate a sale of $10 million to $25 million for his similarly sized business. The modifiers will generally be his company's EBITDA (earnings before interest, taxes, depreciation, and amortization), his net margins (profitability), and some elements of relative demand, bidders, and industry.

Little wonder that investors, then, put so few dollars into consulting businesses and so many into software companies. And little wonder, too, why at Moz, once we started to understand these numbers, we quickly doubled down on software and put less energy into expanding consulting.

I'd Like Some Services, Please

Should every consultant or services-based business try to shift to a product/subscription model? Definitely not. Despite the example in the previous section, the delta in outcome for many product-based businesses isn't nearly as dramatic as the technology media makes it out to be. It's true that product companies usually get more attention and coverage—Salesforce and MailChimp have numerous write-ups in national papers and fawning descriptions of their founders' brilliance. That seldom happens to consultancies. But services-based businesses still have many great strengths that deserve consideration:

- Little to no startup capital is required; you can build these companies from home, with nothing but your own time, energy, and effort.
- You can entirely control the scale, expenses, and profitability of your business with far greater precision by taking on more or fewer clients, raising or lowering prices, and doing the work yourself versus hiring or outsourcing.
- If and when you choose, you can take time away from the business with far less harm to its long-term potential. No new clients for a month and no deliverables committed means a month with family or on vacation.
- You will almost never need to give up ownership or shares in the company, which has tax benefits (using an S corporation or LLC, which most consultancies do, means neither profits nor salaries get taxed twice) and leaves you in full control. This isn't to say that

a software/products business cannot do this, just that it's much less likely, especially if you want/need to raise capital.

- In general, hiring costs are much lower in consultancies (because most types of consultants tend to have lower salaries, on average, than software/product engineers, designers, and marketers), people retention is less challenging, and the benefits/perks are not expected to compete with those of Google, Facebook, and others of their ilk.

- Most surprisingly: services firms are often a superior financial deal for a founder.

Don't believe me on the last point? Let's go back to our comparison of Niki and Silvio:

As Niki started her software business, she raised two rounds of financing, $500,000 from angel investors in exchange for 30 percent of the company's equity, and later, a Series A round from a venture investor of $8 million in exchange for an additional 40 percent of equity. These modest investments and the 15 percent of shares in the company she put in the employee option pool and distributed to team members meant that, upon sale, she owned 15 percent of the company she started. That's slightly higher than the median startup founder, who owns only about 11 percent of his or her company's shares at exit.

Silvio, on the other hand, didn't seek outside investors and retained 100 percent ownership of his consultancy (standard for businesses of that type). So who is ahead when it's time to sell? If we presume each got the median valuation for their sale, Niki made 15 percent of $40 million ($6 million) and Silvio made 100 percent of $15 million. Despite the massively higher valuations of software revenue, Niki made $9 million less than Silvio. Here's all that in side-by-side chart form:

	SILVIO'S CONSULTING BUSINESS	NIKI'S PRODUCT BUSINESS
Investment Raised	$0	$8,500,000
% of Business Owned at Time of Sale	100%	15%
Total Revenue at Time of Sale	$10,000,000	$10,000,000
Revenue Multiplier at Sale	1.5X	4X
Total Sale Price	$15,000,000	$40,000,000
Founder's Share of the Sale	$15,000,000	$6,000,000

That is a lot of money. In fact, my friends, it's twice what the original Adam West TV series Batmobile sold for at auction in 2013. Silvio has two Batmobiles more than Niki! Which, I think we'd all agree, is the single greatest indication of wealth.

However, if as a founder of a product company you're able to retain a larger-than-average share of your business, it's a great deal. If Niki held on to 60 percent of the company she started, again presuming the two founders got the median valuation for their sale, she'd make $24 million (60 percent of $40 million) versus Silvio's 100 percent of $15 million.

The point is, you could get an extra Batmobile if things go right. Maybe two.

But this conversation is moot if the business fails. Fifteen percent of zero is bupkes. And tech startup failure rates don't apply to the services category with nearly the same ferocity. In 2012, Scott Shane of Small Business Trends analyzed US Census Bureau data and found that services firms have some of the best survival rates among small-business types: 47.6 percent make it past year 5 of operation. Contrast that with the less than 25 percent of tech startups that do. *You are, statistically, almost twice as likely to "make it" as a services business than as a technology product firm.*

But, weirdly enough, you'll almost never read about acquisitions of services firms in the tech press. You'll almost never see a seven-, eight-, or even nine-figure merger or acquisition from the consulting world make it to even the bottom of Techmeme, or get a tweet mention by a prominent figure in the startup world. The focus is almost entirely on product companies, VC-backed companies, and those few in the United States with connections to the major media outlets of tech's insular ecosystem. In my opinion, this isn't just correlated with the perception of services firms; it's causal.

I have a lot of friends and colleagues who run consulting companies. Whenever we talk finances, they're blown away that, with a few hundred thousand or million in revenue, they are often personally much, much better off financially than my wife and I.

"How can that be?!" they'll ask when I share our fiscal situation.

"Well," I say, "I have a salary at Moz. And I have my stock. But I can't pay myself any of our profits, and until/unless the company sells or goes public, my stock is illiquid."

"Damn"—they always shake their heads—"a forty-five-million-dollar-a-year business doesn't make you rich. Weird."

I'll dive more deeply into the monetary machinations of venture-backed founders in chapter 8; stay tuned.

How to Push Your Product

I don't mean to unfairly or irrationally condemn a product focus. There are a number of good reasons to choose a product business over a services one:

- Your passion is to build product, not to do consulting.
- You love marketing to a broad, diverse audience, rather than networking and building a reputation among a more niche group.
- You will not be satisfied with yourself or your accomplishments until you try the product path.
- You accept the larger risks, higher failure rates, and more intensive capital demands in exchange for the potentially larger rewards that come with a product-centric company.
- You crave the attention, press, and long-shot odds of becoming wealthy enough to make Solomon blush.

This was the case with Moz all those years ago, and so a transition to product made sense. If you're in the same boat, here's the best advice I have on how to make this transition go smoothly.

Start with a product that's informed by your consulting. The services you provide expose you to real-life problems that consumers and organizations face. You have solutions, in the form of applied knowledge, for which people are willing to pay. Your experience can inform a product's design, content, marketing, amplification, and even the early parts of audience building. Moz's consultancy certainly did that for me—it showed the real challenges organizations of all sizes faced with SEO. It exposed me to hundreds of scenarios and problems, many of them overlapping, and gave me the knowledge of how to solve them that I could share transparently with others (which built the basis for my blog). Before I ever designed a tool, I knew exactly what issues I wanted to solve, and more important, I knew there were many others like me trying to solve those same problems. Thousands of them had already commented on my blog (and, helpfully, opted in for email messages).

Build a scalable marketing practice that attracts your prod-

uct's audience. Because so much of consulting business is driven by small-scale marketing and word of mouth, it's rare to find a consultancy seeking to build a sizable audience. But this is precisely what gave Moz the ability to scale its software product after launch, and if you can leverage marketing channels for your consultancy in the short term, with an eye to your product business in the long term, you'll be vastly ahead of the game. The key is to find channels of attraction with enough overlap to accommodate both the audience you need now—services clients—and the ones you need to reach in the future—product buyers.

Use the services revenue to fund the product's creation and testing. Don't let obsession with your new idea overtake your focus on the consulting business's success. It can be tempting to devote the majority of your time and the business's resources to product development, especially when you're excited about what you're creating (and you better be damned excited, because that passion will be needed to get through the ugly parts of product scaling). But if you cut short your consulting revenue, or fail to fill your pipeline with new clients, or let your work quality suffer, your adventure could be over before it begins.

When I talk to founders who've attempted this shift, three big things are almost always holding back a successful transition.

1. Comfort with the existing model, and the reliance on services income to survive.
2. The undistracted time needed to build a great product.
3. The difficulty of finding enough of the right customers for that product. It's rare that your services clients are the perfect match for your product (because fundamentally, they need services, not a product; that's why they're your customers!). This is why you

can't simply transition services clients to product customers, despite the seeming appeal and overlap.

If you internalize these challenges ahead of time, you can form testable theories of how to overcome them. If you recognize the odds, the sacrifices, and the upsides of both models, you can wisely choose between them. And hopefully, you can learn from Moz's experiences and make use of our tactics to ease a potential pivot.

Consulting Isn't the Enemy; Biased Thinking Is

So which model is right for you? Let's directly compare the two:

	SERVICES BUSINESS	PRODUCT BUSINESS
Startup Costs	Low	High
5-Year Average Survival Rates	Mediocre (47% according to US Census data)	Miserable (<10% according to NVCA data)
Marketing Demands	Low	High
Limits to Growth	People, Marketing, Retention	Capital, Engineering, Customer Acquisition
Competitive Barriers to Entry	Low	Medium to High
Scalability	Low	High
Staffing Requirements	High Ratio of Staff to Customers	Low Ratio of Staff to Customers
Gross Profit Margin	Low	High
Net Profit Margin	Medium	Low (often due to reinvestment for growth)

Clearly, the answer to the product versus services debate is "it depends." Smart founders need to use their best judgment about their strengths, their goals, and their market to determine whether one model is a clear winner, and/or whether it pays to experiment with some of each. Unless you're expressly seeking to raise money from venture investors, nothing's stopping you from offering a subscription product to your services clients, or from adding consulting services to your product business. Don't let Silicon Valley culture's traditional thinking on this bias you away from the right decision for your company and your customers.

CHAPTER 3

GREAT FOUNDERS DON'T DO WHAT THEY LOVE; THEY ENABLE A VISION

Your work is going to fill a large part of your life, and the only way to be truly satisfied is to do what you believe is great work. And the only way to do great work is to love what you do.

—**Steve Jobs, 2011**

Can I geek out for a minute?

I love SEO.

I love how small changes to a web page can make a marked difference in how it appears in search engines and how that drives hundreds or thousands of people to visit my site. I love the combination of technical skills and creativity required to overcome the competition for a tough keyword. And I love the mystery of how search engines rank pages and the process of uncovering each little piece of that puzzle.

When I find a new tactic or uncover a subtlety in Google's ranking process, my eyes light up. I do my best, deepest work, going for hours on the pure delight of discovery and intrigue, desperate to prove my hypothesis about what's happening in the millions of mathematical calculations that drive visibility on the web. If I get enough evidence, and can repeat the experiment consistently with ranking success, I'm elated. I'll run around my apartment, fists pumping in the air like a scrawny, nerdy, Jewish Rocky Balboa (avert your eyes, neighbors; not all our windows have blinds). I'll spend hours more writing up and visually documenting my work for a blog post or a presentation. When I finally hit "publish" or step onstage to share my findings, it's the pinnacle of my professional endeavors. Sharing that knowledge and removing that shroud of opacity from how these systems that govern what billions of people experience every day through search is what I love to do.

So, obviously, as CEO of an SEO company, I should be happy as a clam, right? I'm living the (admittedly, nerdtacular) dream, aren't I?

CEO Is a Real (Shitty) Job

Early in my career as an SEO consultant, a majority of my days were spent actually doing the work I loved. But after the company started on a serious growth trajectory and I assumed the role of CEO, I probably spent less than 20 percent of my time doing those things, and it often dwindled to less than 5 percent for months at a time.

We grew fast. And it was my first time doing anything (and everything) a CEO has to do. The learning curve was steep and uncomfortable. I didn't just have to learn; I had to immediately apply that knowledge and iterate it until I got it right. The stakes were high. Employees were relying on me to assign the right projects that would help make our software better or help us reach a broader audience. Customers were relying on me to build and support SEO tools that were better than their manual alternatives (or our competitors' tools). Investors relied on me to hire staff, to execute on projects, to report how things were going, to maintain financial discipline, and, most important, to grow fast. And, of course, our community of hundreds of thousands of marketers relied on me to investigate, educate, and publish nightly about the search and web-marketing fields.

No big deal, right? (Cue hyperventilation.)

I remember a single week in October 2009 when I was recruiting a new CTO, grasping at the desperate end of a failing fundraising process with a number of Silicon Valley VCs, preparing presentations for two upcoming conferences, negotiating new salaries and stock compensation with senior members of our engineering and operations teams, designing the wireframes for a major new product initiative (Open Site Explorer, which would go on to be one of our most popular products), promoting a book I'd coauthored for O'Reilly Media (*The Art of SEO*), and, unbelievably, meeting with some senior tech staff from the United Nations to talk about how search visibility might be helpful to them.

(Also, figuring out what I was going to be for Halloween. I ended up going as a red-shirted ensign. You know, the guys who are first to die tragically on *Star Trek*? Let's not read into that.)

I did virtually no hands-on SEO.

The myth of "founding a startup so you can do what you love" is at least as enshrined in the tech world's popular culture as the myth of getting rich. It deserves to be unpacked and examined. There's a grain of truth that lies within, albeit a grain buried under layers of maddening falsehood.

Passion Does Not a Manager Make

If you didn't have a preexisting notion of what startup entrepreneurship looks like, it might seem logical to imagine a series of events something like this: the entrepreneur graduates college; works for a year or two in a field that provides broad exposure to many different types of businesses (perhaps consulting); gets an MBA; does a thorough analysis of potential opportunities in a variety of fields; identifies the one with the least competition and highest demand potential; creates product, marketing, and scaling plans; fundraises; and then starts a company.

Hell, it sounds reasonable to me.

But we know from data, and from experience, that most entrepreneurs, and an overwhelming majority of the most successful entrepreneurs, don't start out with anything close to this level of deliberate evaluation. Instead, we dive headfirst into the thing we're passionate about, without even considering the alternatives, the market risks, the competitive landscape, the long-term demand curves and macroeconomic forces that might indicate it's a terrible time to start a new science-of-pasta-making website that relies entirely on cheap ads for revenue (but maybe someday we'll also make our own pasta and sell it on the site). Because, damn it, we love pasta! And we want to share our passion with a world of people who love it, too, but don't know what to buy or how to cook it. People who have yet to learn the handful of little secrets that transform *cacio e pepe* (a Roman pasta with cheese and black pepper) from a five-ingredient bowl of mush to the most satisfying, addictive, and unbelievably delicious dish you can make in twelve minutes flat.

Entrepreneurs start out doing what they love. Not because it makes sense, or because it's a great market, but because they cannot imagine themselves doing (or eating) anything else.

On the one hand, that passion and commitment is an asset. It can help early-stage companies push through the ugly barriers that make it so difficult to find a business model. On the other, once there's a small, working operation that's found revenue, the leadership needs to refocus on all the tasks a growing organization demands. Testing ingredients, taking photos, finding obscure, forgotten recipes, and sharing them with the world may have gotten you where you are, but it won't take you from food blogger to media empire.

When your startup is growing, the tasks and competencies change every six months. From 2007 to 2014, the most important things I did were never the same for longer than that. There were parts of each new job I enjoyed, but I clung for far too long to elements of work I should have delegated, reasoning, as almost every entrepreneur I've talked to does, that it was a core competency for the business. That I could do it better than anyone else. And that I could handle that work plus my other responsibilities.

I held on to near-complete control of our blog, using the logic that my posts were what had built the company's reputation, even though diversity of content and more of my freed-up time could have seriously bolstered our product and engineering. I maintained ownership and reviews of our consulting work (which we kept up until 2010). I insisted on being our primary product designer, and on having final say over every nook and cranny for years, which held back growth from other team members and slowed down product improvements dramatically, too.

Unless what you love is managing people, handling crises, delegating, holding people responsible, recruiting, setting, then constantly amplifying and repeating the company's mission, vision, strategy, and values, being a startup CEO may not provide you with the work you love to do.

Instead, a startup provides the ability to create a vision you love and to see it through to fulfillment. You get to say "today, the world works this way, but once the company I'll build exists, and once it reaches the scale to fulfill its ongoing mission, the world will change to this." If you can reset your passion from "I want to do *this* work" to "I want to see something I create change the world in *this* way," your expectations will align with reality, and the cognitive dissonance and frustration of being torn away from the work you love can fade.

Note that "change the world" doesn't have to mean "change the *whole* world." Your mission could be to make available and accessible the delicious, neglected pasta recipes of Emiglia-Romana. It might be to give the people of Seattle a better, more fulfilling experience with yoga. Or it might be to eradicate student loan debt and class stratification worldwide by building an affordable educational platform with the rigor and brand respect of Harvard at the cost of a Netflix subscription (side note: please, someone, do this). But if your mission is to "do the work I love doing without letting the business get in the way," I strongly recommend against pursuing growth that demands more people on your team. Hiring people adds organizational complexity, the mortal enemy of heads-down, passion-focused, deep work.

How to Be a CEO in 6 ~~Easy~~ Infuriatingly Challenging Steps

If you're ready to accept this limitation in the work you'll get to do, and to put shepherding your vision ahead of doing what you love, you have a new set of challenges ahead. Great startups aren't built by people who never gain competence beyond their particular field—they demand proficiency in financial strategy, task planning, human resources, conflict resolution, office management, fundraising, customer support, payment collections, business intelligence, and dozens of other functions founders rarely consider in the early stages. You'll get to learn each of these through a process the startup world affectionately calls "muddling through." I prefer the more accurate description: "wading into a painful slog of failure, learning, and repetition."

In essence, you'll:

1. Realize, frustratingly late, a particular pain point that's holding your team back from effectively or efficiently accomplishing a goal (e.g., you can't run the A/B tests on your website because you have no framework for measuring results, nor any expertise in how to build effective tests).

2. Attempt a variety of techniques to overcome that pain point (hiring people with previous competency in the practice, researching and learning it yourself, delegating the learning to other team members, acquiring technology or data, implementing a rigid new process, etc.).

3. Determine that most of the things you've tried have failed, and cycle through many more until you . . .

4. Experience the elation of breaking through, at least partially, and finding some success.

5. Uncover new frustrating side effects and unintended consequences of your solution(s).

6. Half the time, settle for partial implementation and a set of compromises that work well enough to become the new norm; the other half, realize that the solutions are worse than the problem and determine a way to simply avoid or ignore the pain point,

possibly by refocusing your strategy so you simply don't have to deal with it.

I'll share an example from Moz.

From 2004 to 2012, project planning followed a very informal path at the company. I'd sit down with one or a handful of our team members, talk about what they could be working on, what they wanted to work on, what we thought would be best for the business, and through those weekly or monthly conversations, establish a road map. Sometimes we'd change it over an email thread or through a hallway chat. And sometimes we'd do a decent job of broadcasting the plans to the rest of the company. But things were small enough (at least when we had fewer than thirty people across our four functional teams) that this informal process mostly worked.

But by 2010, the forty(ish) folks inside Moz got frustrated that knowledge about what each person and team was working on was mostly held in a janky combination of (a) Rand's memory banks, (b) random email threads, and (c) a wide variety of project-tracking systems, some of which were used by only one person. The frustration amplified when projects would cross teams and drag people off their individual tasks to collaborate at inconvenient or unexpected times. To combat this, we tried a quarterly cadence of all-hands meetings, during which I or the department head would run through all the projects on the calendar for the next two to three months. This alleviated some pain but created plenty of new ones.

So we tried a series of weekly emails: each team would send out their in-progress projects and next set of expected work each Friday. By the time we had broad adoption of this practice, there was a massive amount of all-staff emails going out each Friday, most of which were ignored by most people in the company. Complaints about this glut of no-one-reads-them emails led to a consolidated process where each week, one technical project manager (TPM) would get all the teams' reports and put them into a single, very long, Friday email. If you were diligent enough and had the patience, you could scroll through that list and see what everyone was doing and what they had planned next. It basically only worked well for one person—me. I love email, I'm good at it, and very often, I'd be the only person replying with questions and clarifications on those threads.

As you might imagine, that practice neither scaled nor worked well for anyone else. When Sarah Bird become Moz's CEO in 2014 (more about that to come), she implemented a new system of quarterly planning meetings with facilitated discussions between teams over two to three days in a large room filled with poster boards on which each team's projects were listed out for discussion and markup. For those few days, representatives from each team, along with managers and executives, would huddle together and talk through every project and plan, determine work sequencing, and argue over priorities, and many times Sarah herself would have the final say about which piece mattered most.

First to go were the outside facilitators, which many, myself included, felt were inauthentic and created more complexity and process than necessary. Then the meetings shrunk to one and a half days as additional elements of discussion and negotiation were pared back. And, finally, after realizing that the process was simply too demanding and didn't provide enough value to justify its ongoing existence, Sarah eliminated it altogether. She reorganized the company into functional business units, with a smaller number of shared services departments, and shifted to a model where broadcasting everything everyone was working on was no longer required. Each team was given more autonomy to determine its own road map, and less reliance on other teams to get their work done. The pain subsided. The pace of progress increased. And despite (or perhaps, by virtue of) not always knowing what everyone else was doing, Moz's employees felt less frustrated, less overwhelmed, and more focused.

I'm skipping over a ton of the incremental steps, hard decisions, and tedious changes designed to address the struggles that arose throughout this process, but the narrative remains. It's probably familiar to anyone who's worked in a scaling organization, and it's critical to understand if you're going to build a company designed to grow. It took six years, more than ten iterations, and two CEOs to find a process that worked for product planning at Moz. In the end, Sarah made the tough but smart choice to avoid the problem altogether by restructuring the company.

The Best Leaders Know When to Lead— and When Not To

Many founders believe they can delegate key business functions to other people on their team—and often they should. But your first hires in any of these roles will need guidance, support, input, and occasionally you'll need to dig into the details yourself because you can't find the right person or you had to let them go, or you simply need to know more about the issues before you can determine whether the problem lies with your people, your management, your processes, or something else.

I hired multiple CTOs to run the technology side of our business, but never got to know the processes well enough to support or mentor a technology leader. Sarah did likewise, but finally buckled down and decided to dig into the role herself. We actually fought about it . . . a lot. I was angry that she wasn't recruiting a CTO after we lost

Anthony, our fourth engineering leader in six years. She countered that until she spent time understanding and leading that part of our business herself, she didn't feel confident in hiring an effective outsider. It was a point of contention for more than a year between us, but she proved to be totally right. Her insider knowledge of the teams and people, the work needed, the relationships and conflicts proved instrumental in finding a great tech leader, hiring him, and then eventually promoting him to the position of CTO.

Sarah and I both delegated a set of work we weren't cut out for (neither of us have particularly technical backgrounds), but we didn't get it functioning smoothly until she invested the time to understand the practice herself.

This is the work entrepreneurs do in growing organizations: digging into problems, untangling conflict, freeing people from the mind-sets or structures that hold them back, crafting (and refining, over and over) the pillars and policies of how the company functions. The hours you spend on the business will shift from doing what you love to enabling a vision and navigating whatever impediments arise along the way. Expect to do work you don't love in order to allow what you do to flourish. If you don't, the disappointment and frustration can kill your motivation.

Embrace that reality, though, and you'll come to see the CEO role as one of enabler and problem solver. For those who love helping others get unblocked and watching progress scale far beyond what they could achieve alone, this can be an immensely rewarding job.

CHAPTER 4
BEWARE THE PIVOT

Ideas are worthless. Execution is everything.

—Scott Adams,* 2010

There's an idea floating in the mythos of Silicon Valley's hallowed halls that the "pivot" is a fundamental right bestowed upon all startups, designed to help absolve the sins of your past incarnation and allow you, too, to go from Tote to Pinterest, Odeo to Twitter, or Glitch to Slack. If the decisions upon which you founded your business prove foolhardy, never fear, the pivot will save you! It's more important to get started than to spend months evaluating and choosing a wiser path. The path can never be known! The path must be discovered by trying and failing and . . . you guessed it, pivoting.

---

* Fittingly, most of Scott's own ideas about ethics, politics, and humanity are complete crap. Don't read his blog unless you're ready to watch a talented cartoonist reveal himself to be a shitburger of a person.

Bollocks.

In the annals of startup history, there are tens of thousands of companies that achieved remarkable success—hundreds of millions or billions of dollars in returns, a lasting impact on their ecosystems or industries, delighted customers and users, and a financially well-compensated founding team that now spends their days swimming in a pit full of gold coins (side note: everything I know about the lifestyles of the wealthy comes from Scrooge McDuck).

But among all those successful companies, how many great "pivots" were there? If we're using the formal definition of migrating completely from one business idea to a radically different one, all my research could uncover only a few dozen. Slack, Flickr, Twitter, Pinterest, PayPal, Groupon, and Instagram aren't just among the most famous, they're among the *only* ones (at least of those that have achieved truly lofty, founders-now-have-a-gold-coin-filled-swimming-hole success).

This should come as no surprise. Pivots don't happen on a whim. You change your business model, your product, your market, or your entire idea only if things are going very poorly indeed. Anything else would be foolhardy (if it ain't broke, don't pivot). It's nasty, ugly, hard, grueling work building these things in the first place, and if you've achieved any progress whatsoever, you're likely to stick with it, learn, and improve.

Given this reality, it might pay to be less cavalier and more analytical in your approach to choosing an industry, an idea, a product, and a target customer. It may also pay to choose a field others ignore because it's perceived as unsexy, sketchy, or uninteresting by some other vanity-centric logic.

In my case, Moz picked a field experiencing massive growth

(being found in search engines during Google's dramatic rise) and a model that scaled wonderfully (software to help marketers and SEOs do their work more efficiently, with better results), and we spent our energy iteratively improving. We got better at marketing, at building software, at collecting data, at designing product interfaces, at retaining subscribers, and at all the other things core to our business. We favored improving execution over changing our model, market, or fundamentals. From 2007 to 2013, that brought us 100 percent year-over-year growth, leadership in our space, a variety of accolades, and the adoration of our customers and investors.

Execution Is More Malleable Than Market, Model, and Idea

I started writing about SEO in 2003. Back then, very few people were doing so, and even fewer were doing it in a transparent way that helped others learn the practice. There was a pervasive belief in the field that sharing too much about how search engines worked or what tactics earned rankings could put you out of business. Many SEO consultants perceived their "secret sauce" knowledge to be more important to their clients than the work itself.

That secrecy, combined with the unpopularity of the industry, gave my blog a unique advantage—it stood out among the available offerings for its open, transparent approach to the subject matter. The writing certainly wasn't anything special. The advice itself wasn't vastly superior to what others had. But while our competitors were mostly unwilling to share this kind of information without a signed NDA and a consulting fee, SEOmoz.org required nothing but a browser visit. As a result, other sites linked to me. Press outlets cited my posts. Consulting clients found their way to our contact page. And thousands of industry practitioners, hungry for knowledge, signed up for daily updates.

Fast-forward to 2007, when we launched our subscription business. The tools contained there weren't especially great. They were often broken or overloaded. The data they gave back was mediocre at best. But digital marketing was a fast-growing field. SEO was heating up as a practice. And there were almost no other sources of automation for folks who couldn't write their own software, so Moz stood out.

In both of these cases, we were mediocre providers who, over time, dramatically improved our offerings. My writing in 2004 was pretty sad (you can still find those early blog posts on Moz.com/blog and see for yourself). It was at least a few years in before I was producing anything that could be called "high quality." Similarly, when we launched our software via a $39/month PayPal subscription, the tool set was lackluster, the features subpar, and the usability just a hair better than atrocious.

What did we do right?

We picked a good market. We stumbled onto a compelling communication medium. And we chose a good business model. These inadvertently wise choices covered up a tremendous number of mistakes and a steep learning curve.

I published no fewer than one thousand blog posts before my posts achieved consistent, broad readership that earned the kind of value we see with published content today. From late 2003 to early 2007, I wrote for an hour or a few, five nights a week, Sunday through Thursday, and I'd spend additional hours the next morning promoting the posts, replying to comments, and finding new topics to cover. By the time the blog appeared on "must-read" lists, I'd invested hundreds of hours researching and writing. I started out an amateur but today have a massive following and the ability to generate tens of thousands of visits, resonant messages, and powerful business impacts via my blogging.

The software side of Moz has uncanny parallels. Our first tools were barely worth the subscription prices. But over many years, we got better at software development processes, at affording and hiring great engineers, and at designing more useful applications. From a few dozen subscribers to tens of thousands, from an average customer lifetime value of a couple hundred dollars to more than $2,000, we improved in every facet of the SaaS model (Software-as-a-Service, wherein subscribers are charged on a recurring basis to access software via a website or Internet-connected app).

We love to praise execution, as if executing well on any dumb old idea would take us somewhere. Sure. Immense dedication, skill, and the hard work of great people can overcome most obstacles. But choosing wisely at the start—the field, the approach, the customer target, the economic model, and the marketing methodologies—has a massive impact on the difficulties you'll face and how forgiving the journey will be. Not everyone can afford the costs of starting over. Not everyone has the privilege of being able to test hypotheses willy-nilly. If you have a family, if you have debts, if your cost of failure is anything but zero, it makes better sense to tread carefully.

The Switching Costs Can Kill You

Here's the weird thing about this argument in favor of pivoting: execution is far more fungible than your idea, your business model, the industry you choose, or even your team.

What happens as a startup makes progress? The team improves the quality of its work. Customer service folks improve their response times. Product features and functionality catch up to customer needs. Engineers deliver better technology. User experience goes from bare bones to impressive. The marketing funnel widens. Conversion rates go up.

If you're prioritizing execution and learning from your mistakes, you're already doing this.

Now imagine how hard it is to move from targeting one market to another. Many of the hard-won lessons your marketing team or salespeople or business development folks have earned are useless. You're back to square one on how to attract customers, how to close deals, how to retain their loyalty. Yikes.

Say you switch your idea or product. You'll throw out months or years of sweat and toil validating a concept, earning customer buy-in, and attracting influencers, press, and perhaps even investors. Maybe this new product or service will be easier to build than your last one. But it's not free. And it's certainly going to set you back on every other vector—including customer traction and acquisition.

Or maybe you're changing from one business model to another. It may be a smaller shift than the two above, but it still takes a vast degree of energy, and likely means migrating your customers (if they'll come) from one system of compensation to another.

Don't believe the hype—execution isn't everything. You can be the tortoise, rather than the hare, and by picking the right race and the right route, win over far more talented teams because you're constantly improving in a less crowded space no one else has chosen.

Some Unorthodox Tips on Choosing Your Market and Your Idea

If you haven't already read Eric Ries's book *The Lean Startup*, go do that now. Then pick up *Sprint* by Jake Knapp and the Google Ventures team. The first one will help you nail the basics of choosing and validating a market, and the second shares my favorite method for nailing new products and features.

Now that you're analyzing competitors' UVPs* like a boss, and rattling off sarcastic product/market misfit jokes with the best of 'em, I've got a few additional suggestions:

1. If you can keep your ego and your aspirations below the need to pursue venture capital in order to aim for a billion-dollar unicorn, you can ignore a lot of the advice about choosing a giant, fast-growing market ripe for "disruption." Instead, it's totally cool (and may make your life vastly easier) to chase after smaller markets where you have unique knowledge and passion, and where ongoing, smaller amounts of innovation can separate you from the pack. There are thousands, maybe millions, of opportunities like these with dramatically fewer venture dollars and Harvard MBAs (or Stanford CS dropouts) chasing them. Because let's face it: most of us aren't going to be innovators in humankind's quest to explore outer space. But we might be able to develop a better way to clean out a garbage disposal than, say, sticking your hand down it.

2. Great ideas and products are often born from mediocre ones. The keys are time (enough to iterate and evolve into something remarkable), humility (enough to see what's wrong and admit a

---

* Unique Value Propositions

failure so you can move forward), and survival (a profitable services business can be a godsend here).

3. Your business will be even more likely to succeed if the market you target is served by incumbent solutions that are some combination of (a) hated by their customers, (b) unwilling or unable to evolve with their customers' needs, (c) protected by competitive advantages you can unravel (or that a shift in market dynamics or regulation is unraveling for you), or (d) in their early stages and not yet dominant (i.e., a non-mature market). If you find a market with two or more of these (think vacation home rentals before Airbnb or crowdfunding before Kickstarter), your odds rise exponentially.

4. Keyword research (wherein you uncover what words and phrases people are searching Google for and in what quantities) will almost always uncover untapped opportunity. Move beyond the solution keywords, and look for searches that indicate problems—the quantity of monthly searches for "cityname+taxi" helped Uber figure out which cities to launch in, just as the monthly searches for "best restaurant in cityname" helped Yelp pick their expansion markets. Two good tools for this—Google's AdWords program (you don't need to buy ads; just sign up for free) and Moz's Keyword Explorer (a shameless plug, but it really is the best tool out there).

All that said, if you have to compromise on several elements (and you almost certainly will), I'd urge you to sacrifice market size, lack of (or weak) competition, and sales and marketing tactics, in that order, before you endeavor to tackle a field where your abilities don't create a competitive advantage and a unique value proposition. It's that important.

CHAPTER 5

STARTUPS CARRY THEIR FOUNDERS' BAGGAGE

Writing code? That's the easy part. Getting your application in the hands of users, and creating applications that people actually want to use—now that's the hard stuff.

—Jeff Atwood, March 2010

It's probably no big surprise to hear that a company inherits its founder's attributes—whether they be good or bad. Install a misogynist as CEO, and you'll find that the company has misogynistic practices (cough—UBER—cough). Back a founder with self-worth issues and they'll often overcompensate through political power plays and a lack of sharing credit. Study enough startups and you'll see this pattern over and over. Amazon inherited Jeff Bezos's passion for logistics just as surely as his thriftiness with employee pay and benefits and proclivity for causing burnout. Craigslist reflects founder Craig Newmark's near-luddite innovation sensibility alongside his desire for inclusivity. Slack has Stewart Butterfield's focus on visual design, user experience, and delightful Easter eggs baked into numerous features.

One of my favorite examples of this is Jessica Mah's startup: inDinero.

In 2008, Jessica enrolled in UC Berkeley's Computer Science program. She had a passion for coding, but a couple of years in, knew she was in the bottom cohort of her class. It's not that she lacked the skills or intelligence to be a great engineer, but she (to use her words) "lacked the patience." Jealously, she watched classmates attract six-figure offers (with sizable stock bonuses) from Google and Facebook. Resolving to leverage the skills she did have—a penchant for writing, for attracting press, and for inspiring people with her explanations—Jessica started a blog (http://jessicamah.com/) where she wrote about software development, team building, and startup culture.

Paul Graham, the founder of Silicon Valley's most famous startup accelerator, Y Combinator, and a demigod in the eyes of many entreprenerds (what? I can make up dorky portmanteaus), was one of her early readers. He found her writing and invited her to apply to the program.

As Jessica put it: "It was literally the day after graduation that I went to Mountain View and started at YC. I have high standards for myself, and for people around me, but I wasn't focused on my coursework. I hate being told what to do. I started inDinero because I value freedom and flexibility."

Over the next six years, inDinero grew from two people to two hundred, raised $20 million in angel money (Jessica abhors the venture model and turned down multiple offers to raise VC), and became a media darling in the B2B startup world.

I asked her what the hardest parts of growing inDinero were, and her response was immediate: "People management. Mentoring. I hate it. I don't have the patience for it.

"When we were ten people," she continued, "I thought we wouldn't make it. I hated coaching and giving feedback and being patient while people made mistakes. As we got bigger, I got rid of all my reports except two; I do as little management as possible and it's worked great."

The other big struggle for inDinero was marketing. While Jessica's a great writer and evangelist for the business, she never found a groove with web-marketing channels like search, social, or content. But she was able to leverage her immensely compelling interpersonal skills, alongside her contrarian leanings, to build a powerful PR machine. InDinero's been featured in dozens of publications, and Jessica herself has been interviewed for hundreds of articles over the years (I do an excited dance every time I see her on the cover of some national tech or financial magazine). Each new piece is an opportunity to expose her business to exactly the kinds of customers (and influencers of customers) that inDinero's chasing.

Jessica struggled in the early days, just as many founders do, because her skills and proclivities had giant gaps with what her business needed. But despite nearly failing multiple times (including once when she and her cofounder were forced to spend their personal savings, down to the last penny, to keep the business afloat), inDinero survived and thrived. How? By Jessica's gaining awareness of her strengths, weaknesses, quirks, and motivations and then structuring her startup to work with (or around) these attributes.

The near collapses of inDinero and the actual collapses that many startups suffer are often because founders don't understand themselves and how their companies inherit these traits. If you can identify and balance (or work around) the DNA that founders pass on to their startup children, you can build on your strengths and avoid many of the journey-ending pitfalls.

The Outsized Influence of Founders

Moz has always been marketing-centric. For us, the easy part is getting millions of visitors to our website who care about the problems we're trying to solve and are seeking answers to questions about SEO. These are the very people our products serve, and we're one of the best-known, most-respected, and most-trafficked destinations for this challenging-to-reach B2B audience. Marketing has never been our problem, at least never for long stretches. The hardest nugget for us to crack has always been the product itself and the technology underlying it.

We've struggled, since inception, to create high-quality software. Perhaps when this book is published, that will have changed (or maybe giant penguins will have taken over the earth. I mean, honestly, either would be an improvement). Certainly, we've made progress over the years, but it has never been fast enough or high-quality enough to outrun far less-funded, less-experienced, less-well-known, and less-well-regarded competitors. I've literally had professional SEOs who want desperately to be our customers tell me they can't wait for Moz to build or improve upon a particular feature so they don't have to give another player in our field their money. With loyalty and brand preference so strongly in our favor, I figured it would be easy for us to hire a few more developers and build software our customers loved.

Almost every founder believes this to some degree: hire the right people to bolster your weaknesses and you can focus on your strengths.

Cut to grainy film of me, sitting alone in a dark room. My eyes are bloodshot. I shake my head sadly, as I stare into a glass of whiskey.

"If only it were that easy," I whisper.

Er, sorry. It's easy to get melodramatic about this stuff.

The thing is, it is absolutely true that a balanced team, in which one person's weaknesses are covered by another's strengths, can be tremendously successful. What's not well understood, and usually only gets uncovered after years of operations, is how founders' attributes instill themselves with near-permanence in an organization, while the attributes of the supporting team fluctuate over time. Partially, this is because founders tend to be around much longer, exerting more influence over more time. The average tenure of an employee in the startup world is only about two years. But even if you retain that supporting team, there's an undeniable, indelible imprint sourced from the founders' biases, the structure of the business they created, their recruiting, their delegation, their assignment of resources, their passions, and their blind spots.

Time and again, I see this pattern play across companies of all sizes, industries, and makeups. Founders (and CEOs) determine not just the personality and culture, but the fundamental strengths and weaknesses that govern an organization's trajectory for years or even decades. Take, for example, Virgin brands, which bear a striking resemblance in tone and style to Richard Branson himself, but also carry his particular strengths (willingness to take risks, strong brand marketing, an affinity for youth culture, customer experience as the cornerstone of competitive advantage) and weaknesses (prone to short-term thinking, unconcerned with underlying technological or product innovation versus cosmetic upgrades, inconsistent financial underpinnings).

It should come as no surprise, then, that Moz's founders—me and my mom, Gillian—had no formal programming or software development experience or education. We fell into the software world through our marketing backgrounds and exposure to the field, leaned on our writing and business development skills, and managed to hire a few great folks early on who helped us build some revolutionary software. One story illustrates this perfectly.

"Never Leave Me" Is a Weird Thing to Say to an Employee

Geraldine had a classmate in high school named Ben Hendrickson. Ben is an unusual guy. He's six four but weighs about 160 pounds. His professional demeanor is equal parts programming savant and absentminded professor. Think Ichabod Crane meets Anthony Michael Hall.

In 2007, just after we'd raised our first round of funding from Ignition, Geraldine connected me with Ben. At a Greek restaurant near our offices, over avgolemono soup and gritty coffee, I explained my outlandish dream to him of building a web index to mimic Google's. Every other person I'd talked with about this plan dismissed it as impossible or, at least, impossible without the hundreds of millions of dollars Google had at their disposal. But Ben inclined his head, stared into space for an uncomfortable few minutes, and then replied in his booming baritone, "I think I can do that."

He started solo. First, by crawling, indexing, and storing all of the Wikipedia website (which, by itself, has tens of millions of pages). Then, in early 2008, once the prototype was proven to work, he and I recruited a second engineer, Nick Gerner, through a friend who worked at Google with Nick's wife. That friend—Vanessa Fox, creator of Google's Webmaster Tools program—was someone we consulted on the web index concept. Ben, Nick, and I sat down with her over Indian food, described our plans, and listened as she explained why it couldn't work and would be folly to try. Undaunted, the three of us sequestered ourselves in the dark back room of the Moz offices and, for another six months, worked on the project we'd code-named "Carhole" (a reference to an old episode of *The Simpsons*. Moe the bartender suggests Homer is an elitist for using the term "garage," because "carhole" was just as good. The name perfectly encompassed what we were trying to do: create a less fancy version of Google's index that was just as good). I advised on the product's structure, design, and outputs, while Ben and Nick did the hard work of building the crawl, indexing, and data-serving infrastructure, as well as most of the front-end application.

We were burning cash from the investment at a healthy clip on salaries, hosting, and operations. Our revenue was growing, too, but not nearly as fast as expenses. The Carhole project (renamed "Linkscape" at launch, and later "Mozscape"), was, we hoped, our ace in the hole. We knew our customers desperately wanted the competitive information about who was linking to whom on the web, and that Google had, a couple of years prior, removed that information from their search engine (historically, you could use the command link:websitename.com in Google Search to see the links Google knew about pointing to a particular website or page). We bet heavily that giving this information back to marketers and website owners would be a big driver of paid subscription growth.

October 7, 2008. I woke up in New York, excited to launch our new project at a major search marketing conference in the city (SMX East). I went downstairs to the hotel restaurant, where a crowd was gathered around the television at the bar. Many of them were clearly nervous or entirely distraught. Lehman Brothers had collapsed. Banks across the United States and Europe were waking up to their exposure to credit-default swaps in the housing market. Stock markets were crashing. My email inbox had messages from a handful of reporters who'd agreed to cover our product launch that day, canceling their interviews at the conference, explaining that they had bigger issues to cover. I walked through midtown to the conference center dreading what might happen.

The conference was a blur, but the launch, at least inside our tiny pocket of the SEO world, was a hit. Customer signups accelerated. Our revenue grew. That December, we had our first profitable month since taking investment. Ben and Nick added a third member to their crew, Chas Williams, who'd built a prototype project in college that Moz bought from him and added to our suite.

It was the startup dream come true. Raise money to build a big, challenging piece of technology everyone said was impossible, finish on time and within budget, launch, and attract real customers who used what you built. We celebrated with the company's first holiday party. We put on funny hats and fancy clothes (okay, fine, it was more like ill-fitting sport coats with shiny shirts . . . we were young). We took photos and drank champagne. We invited our investors, and they actually turned up to celebrate with us!

For the next two years, our product got better, and our revenue grew at a fast clip. But in 2011, Nick left the company. A year later Ben got an offer he couldn't refuse from Google. Chas left not long after. We'd hired other engineers to help manage the link index project, but made only incremental gains and suffered a lot of challenging problems as we tried to grow the index's size and freshness. Over the next five years, we invested near-insane amounts of effort, dollars, and engineering time trying to improve, but fell short. We hired more than a dozen folks to work on just this one project. Some worked out and stayed, others didn't. Parts of our software improved during that time, but our link data stagnated.

Simultaneously two competitors in the market—one, a secretive operation based in the Ukraine and Singapore called "Ahrefs" (pronounced "A. H. Refs"), and the other, a British firm founded by a passionate Russian engineer whose initial goal had been to build an alternative to Google's search engine called "Majestic"—grew to market dominance. After years of leading the industry, Moz became an also-ran in the field of link data.

What the @#$% happened? We were the pioneers and now we were being outdone? We'd done the impossible but now we couldn't maintain it? Is this why Usain Bolt didn't run marathons?

I've spent years agonizing over this failure. Night after night in bed or at my computer wondering how things went so wrong, what I did to cause it, how it could have been avoided. I spent hours in meetings with engineers after another quarter or two of work produced subpar results, trying to unpack our missteps and figure out how things went sideways. But I'm not a software engineer, so I couldn't even properly assess what had gone wrong. It was like trying to diagnose an illness without a medical degree. On an alien. With three heads.

Retrospectives, analyses, comparisons, competitive intelligence, anger, sadness, frustration. And the worst one of all . . . helplessness.

Jeff Atwood said that writing code was "the easy part." Maybe for you, Jeff. I'd say it's been the hardest, most mind-numbingly difficult part of Moz. For me, marketing, reaching our target audience, and getting our product into the hands of customers has been the easy part. That's a language I speak.

Impressing them with the product we provide? *That* was the nightmare.

I was lucky when I found Ben, Nick, and Chas. Their success at building a product others told us was impossible gave me a false sense of confidence. I thought I could concentrate on my strengths and hire to fill Moz's weaknesses. That didn't work out. Through multiple CTOs and numerous engineering teams of varying sizes and compositions, we were never able to recapture that magic Ben and crew brought to the link problem.

Well, not until we got them back.

In 2016, five years after Ben had left Moz, he'd founded his own startup, Idina, alongside his prior compatriot Chas Williams. Ben and I had breakfast together after I'd made a number of introductions to help him sell his fledgling company. It turned out that Ben had exactly the opposite challenge that I did—marketing and customer adoption were nonexistent despite impressive software under the hood.

We talked about the potential offers, and about the technology he'd built with Chas at Idina. Upon hearing Ben describe the data ingestion and processing system, I wondered aloud if Moz should be making a bid for the company. Ben stared off past me, *hmm*'d for a few awkward moments, and then replied: "Well, have you solved the link scaling problem yet?"

"I only wish."

"Then, yeah, Moz should probably buy us."

"You know . . . you could have told me that before I introduced you to all these other bidders."

Fast-forward three months and, via a creatively structured (and lucrative) acquisition, the band was back together again. Ben, Chas, and the Idina infrastructure were part of Moz. Another year later and we were, once again, leaders in the field of link data, with an index to rival our competitors and a lot of happy customers.

I cannot say for certain that if I'd had an engineering background, and counted big data software design and execution among my personal strengths, that Moz would have maintained its leadership and quality in that field. And I don't know for certain that if Ben and Chas had been more experienced marketers, whether their startup would still have struggled to attract users. But I know that these are not isolated stories. They're practically universal.

It's Hard to Pick the NFL's Draft Order if You've Never Played Football

Every founder (or set of founders) has a different take on the hardest parts of building a company. And those same founders will have different takes on the easy parts. Talk to two talented software engineers who founded a company and you may find that recruiting, managing, or marketing are perceived as the most difficult issues. Talk to the marketer and people manager who founded a company down the street, and you may hear just the opposite.

The uncanny truth is that those "hardest parts" and "easiest parts" say less about the challenges and more about the strengths and weaknesses of the founders themselves. We all believe the problems and experiences we face are the most common ones, the ones every founder must struggle against. It's inherent in the psychological principle known as availability heuristic bias.

And while that phrase is daunting (seriously, do not try saying it while drunk), the concept is a pretty simple one: our exposure dictates our perception. If you've ever tried convincing someone whose politics differ from your own about the statistical reality of something they've experienced personally, you know the power of this principle. (Just think about how many times you've had a miserable experience at a restaurant only to find that the 238 Yelp reviews are all five-star.)

The conventional wisdom that you should bolster your weaknesses with great hires who can give you that strength isn't totally wrong, but every time this advice is passed on, it should contain these three caveats:

1. Lacking deep knowledge and understanding of an area means that you are less likely to have connections in that field, less likely to identify right versus wrong hires in that field, and less likely to successfully recruit and convince great talent to join. You might not even realize which knowledge you lack (unknown unknowns, amirite?).

2. A founder's weaknesses are often baked into the company's DNA and create a figurative kind of debt (nonideal practices or systems) that must be addressed before progress can be made. If you lack engineering skills, this often manifests as technical debt that must be remedied through re-architecting and rebuilding core systems before adding features or enabling scalability. If you lack people management skills, it's likely organizational debt that requires months of digging into interpersonal and intra-team conflicts, letting go of some staff, rehiring, and creating processes for engagement and teamwork that build trust.

3. When you rely on someone (or several someones) to bolster a weakness, their departure from the organization creates risk that the wound will reopen. This risk is greater in smaller and less-experienced teams where the senior leader is often the glue keeping things together with their presence, and lessens as organizations grow (so long as that leader has created consistent quality through redundancy of great people and great processes).

Hiring or finding a skilled cofounder is not the only way to bolster a weakness.

If you have great confidence (or considerable fear) that an area of weakness could be your company's downfall, you can invest in that attribute. But first, you have to know it exists.

That process is eminently achievable, but few entrepreneurs have the self-awareness or take the time to diagnose. I've fallen prey to this too many times. My advice, therefore, is to be prescriptive and deliberate in examining your own strengths and weaknesses. They will, almost always, map shockingly well to those of your company's.

Make a list of the primary functions in your organization. Now apply the following scale to those functions based on your personal aptitude for each:

Level 1: Theoretical knowledge (or less)—You have friends who've worked in the field, and in theory, understand the raw elements of the practice through lots of reading and a strong degree of interest in the subject. But you've never directly worked in the field (occasional volunteering or pro bono assistance doesn't count), never managed anyone directly who was responsible for this sort of work, and haven't done any formal training, either.

Level 2: Managerial knowledge—At this level, you've had direct reports who did this work, and completed a few successful projects. You've overseen retrospectives, heard the conversations, been involved in some tough decision making, and reviewed a lot of results. But you can't do the work yourself, at least not with any degree of certainty or confidence. You have to rely on what others tell you is achievable and the reasons others give you for why something worked or didn't, and it'll be hard to call bullshit with credibility.

Level 3: Practical, applied knowledge plus working experience— You've done this work yourself, possibly alongside a team. And though you may have graduated to managing others who did most of the heavy lifting and details, you could still pick apart and identify pitfalls, potential issues, poor assumptions, or mistakes. You may have completed classes or gone through formal training, though in general, hands-on experience is the hallmark of this level.

Level 4: Deep, working expertise plus ability to teach—You've not only done the work yourself but managed people doing it, achieved high-quality results consistently over multiple years, and taught these practices to others.

Let's use software engineering as an example because it's something so many founders and would-be founders in the startup world struggle with (just look at the thousands of questions on startup-focused forums that begin with "I want to start XYZ but am not technical . . ."). Assuming you're like me, and this skill is currently a level one or two, your options to make this a strength are straightforward:

1. Learn the process and do it yourself.
2. Start the company with cofounders who have this strength already.
3. Invest in the knowledge necessary to hire, retain, focus, and manage great talent in the field.

Nearly every piece of advice I've ever seen ignores the last one and focuses on the first two. But after Sarah Bird became CEO, I watched her go from the low end of level one to the top end of level two, and turn a fundamental weakness we'd had at the company throughout my tenure (with only occasional success stories like the early link index) into a core strength in her first eighteen months leading the company.

How did she do it? I asked Sarah to contribute so we could hear directly from the source:

Before Moz, my only software engineering experience was a Computer Science 101 course many years before. My lack of technical depth made me feel insecure about managing engineering leaders and teams. It was pretty easy to discern when development wasn't going well, but it often wasn't clear why. Was it because I had the wrong CTO? The wrong engineers? Perhaps the technical problem we were trying to solve was harder than we imagined? Maybe we didn't have enough resources? Or the right resources? Were we underinvesting in development infrastructure and tech debt? I can spin myself in circles trying to understand the why.

Here are the top things I did to become a better leader of technical people and teams:

- Ask questions during skip levels (meetings where a senior manager meets with team members who report to the managers below them) with engineers that go beyond identifying problems and into concrete solutions. For example, asking, "What good development practices did your last company have that you don't see in play here?" surfaces best practices.
- When you find an engineer on the team who can articulate different strategies she has tried, and the why behind them with conviction and clarity, give her power to try implementing some of those changes here. Be her champion, even when she ruffles some feathers making change. If some of the strategies don't work out, praise the effort.

- Read everything you can about different engineering cultures and best practices. Read dev blogs for companies like Spotify, Netflix, and Airbnb. There are a lot of great books, blogs, and conference talks about best practices. Invest time to consume as many of these as possible. For example, I follow Edmond Lau (a software engineer who worked at Google and Quora, and runs the EffectiveEngineer.com blog) and Jez Humble (who works at UC Berkeley and runs ContinuousDelivery.com) pretty closely. Go beyond the slogans into the meetings, habits, and platforms high-performing teams employ.

- Take notes about the technologies and practices that you hear about in design reviews and one on ones. Then go back to your computer and google them like crazy. Read everything you can about the technology. While reading, keep in mind that engineers are famous for indulging in so-called religious wars about why a particular technology is "so much better" than another one. Learn to spot it when an engineer moves beyond advocacy to naive devotion to a particular tech. Take everything with a heaping spoonful of salt. You need to know the lovers, the haters, and the companies that are using the tech. There's no such thing as the "perfect solution," and beware anyone who tells you otherwise. It's all trade-offs.

- Recruit technical leadership with a teaching orientation. The best way to ensure that your CTO is going to make you a better CEO is to hire a CTO who likes to teach. Make it clear that you're looking for someone to drive change and educate you and the team. Beware CTOs who try to "shield" you from the details. Being able to explain complex things simply is a job requirement.

Ultimately, leading technical teams comes down to curiosity and courage. You must be humble, ask questions, and read a lot about engineering. If incremental changes aren't getting better results, you need the courage to change technical leadership. Keep changing and trying new things until you start seeing positive momentum, and then get out of the team's way.

Sarah Bird, CEO of Moz

This is the power of knowing your weaknesses, personally and organizationally. You can invest in them. Double down on them. And benefit your entire company in the process.

If You've Got Strong Roots, Might as Well Grow Tall

Thankfully, founders don't just come with weaknesses (despite what our brains tell us while we're trying to fall asleep). A founder's strengths and passions will often become the organization's strengths. Smart organizations should use this to their advantage by crafting a business model, a team structure, a product, and sales/marketing channels that lean on these strengths and minimize (but don't ignore) the weaknesses.

We did this unintentionally at Moz, but with great results. We'd created a community of hundreds of thousands of marketers, a website with millions of monthly visits, and an authoritative, trustworthy voice in the industry. It would be foolish, given that strength at the top of the funnel, to have an enterprise-exclusive offering that served only a tiny swath of our audience. Instead, we used a self-service model, with a low friction signup and onboarding process, to attract thousands of free trials to our software each month.

Moz aligned the strength of community and high volumes of relevant traffic to a business that maximized the value given and received. Recall that we'd started as a consulting business, serving only a tiny fraction of our potential audience (literally a half dozen clients a month at most). Transitioning to a free-to-try software subscription gave us massive improvements in gross margin, growth potential, and connection between our strengths and our structure.

Know Thyself: Not Just a Biblical T-Shirt Slogan

There's a crucial prerequisite needed to double down on your strengths or combat your weaknesses as a founder, team, and business: self-knowledge.

Tragically, most of us have a poor understanding of our own strengths and weaknesses. For me, this lack of self-awareness led me to grow muttonchops, to teach myself how to drive a stick shift while watching exactly one YouTube video in a Belfast hotel room, and to start a software company with virtually no programming experience.

Short of nearly killing yourself on winding Irish roads or going massively into debt, how do you figure out your weaknesses? I've listed a few of the most useful ways below. If only I'd known of them before I grew out those damn sideburns.

- If you're a founder, make a list of the previous successes and failures you've had in your career, and of the elements of running a business with which you're familiar and comfortable. Chances are high that your weaknesses will be the items not on that list.

- Keep a running record of successes and failures. A shared document where people and teams record initiatives and investments that kicked butt or went off the rails won't be useful right away. But over time, you can categorize and analyze these and recognize useful patterns.

- When problems arise on a team, a project, or an area of investment, do you/could you (or your founders) personally step in to provide the remedy? When you/the founder(s) do the work in this arena, does the issue generally get fixed, or does your position get stronger? If the answers are consistently "yes," you've found a strength. If it's "no," you've got a weakness.

- List functional areas of the business (ignore how you're actually subdividing the teams/people) and record which teams or roles have high turnover versus strong retention, which have an easy time recruiting versus a tough slog getting qualified applicants. These recruiting and retention numbers have strong correlation with strengths and weaknesses.

- If you haven't yet started your business or are in the early stages, use your strategic plans to identify hits and misses. Chances are, some aspects of the plan are fully formed, with high confidence, and a strong road map of tactics. Others will have a lot of hand waving and hopeful eventualities, with the details left to be filled in by either the people you hope to hire or a model of execution, learning, and iteration. That latter group will almost certainly be what trips you up.

- Ask. Question your team. Your investors. Your friends and loved ones. Your customers. Your past managers and coworkers. So often we fail to see ourselves clearly, leaning too far in the direction of pride or false humility (sometimes both at once on different aspects). If one person mentions an attribute of yours as a virtue or a failing, consider it. If multiple people mention the same one, you've got a more concrete answer. And remember: the more receptive you are, the more honest people will be.

These tactics are not exhaustive, and they might not uncover all the risks or opportunities you'll need. Vigilance and ongoing reflection are equally essential and equally difficult. Those same strengths a founder shows in the early years of a company may turn to weaknesses at scale, just as practice and experience over years of failure and learning can turn a weakness into a strength.

CHAPTER 6

DON'T RAISE MONEY FOR THE WRONG REASONS OR FROM THE WRONG PEOPLE

The best entrepreneurs . . . know how to tell an amazing story that will convince talent and investors to join in on the journey.

—Alejandro Cremades, 2016

If you want a better-than-average shot at being counted among the world's most admired, most successful entrepreneurs, you'll almost certainly need to raise money from investors (unless you're independently wealthy, or your father's last name rhymes with "rump"). Fundraising is glamorous. The press writes about you. Your friends congratulate you. Your competitors fear you. The office and the perks improve. Salaries go up. And, supposedly, everything else about your business (customer growth, recruiting, marketing) benefits, too. Plus, it can win you new friends. My wife once physically stopped me from shouting "Drinks are on me!" at a bar on St. Patrick's Day, because I'd just received a funding offer over email. Keep in mind, the money wasn't in the bank, but I was already drunk on the idea of it (and two Moscow mules).

But there are a multitude of reasons why, if you're not building a business 100 percent aligned with their model, raising money from institutional investors is a terrible, no good, very bad idea.

We raised our first round of $1.1 million in 2007 with Michelle Goldberg from Ignition Partners and Kelly Smith from Curious Office. Since then, Moz has raised two subsequent rounds totaling another $28 million. I was privileged to spend a few years on the board of another venture-backed startup, San Francisco's Minted. I was also, unfortunately, the beneficiary of months of fruitless fundraising attempts nearly every six months from 2009 to 2012. And I've spent countless hours over the years with dozens of other venture-backed CEOs and founders, hearing their stories. My exposure to the startup investment world hasn't been as deep as some, but it's been enough.

Venture capital changed Moz. It changed me. It made me a better, more focused, more ambitious entrepreneur. I learned more in my first two years as CEO of a VC-backed startup than I did in the seven prior years at a struggling family-run business with my mom.

The money we raised at Moz and the help of the partners who joined our board were remarkable gifts. I couldn't have come this far in my professional career or written this book without them. But when asked if I'd raise money again in any of my hypothetical future business endeavors, my answer has changed over the last few years, from "Yes, definitely" to "Oof . . . I really hope not."

Why? Two reasons. The odds. And the cost.

I Mean, You Don't *Technically* Sign the Deal in Blood

Founders usually think (I certainly did) that when investors put money into your company, there's alignment in the outcome. You're on the same team. Everyone's cheering for the company's success, and everyone's willing to put in hard work to make that happen.

Forgive me, but I have to take a little reality hammer and smash your founder delusion.

Look, investors aren't jerks (I mean, some of them are. Looking at you, Caldbeck. You too, KPCB.). They aren't lying when they loudly proclaim that they're 100 percent behind you and want to do everything possible to help. It's true. In the beginning. But over time, their incentives change according to your performance versus the rest of their investment portfolio. That's when misalignment occurs, and if you and your company, especially your leadership team, aren't prepared for it, reality can hit hard.

Institutional investors and angel investors alike face long odds with any individual company. That's why they place a lot of bets. A tiny number of companies will make them money, and the rest will lose money, break even, or deliver returns too small to "beat the market" (i.e., earn more than the 8–10 percent compound, year-over-year growth of the S&P 500). Realistically, the distribution for the average venture fund looks like this:

- Out of ten investments, five will fail.
- Another three will return an insignificant amount.
- The final two will combine to form the bulk of any gains.

Startup investing follows the Pareto principle: 20 percent of the investments return 80 percent of the fund.

If you go into the fundraising process, or come out of it, even successfully, thinking that you now have a partnership of equals, a partnership of aligned interests, a partnership where their success is tied to your own, you will have a shit experience. I don't want to spoil the end of the book when we're only in the middle, but trust me, it happens a lot (if you can't handle the suspense, flip to chapter 17).

Here's what I wish investors would tell founders before they put money into their company:

- "I invest in dozens to hundreds of startups. Eight out of ten don't return any money, but I don't know which ones those will be, so I have to place a lot of bets."
- "If you end up looking like one of the companies that will be that big moneymaker, I'll lavish you with attention, as will the rest of my partners. We'll make you feel important, powerful, respected—like a dear friend and close confidant, and maybe the kid I never had."
- "If things go the other way, and you look like one of the duds, expect that our attention and interest will fade; it may start to feel like meetings with you and requests from you are more of a chore than a shared mission."
- "One of our biggest tools in either preserving a growing company's prospects for success or attempting to recover a flailing startup is to replace the CEO. If things are going well, that's very unlikely. If things go poorly, especially for an extended stretch, it's much more likely."
- "If you would be happiest building a strong, stable business that's profitable, that makes you wealthy and happy, that has reasonable harmony between your work and the rest of your life, we are absolutely the wrong choice."
- "If you cannot imagine doing anything but grinding as hard as you can, with relentless focus, and demanding the same from the team around you in pursuit of becoming an incredibly rare moonshot of a billion-plus-dollar business, even though the odds suck, congratulations, our model is a match."

- "Personal happiness and successfully raising venture capital are rarely correlated."

I don't mean to be overly negative on the venture model. If I seem harsh, it's because the tech media and startup culture has done such a miserable job portraying reality. And VCs themselves—whether on Twitter, onstage at tech events, or in the coffee shops where entrepreneurs meet them—don't, either. Most will downplay the odds of failure, oversell the value they bring, and, if they're truly excited about your business, make you believe you're a world-conquering genius. For a very brief window of time, they are the ultimate optimists. And for a brief window of time, you'll be one, too.

How VCs Lose, Even When They Win

According to statistics from the National Venture Capital Association, an estimated 30–40 percent of high-potential US startups fail completely in the sense that investors lose all their money. But if you define startup success as delivering an expected return on investment, a whopping 95 percent of startups would be considered failures. That often also means they fail to deliver meaningful compensation to founders or employees, as well. Considering the countless hours, stress, and effort it takes to start a company, receive investor backing, and put that money to work, that failure rate seems almost unbelievable. It's like agreeing to exclusively produce movies starring Nicolas Cage. Who would willingly sign up for such a painful journey with such awful odds of success? And why would so many billions of dollars go into it?

(Also, have you seen *Ghost Rider*? Don't.)

To understand this quandary requires understanding the world of venture itself—how VCs get their investment dollars, what their goals are, and how their funds operate. Just as it pays to understand the motivations and attributes of a supplier, a partner, a contractor, or a potential customer for your business, so, too, it pays to know how institutional investors operate. In fact, it's actually more critical than many of those others because once you sign up for venture capital, you're usually locked in for the life of the company (or until/unless you become part of the 5 percent that meets your investors' return expectations).

Venture firms generally get money from four places: large endowments from very wealthy individuals or families; pension funds from big employers; well-endowed university funds; and evil billionaire masterminds.

(Technically, the billionaires don't have to be evil, but then they just fit into the first category.)

Together, these sources of capital are called limited partners, or "LPs." Much as startups raise money from VCs, VCs raise money from LPs. The venture capitalists will try to convince an LP's investment committee that their approach to startup investment opportunities, their team's judgment and experience, and their fund's assistance will produce a winning ROI.

The best VCs are good people as well as good investors. But they're only human and beholden to commitments they've made to their own investors. Incentives matter, and until you can empathize with theirs, it will be a struggle to understand their (mostly logical) behavior.

Their goal is to improve upon the rate of return that would have been achieved through putting the money into public stocks, bonds, or other investment vehicles. The target is 12 percent annual growth, which, over the life of a ten-year fund, means returning three times the fund size (e.g., $300 million on a $100 million fund). Beating the market is hard. Like, really, really hard. Only about 5 percent of venture investment firms actually succeed at it. A further 10 percent will return two to three times, the next 35 percent will return one to two times, and the bottom 50 percent return less than their initial fund. Thankfully, for all those employed at the 95 percent of firms who don't deliver on their goal, it can take fifteen-plus years to determine whether a fund is successful due to the extended time it takes for them to make investments and for those companies to die, sell, or IPO.

The only way the 5 percent of successful VCs make their returns is through enormous outcomes from a tiny number of companies. It's usually one or two investments out of dozens to hundreds a fund might make that deliver almost all the gains. This makes intuitive sense if you're a close observer of the startup world—for every Google, Facebook, Snapchat, or eBay, there are thousands of startups most of us have never heard of, and never will.

Moz and its investors can serve as a good example of why only "enormous outcomes" fit the model.

In 2004, Ignition Partners raised $300 million from their LPs. Those LPs expect that, over the next decade, Ignition will return at least three times the amount invested. That's $900 million.

In November 2007, Ignition used $1 million of that $300 million fund to invest in Moz. That deal valued Moz at $7.1 million, making Ignition's ownership about 14 percent of the company's shares. Let's imagine that in 2011, Moz sold to an acquirer for $40 million (a not-so-far-fetched scenario that we'll talk more about in chapter 9 while I cringe at my past decisions). The returns would look something like this:

PARTY	AMOUNT INVESTED	% OF COMPANY OWNED	AMOUNT MADE IN A $40 MILLION ACQUISITION
Rand	N/A	32.3%	$12,920,000
Gillian	N/A	32.3%	$12,920,000
Moz employees	N/A	20%	$8,000,000
Ignition Partners	$1,000,000	14%	$5,600,000
Curious Office	$100,000	1.4%	$560,000

Technically, in the scenario above, Ignition's partners are beating their model's forecast. Their investment is returning 5.6 times the capital back to the fund and doing so earlier than the LPs need or expect. But for Ignition, this would be a useless return. It sounds absurd, but it's true: following this example, the partners would need to fund three hundred companies with a guarantee of the same successful outcome on each to hit their goal.

There's no way the fund can make even half that many investments, and the success rate, as we discussed, has a nonlinear distribution that's strongly weighted to the top few companies. In the dispassionate eyes of a mathematical, dollar-focused analysis, it would be better to have put that $1 million and, more important, the time one of Ignition's twelve partners spent (sourcing the deal, making the investment, sitting on the board, and helping the company) into another startup.

Read on and tell me this doesn't sound like an insane game of high-stakes craps in a Bond film, only with nerds.

We're starting a venture capital partnership together. We'll call our firm "Scorpio Ventures"; it has a nice, subtly evil ring to it. We pitch some LPs and convince them we're investing geniuses, raising our first fund of $400 million.

After a few months of driving around in our Teslas, meeting entrepreneurs at hipster espresso shops, and crafting our Internet of Things market thesis, we find a company we love: the Globex Corporation. We negotiate with the founders, agree on a pre-money valuation of $45 million, and invest $15 million from our fund in their Series A. For the next two years, we watch them grow like a weed, supporting the team by leveraging our networks, our wisdom, and our time. At our ninth board meeting, they announce they have an offer from industry giant C. M. Burns Inc. for a whopping $450 million. The founders are ecstatic! Their company is worth ten times what it was just two short years ago. But the Scorpio Ventures team is having a bad day. Why?

Because $450 million returns only $112 million to us. That's almost ten times our original investment, which sounds phenomenal, but to reach our promise of three times the returns on our $400 million fund, we need to get to $1.2 billion. The math of startups is now working against us, because Globex was our hottest investment, and with them out of our portfolio, the odds of making up the other 90 percent–plus of our needed returns are considerably worse.

We might even be tempted to fight the founders on the company's sale, arguing that in another four years, Globex could be worth five to ten times as much as it is today. The founders' families and friends (and those of their stock-option-holding employees) might say they're foolish to give up a surefire, massive payday on the outside chance of an even bigger one years from now. After all, once you've made $100 million from selling your company, does a few hundred million more really mean all that much?

But for us, letting the sale go through (and it's up to us, because our investment terms with the founders give us veto rights over any transaction) is almost equally foolish. Upon hearing that we okayed the purchase, our own family and friends, at least the ones who understand the mathematics of venture, would be fully justified in telling us "You're totally mad, Scorpio!"

(Did I squander my youth watching *The Simpsons*? No. It was clearly time well spent.)

From this overly simplified model, anyone considering entry to the world of venture-backed startups should have at least this one crucial takeaway: unless your business is in alignment with the venture model of investing in many failures to find a small handful of absurdly successful mega-winners, this path is not for you. Get comfortable with the odds, or don't roll the dice. The venture business is about outliers.

If you want to raise money, or if you're joining a startup that's planning to raise money (or already has), you *have* to understand these odds and this risk model or you'll be an unwitting pawn in a game where the deck's stacked against you. If your startup raises VC, but you're unwilling to do high-risk things that could kill your business nine out of ten times but might make you a unicorn, you're not aligned with the venture model. That misalignment can mean losing your job and your company, or getting in a nasty stalemate with your board of directors.

Alignment means that you and your company are in this for the long haul, and recognize that only an exceptionally unlikely, multi-hundred-million- or billion-dollar outcome constitutes "success." It means you have a plan for how to turn your idea into a company with either hundreds of millions of dollars in revenue or tens to hundreds of millions of users. It means saying no to the early offers (that may or may not materialize) that could make you, your cofounders, and your early employees into millionaires so you can play the long odds of the future.

This journey, by the way, is getting longer. National Venture Capital Association data showed that the average time from funding to exit (via an acquisition or an IPO) increased dramatically from 3.1 years in 2001 to 6.8 years by 2014. Those figures count all exits, including many that did not generate a positive return for investors or founders. When EquityZen limited its analysis to only those startups that had an IPO (and thus, almost definitely generated returns for at least its investors and probably most founders, too), it found that from founding to public offering takes an average of eleven years.

In the startup world, even if you raise money, becoming an overnight success doesn't happen overnight.*

---

* While this chapter has focused on venture capital, there are some alternatives for aspiring startup builders. I've covered these a bit more (along with some resources) in the book's afterword.

CHAPTER 7

SO YOU'VE DECIDED TO ASK COMPLETE STRANGERS FOR MILLIONS OF DOLLARS

For the first seven years of Moz's life as a venture-backed startup, we had it pretty sweet. With growth rates of 100 percent year-over-year, operating with a model that investors and acquirers valued at many multiples of revenue, we got a lot of attention. My inbox was regularly filled with invitations to connect with people and participate in events that seem outlandish even to this day. A dinner at Sheryl Sandberg's house (thanks to an invitation from her immensely kind late husband, Dave Goldberg). An evening soiree with UN Secretary General Ban Ki-moon (at the home of one of the partners from our Seattle investors at Ignition). I'd travel to Silicon Valley and be swarmed with offers of coffees, dinners, drinks, come-by-the-office-and-let-me-show-you-arounds from companies and people I idolized. I felt important. And wanted.

But years later, when our growth rate slowed to 20 percent, then 10 percent, and it had been a long time since our big fundraising rounds, that professional and social validation from my fellow VC-backed startups waned. Our board meetings went from the most important thing on our investors' calendars, never to be missed, to getting rescheduled three times and being attended via video calls rather than in-person. The technology press stopped writing about us. Potential investors stopped emailing. Sure, our products were getting better, our company was still growing, and we were technically more profitable, but startup culture is about one thing: growth. As fast as you can. At all costs.

If I haven't scared you away from venture capital yet, don't worry—it gets worse. Because we're about to dive into the heartrending, ugly, unfair, why-does-everyone-get-it-but-you process of fundraising.

I kid! I kid! Sort of.

For some entrepreneurs, fundraising is part of the fun of building a company. They relish the exposure to critical feedback, the social aspects of those hard-to-get introductions, the prestige of being in meetings with seven- or eight-figure outcomes, and the congratulatory press and celebratory experience of finally closing the deal.

That's not me. I loathe the concept of direct sales—of convincing someone to back you or buy from you, rather than earning their interest and attention through your good works and organic marketing. Little wonder I love SEO, eh?

But regardless of your predilection or aversion to fundraising, the process is incredibly tough, with dismal odds. My goal is to improve yours by making my experiences transparent and providing a road map for how this insular, seemingly inscrutable world works.

In 2009, Moz was growing fast, profitable, and, at least in my opinion at the time, in need of another round of funding to help us accelerate that growth and dominate the SEO software market. From April to October, I talked to dozens of venture capital firms, most of them on or near Sand Hill Road, an arterial connector between Highway 101 and I-280 in Menlo Park, California, famous for its density of low-slung office buildings housing many of the world's best-known VCs. I'd spent the better part of the spring earning introductions to these potential investors, almost entirely through other CEOs who were familiar with or fans of Moz (over the years, I'd helped out a lot of these folks with SEO issues or recommendations, and they were, in turn, very kind to me).

I was twenty-nine years old at the time, and had as much impostor syndrome as I would have had pretending to belong in the Batcave. In my first few meetings I was so jittery and nervous that I can't even remember what happened (which is probably a blessing; I didn't hear back from most of those investors). But by meeting four or five, I was getting the hang of things.

You start with an email introduction, best delivered directly by one of the VC's current or prior portfolio CEOs. The one below (as near a prototype as you'll find) came via Mike Cassidy, whose company Ruba was later acquired by Google, and connected me with James Slavet, a partner at Greylock Capital, whom I'd meet that summer.

Subject: intro SEOmoz

Mike Cassidy < ▓▓▓▓▓▓▓▓ >   6/12/09

To James, Rand

Hey James,

I had dinner with Rand Fishkin, the CEO of SEOmoz, a few nights ago. Great guy with a very interesting business. He's been approached by a few VC's, but he's really interested in the right chemistry. I thought of you. I'll let you two chat if there's mutual interest.

Hope all is well with you!

Mike :)

Mike Cassidy
CEO, Ruba

The email connection usually kicked off an introductory phone call between me and the investor. If that call went well, they'd ask when I would next be in "the Valley," a.k.a. Silicon Valley. My 2009 fundraising attempt dictated no fewer than four separate trips to that valley, most with four or more separate meetings spread over a few days.

I'm most comfortable eating homemade cookies and watching the Die Hard canon while my wife shouts advice to the characters on-screen. This was not my world.

Just driving into the parking lot was humbling. I'd be in a bare-bones rental car, surrounded by shiny, six-figure automobiles. The lobbies were always an indescribable combination of low-key and utterly terrifying. The furniture didn't look ostentatious, but it clearly cost a fortune. The names of companies and founders on the walls weren't flashy but were meant to impress upon visitors the billions of dollars of wealth that had come through these premises. To me, these complexes were always asking "who the @#$% do you think you are, coming here?" I can't imagine how doubly intimidating it would be as a woman founder or a founder of color to see only white (and a few Asian) men on the staff, in the magazines of the coffee table, and celebrated on those walls highlighting great exits.

Usually, the partner I was meeting was running ten to twenty minutes late, so I'd wait in the lobby, willing my resolve to stay cool, calm, and confident, double-checking my notes about their bio, past companies, current deals, and anything they'd written or published. The meetings were always an hour, minus whatever time had been lost up front. If we started twenty minutes late, we went forty minutes. Maybe that alone was a bad sign for me. . . . I'd assume the more interesting deals got the overage.

But the fascinating part came at the end of the meeting or in the email follow-up from the investors who seemed genuinely interested. They'd tell me (or I'd ask) to speak to some of their portfolio CEOs and ask about their value as a partner and their support as a firm. Every VC believed himself or (in, unfortunately, only two cases out of almost fifty) *her*self to have strong references from their CEOs. I diligently followed up every time, and talked to at least two or three CEOs funded by a dozen or so venture firms. Of those, the majority did have good, though not always glowingly positive, things to say. And even though it was my first time speaking to these CEOs, many were happy to give me an honest and surprisingly cold or even directly negative feedback about their investors. I found this disconnect between the confidence of the partner and the honesty of the founder/CEO valuable and refreshing.

If you go down the venture funding path, make sure you do the same. And for those of you who get funded or who already are, please carry on this tradition of putting your fellow entrepreneurs first. It helps make the land-mine-laden game of startup investment a little less dangerous and a little more camaraderie-filled.

It's not just this closeness and rapport among founders or the reputation VCs inherit that makes them, more often than not, fair players in the startup game. Deal flow is the other component.

In the movie *The Social Network*, Mark Zuckerberg, portrayed by Jesse Eisenberg, insults a group of investors who hope to put money into Facebook, citing his friend Sean Parker, and walks out. It is indeed true that Facebook's founder arrived late to a meeting with the VC firm Sequoia (whom I pitched on behalf of Moz, twice, and whom, I'd agree, has a fairly deserved reputation for humorlessness). In his pajamas, the Facebook founder delivered a "top 10 reasons not to invest in us" pitch, and mentioned Sean Parker, whom Sequoia had fired from the board of another company (Plaxo).

That's an extreme example of a real phenomenon. VCs develop connections and reputations based on their actions, and when a founder or executive feels mistreated by their investors, word spreads fast. That mistreated founder, and their friends, are less likely to refer other startups to that investor in the future, and if a very hot deal that many VCs are interested in arises, those founders may opt to choose based on reputation and on references from their network. Thus, investors have a strong incentive, one tied to their future success in earning important and valuable deals, to treat founders and portfolio companies well.

My experience with investor Brad Feld of Foundry Group could not have been more atypical. In 2012, I had one phone call with Brad on a Monday, during which he invited me (and my COO) to come visit Boulder at the end of that same week, to pitch their entire partnership. We spent nearly the whole day with Foundry's four partners. Brad took us out to dinner. As soon as we ordered, he told us he wanted to invest. Then he spent another ninety minutes with us after the meal, talking about all the aspects of Foundry's involvement with Moz. I never felt that Brad was playing games with us, or that he ever treated us with anything but the utmost respect and friendship. He was a mensch that day, that evening, and ever since.

One conversation in particular stuck in my head. I asked Brad how Foundry would react if we were offered a deal in the next couple of years that looked great to Moz's founders and employees, but didn't provide the kind of return on investment that Foundry sought. My recollection won't be perfect, but to the best of my memory, Brad said:

> I've worked with a lot of entrepreneurs over the last fifteen years. Sometimes their first company goes well. Sometimes it doesn't. But I'm patient. I pick founders because they're people I want to work with, and I hope I get to work with them again. So if they have a chance to do what they want, we never stand in the way. My relationship is one that spans decades and companies, bankruptcies and exits. It's like a marriage—I want to be there for richer or poorer.

I've never felt so confident saying yes to an offer as I did to his.

No Such Thing as a Free Round of Funding

A question I hear often from aspiring entrepreneurs is: "How much about my company will VCs really control?" The answer is complex.

Investor and founder relations are generally positive. There are always contentious issues (as there should be in a high-growth company), but when things are going well for the company, they're also going well between you and your investors. However, if things take a turn for the worse, and it appears the company is in serious trouble, one of the primary powers a board of directors holds is to replace the CEO. Sometimes, this can only be done with the CEO/founder's consent, but other times, preferred stockholders (a.k.a. investors) have the ability to remove you or your cofounder from the company even against your will. What seemed like a minor point in a giant contract signed in a funding event can have a profound impact on your relationship to your board and your company.

I've spoken to dozens of founders over the years whose companies were "taken away from them" by their investors and boards. In some of these cases, it was probably a wise decision for the company. In others, it may have been a bad faith move that hurt the company's prospects even more. But as a founder, it's critical to keep in mind your motivations and how they align with those of your investors. Even when you all want only what's best for the company's survival, growth, and success, there can be varied beliefs about what will lead to that best outcome. Statistics are on your side—founder-led startups tend to dramatically outperform non-founder-led startups. But being removed from a leadership role, or from the company entirely, is a real possibility founders must face.

When you sign up with an investor, you'll agree to a lot of terms and clauses that can be a peculiar combination of seemingly unimportant and concerningly scary. I have three strong pieces of advice. First, do not attempt to raise money or talk to potential investors without reading Brad Feld's superb, transparent, and surprisingly fun-to-read guide *Venture Deals*. Second, get your investors to explain each piece of the term sheet (the initial offer upon which the final paperwork will be based) to you, then get your attorney (yes, you need one; no, your cousin who watches lots of *Law & Order* doesn't count) and (if you have one) a savvy entrepreneur friend to explain the same pieces to you. If the stories don't align, you'll have a strong answer to my third and final suggestion on this topic: don't sign anything with anyone you don't trust 100 percent and don't believe has your best interests (and not just their portfolio's returns) at heart.

This last one sounds more difficult than it is. Thanks to the interconnectedness of the entrepreneurial world and the general bias that startup folks have to put the interests of their fellow founders (even ones they've never met before) ahead of investors, reputation is earned and transmitted quickly. If your company fits the mold for venture, or even for angels, outreach to other founders in your field or your geography is surprisingly effective. I've been consistently amazed at how willing other entrepreneurs have been to take my emails and phone calls, to make introductions, and to give their unvarnished opinions. Take advantage of this camaraderie, and if you manage to get funding or become successful, pay it forward and help the next generation.

One final, unorthodox tip: if possible, build your expertise before you build your network, and build your network before you build your company. Each one leads elegantly into the next. If you have deep experience and skills in a particular aspect of startup building or technology that makes an hour on the phone with you deeply valuable and valued by entrepreneurs and startup teams, you've got a clear, compelling path to build a powerful network. Assist a handful of people and companies with their issues (as a consultant, a member of the team, or simply an outsider who loves to help others) and you'll have a built-in network to assist in your fundraising process. That network is what takes the fundraising process from near impossibility to potentially achievable.

Yes, it's frustrating that the worlds of startup financing are a closed ecosystem, exclusive and walled-off in their nerd-paradises. But you can make friends with the gatekeepers. And once you do, the inhabitants can be surprisingly affable.

CHAPTER 8
FOUNDING A TOP 5 PERCENT STARTUP MAY NOT MAKE YOU RICH

Economically, you can think of a startup as a way to compress your whole working life into a few years. Instead of working at a low intensity for forty years, you work as hard as you possibly can for four.

—**Paul Graham, May 2004**

About once a month, I get an email from an entrepreneur telling me they're seeking investment and asking if I'd be interested in learning more about their company. My response has been the same for years:

> *Unfortunately, I can't invest in your company, because I don't have the money. Hopefully, someday, Moz's growth will provide liquidity, but for now I just own private stock. Wish you luck!*

As of this writing, my wife and I have about two year's worth of savings in the bank. She still has the used 2003 Kia Spectra she got in 2004, but I've never owned a car myself. I walk to work and back each day, often with an umbrella because we live in Seattle. Our apartment is only a few years old, in a high-density part of town, and plenty big enough for the two of us. We've even been lucky enough to help some family out with money in the past. But owning shares, even a large amount, in a private company like Moz doesn't generate the kind of payout that many folks would assume.

I don't share this story for sympathy; my salary is $220,000 a year, an amount that enables terrific freedom, the ability to help out family, and some reckless spending (mostly on travel) and helps us cover Seattle's insane rent prices. I share it because the startup culture has convinced many, many folks that if you start a company that turns into a multimillion-dollar venture, you've hit the jackpot. That conditioning has been ingrained in the gold-rush mentality of Silicon Valley geographically and of the tech startup field worldwide. But statistically speaking, this isn't the case.

Even Successful Startup Founders Don't Get Rich (Quick)

We've talked about how most startups fail. But it's not just investors who lose out. Founders and early employees are hit especially hard because they tend to take compensation below market rates for the first, riskiest years of a new venture. As is true across the economic spectrum in the first few decades of the twenty-first century, the distribution of wealth in startups goes massively, disproportionately, to the few at the very top of the field.

Conversely, a job at an emerging contender (think Box, Slack, Airbnb,

Snapchat) in the tech world or at a major, public tech leader (Microsoft, Google, Amazon, Facebook) can provide salary and stock that has a vastly better chance of making you a lot of money in a few short years. Here's a comparison of the average tech salaries in Seattle from 2001 to 2015 and my own earnings at Moz during the same period:*

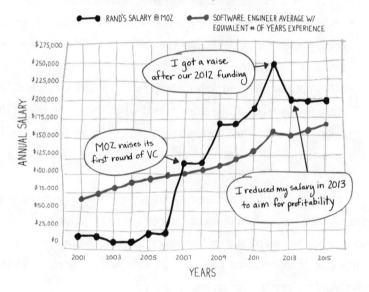

This chart doesn't account for the value of my stock, and hopefully, someday, that stock will turn into an asset that can be liquidated.

---

*In case you're curious, my salary in 2016 was about $205K and partway through 2017, I got a raise to about $220K. Seattle software engineer salaries have continued to grow, and senior engineers' total comp at late-stage startups with at least ten years' experience average just over $180K.

But many would-be startup founders and startup employees have confusion about why, sometimes, ownership of a company makes the founders wealthy versus other times when it may not.

Let's assume a scenario in which you're starting a very traditional startup—one with investors and a board of directors and the goal of a financial exit that returns money to those investors. Initially, you and your cofounders own 100 percent of the company, but once you raise money, the company will issue shares that are divided into several segments:

- Common stock: the kind you and any cofounders own
- Preferred stock: the kind your investors own (which usually grants them some special rights, like the ability to get their money out first in a sale and to have a seat on the board of directors)
- Stock options: the kind your employees own (which gives them the right to buy stock at the price it held when they were issued the option—usually when they join the company or get a promotion or bonus)

If things go well, the value of your company will increase over time, and the stock should, accordingly, have more value, too. But in reality, stock owned by you (or by your employees, should they choose to exercise their options) can only be sold when there's a willing buyer. And willing buyers are rare.

Imagine there's a supposedly valuable painting sitting in your attic. You put it up for auction, but no one bids. The painting may still have value, but it can't be turned into cash unless you find a buyer who wants it, is willing to pay, and has the liquid assets to do so. The same is true of stock in your startup. You own something that, on paper, has great worth, but it can't pay your bills or help you with the down payment on a house.

Private companies, especially startups, are very risky investments. The 90 percent failure rate keeps most types of investors away from the field. Government regulations on who can invest in startups also plays a role—in the United States, in order to put money into a startup like the one described here, you need to be an "accredited investor," meaning you have net worth of $1,000,000 or more (excluding the value of your primary residence) and/or income of greater than $200,000 ($300,000 if married) in each of the last two years.*

If the risks and the regulations don't keep buyers of your startup stock away, the fundamental attributes of private stock very likely will. When investors buy stock in publicly traded companies on an exchange like the NASDAQ or NYSE, there's a set trading price, historical data, and a wealth of information (required and regulated by law) available to everyone. In a private company, those requirements don't exist. The price can be set purely by the buyer and seller agreeing to it. No law provides buyers with a legal claim to information about the company's performance, structure, financials, or other data. Some private transactions may include information rights along with the stock sale, but these must be approved by the board of directors and add complexity and reporting requirements to the company, which can be a drag on the poor accounting/financial team (often an area with thin resources in a startup).

For a variety of reasons, investors frown on private stock sales by

---

*The qualifications required to be an "accredited investor," and some of the restrictions around investing more broadly are changing thanks to Title III of Obama's 2016 JOBS act. For more, see https://aaplonline.com/how-the-jobs-act-opens-deal-flow-for-non-accredited -investors.

founders (with some exceptions). Historically, they've believed that founders should be kept "hungry"; chasing that big exit (a sale or IPO) and knowing that until they do, the value of their stock is locked up. The assumption is that founders who have lots of money already will be less motivated to put all their efforts into the company's growth, and that a large payout may distract a founder as she tries to manage her newfound wealth.

Your personal success—reputation, future employability, financial liquidity—becomes inherently tied to the company's. If the company sinks, you sink. But if the company succeeds, you—depending on how much stock you own and whether or not you find a buyer for it—might succeed, too.

Sometimes, if your company is growing especially fast and multiple investors are interested, but there's not enough preferred stock in a fundraising round to go around, there may be an unusual exception made, and an investor will purchase private stock directly from founders (or, even more rarely, from early employees who've executed their stock options). But this rarity depends on a confluence of forces: an in-demand company with high growth, more appetite than availability for company stock from investors, and buy-in from the board of directors and existing investors because, even in these transactions, some special rights are often requested by the new shareholders (e.g., board observer seats, quarterly informational updates that normally go only to board members, etc.).

But if your startup is making millions of dollars and growing, could you, as founder and CEO, bump up your salary or your bonus and profit that way? In short, no, at least not without the consent of your board of directors. The board sets the CEO's salary and approves the salaries and stock compensation of employees, as well. This compensation is, in almost every startup, a function of the market averages. Worse, if you own lots of stock (even if that stock is illiquid), it's factored into your "total comp," and thus serves to make the cash portion of salary your leadership or board sets even lower.

(I have spent long hours trying to explain this to my brother-in-law to no avail. He repeatedly asks to borrow a couple million. Sorry, Ed. We really don't have it.)

Your investors have access to a diverse set of salary ranges across their portfolio companies, and they often buy additional data from aggregators of salary information, too. Using these aggregated statistics, they'll help you determine compensation ranges for the company. Reasonable arguments can be made on either side: being thrifty and relying on passion and the promise of stock option values to incentivize employees versus ponying up the top echelons of salaries to compete for talent with big companies and other high-paying startups in your field. But arguing for a salary that's far outside these ranges for a CEO or founder will garner contention and almost certain disapproval from your board.

It Takes a Lot of 7s and a Long Time to Win at Startup Roulette

In essence, founding a startup or being an early employee means taking a risk. You're sacrificing the certainty of a potentially higher-paying job with greater benefits at a more established company for what is typically a less-than-market-rate salary, bare-bones benefits, and the hope that if things go very well, and your company is one of the few that survive and thrive, your compensation will rise, the benefits will get better, and someday, if you're *extremely* lucky, your stock's value will exceed the delta between what you could have made in another job.

It's a gamble. But because the stories we hear always focus on the big winners—the Zuckerbergs and the Andreessens—we tend to forget that.

We also forget that startups take a long time to exit. Much longer than what popular culture would have you believe. Moz itself started in 2004. Thirteen years later, it is still going strong but despite moving on from what most would call "early-stage" to "mid-stage," has neither graduated out of the startup need for rapid growth nor returned money to its investors or employees. In many ways, Moz is a lucky outlier: the majority of startup founders' efforts fail entirely. But we are a great example of how foolish the idea that you can "invest four years and become a millionaire" is.

For all these reasons and more, it's often the case that founders of startups, even those that appear, from the outside, to be massively successful—raising large amounts of funding, growing at a fast clip, making a lot of money—may be (at least until or unless an exit arrives) financially worse off than their counterparts working mid-level jobs at a traditional firm. The venture capitalist and blogger Mark Suster gives wise advice to founders on how to talk about options with their team:

> We give out stock options. I hope they're worth money to you some day. But let them be icing on the cake. If they pay off handsomely that's great. But don't count on it. Don't let it be your motivator or your driving decision.

This same advice should be taken just as strongly by founders themselves. Your stock's "value" can blind you to the reality that private company stock is very difficult to sell, rarely appraised similarly to your investors' stakes in your company, and, if that sale ever does come to pass, it's reliant on forces largely beyond your control.

I've met plenty of people who've taken pay cuts to work at startups and then found out their stock is worth nothing. (It's happened to my friends and colleagues, and even to my wife.)

Does this mean you shouldn't found a startup? Or join an early-stage company? No. But it means you almost certainly shouldn't do it exclusively for the promise of short-term wealth. The idea that you can compress an entire career into a few years of work and be directly or consistently rewarded with cash for that compression is insanity borne out over and over by the stats. Yes, startups have better odds than the lottery, but they're dramatically worse than "put it all on red" at the casino. The myth that "founders get rich" has brought thousands of people into the world of startups potentially for the wrong reasons and almost certainly with the wrong expectations.

There are logical, wonderful reasons to start a company or to join a risky, early-stage venture. Chief among these is the freedom early-stage companies provide, especially to founders, to determine what you work on, how to structure that work, who to hire, who to keep on the team, and how every aspect of your organization will operate. Plus, you might have an idea, a product, or a mission that you really want to share with the world. It's an immense, stressful responsibility, but it's also intensely rewarding when it works.

And, many times, even when it doesn't.

One of the great things startups can do is massively accelerate your career path. If you've felt trapped in positions that don't challenge you, or constrain your earnings or influence potential, a few years at a startup, even one that ultimately fails, can dramatically shift that reality. Early-stage companies need people who are self-motivated, mission driven, and can get immense amounts of work done in short periods (by working very hard, by being efficient with their time, or both). Demonstrating that you have strategic vision, the ability to execute, and the qualities needed to recruit, motivate, and lead will make you a rare, desirable commodity in the modern economy. One of the reasons so many early-stage companies sell in small acquisitions (often called "acquihires") is precisely to get these proven, self-driven, multitalented people on board.

Moz has completed six transactions to accomplish precisely this. One of those was a young man who'd just graduated college but had built a useful product in his spare time at school that proved to me, and to our team, that he could be incredibly valuable. We paid a small acquisition price ($18,000) and brought him on board at Moz at a salary, with stock options, and with influence greater than what we'd have offered a candidate who simply applied to a job posting. Another was a pair of SEO professionals who'd built a successful consulting practice and whose skills we wanted internally for our product and engineering teams. We paid $330,000 (plus stock options and retention bonuses) to get them here, a nice multiple on their business in addition to strong salaries and benefits.

A startup can be a great way to visibly multiply what companies are willing to pay to bring you aboard. It might be a great way to level up your skills. And it has the outside chance of making you remarkably wealthy.

Just don't go in blinded by the money. Most of the time, startups are a comparatively poorly rewarded labor of passion.

CHAPTER 9

SCALABLE MARKETING FLYWHEELS > GROWTH HACKS

Growth hackers are a hybrid of marketer and coder, one who looks at the traditional question of "How do I get customers for my product?" and answers with A/B tests, landing pages, viral factor, email deliverability, and Open Graph. On top of this, they layer the discipline of direct marketing, with its emphasis on quantitative measurement, scenario modeling via spreadsheets, and a lot of database queries.

—from Andrew Chen's "Growth Hacker Is the New VP Marketing," 2012

At the start of 2009, in the wake of the great recession, Moz was in remarkably good shape. Following the successful launch of our link index tool, the team was frantically working to double down on our progress. But costs were holding us back. With greater resources, we could grow our data set and ward off any competitive pressures. Without it, we feared a well-funded copycat could easily take the market from us.

I wanted to raise another round of venture capital to help us scale.

I believed that, despite the awful VC climate (investment dollars going to startups had fallen off a cliff after the financial crisis of 2008), investors needed somewhere to put their money, and Moz was a growth opportunity with a steady two years of rising subscribers and revenue. In the first half of 2009 I made multiple trips to the Bay Area from Seattle, spent thousands on flights, hotels, and rental cars, and, after pitching more than forty individual partners at VC firms, had nothing to show for it.

So instead, we turned to the now-ubiquitous "growth hack" model in hopes of boosting revenue. That growth hack, in the form of an email marketing campaign, brought in a tremendous number of new customers and new revenue. But over time I've come to wish we'd never done it. At least, not the way we did.

It's Just a Little Hacking; What Could Go Wrong?

Our hack started with the assistance of a pair of brilliant marketers out of the UK, Ben Jesson and Dr. Karl Blanks, cofounders of Conversion Rate Experts. Their specialty was taking poorly performing web pages designed to sell a product and massively improving the percentage of visitors who converted into customers. This practice, called "conversion rate optimization," or CRO, is a powerful, meaningful part of a web marketer's toolbox. It's easy to see why: if you improve your conversion rate it has a massive impact on your customer and revenue growth (e.g., for every 100 visitors who visit your site today, 1 buys something, but tomorrow you make changes that double that to 2, or heck, just boost it to 1.1).

Ben and Karl, alongside an equally brilliant employee of theirs, Stephen Pavlovich (who'd later go on to found Conversion.com and marry one of my employees—long story, the wedding was lovely), worked with Moz to design three things: an update to our website's home page, a new version of the page that sold our software subscription, and a promotional email campaign. Their process sounds simple but is both ingenious and remarkably effective. I implore you to copy it:

Step 1: Ben, Karl, and Stephen asked us for contact information of three different types of Moz users:

Paying subscribers

Subscribers who'd tried Moz's products but left

Members of the Moz community (who engaged in our blog comments and discussion forums) but who hadn't yet tried our subscription

Step 2: They conducted phone interviews (and a few in-person interviews at conferences and in their offices) with several dozen members of each group, asking questions like:

What do you do professionally? What's your job title? What are your responsibilities?

What made you initially sign up for Moz? What objections did you have, and how did you overcome them?

(For those who were long-term customers) What do you use Moz for? What does it help you do?

(For those who'd signed up, but quit) What did you hope Moz would do that it didn't? What made you cancel your subscription? What would have made you stay?

(And, for those who were free members of our community, but had never signed up for our software) What holds you back from signing up? What would make you try Moz's subscription?

Step 3: They used the answers to identify the right target customers for our products and to craft messaging toward this group. For us, these tended to be professional web marketers who cared deeply about their search rankings and search traffic. They were either consultants (independent or at an agency) or in-house marketers (who worked full time for a single website/brand).

Step 4: They compiled a list of objections that those who'd frequently visited Moz but never tried our software had to signing up. They additionally built a list of reasons subscribers loved the product, descriptions of how they'd overcome objections of their own, and a long set of testimonials based on those interviews.

Step 5: Stephen worked with us to design a new landing page that focused on addressing the objections we heard most commonly among the group that matched our best customers in terms of their traits and professional focus but had never signed up. That new page was almost eight times the length of the original version. You can actually still see a comparison of the two on Conversion Rate Experts' website via a case study they made.

Step 6: Lastly, we all worked together to create a promotional offer that would go out to all the members of our community who'd never tried our software before. This list numbered nearly 120,000 email addresses.

The new landing page was the first big win. When compared with the prior version, it converted visitors into buyers at nearly twice the rate of the prior page, a phenomenal improvement. To this day, I'm a huge believer in the power of Conversion Rate Experts' objection-gathering and objection-addressing methodology. It's something I urge marketers of all stripes to attempt on their own landing pages.

But good conversion practices don't fall under the "growth hacks" umbrella. Our email campaign, however, did. The original email from 2009:

Hi [redacted],

Thanks for hanging out on the SEOmoz blog this year; I'm thrilled you're a fan of our work. As a special thank you for your support, here's a gift that will (in my humble opinion) have an enormous, positive impact on your SEO performance in 2009: **a full month of SEOmoz's PRO membership for only $1.**

There's only one itsy bitsy teeny catch: because we offer one-on-one Q+A with the SEOmoz staff, we've had to limit the number of places available at the discounted rate. So while we're sending this offer out to 122,451 SEOmoz members, it's only valid for the **first 5,000 people who respond.** Don't delay—we'll be promoting our once-in-a-lifetime $1 offer on the blog on Monday, February 9th. So act now, before the riotous, can't-be-tamed masses hear of this.

To claim your first month of PRO membership for just $1, visit www .seomoz.org/trypro and enter **SUCCESS09** as your promo code. The code expires February 13th (that's next Friday), but remember, space is limited.

IF YOU DECIDE YOU DON'T WANT TO CLAIM THIS SPECIAL $1 OFFER . . . then please send a reply to this email with a brief explanation of why you aren't interested (and don't worry about hurting my feelings; my wife says it "builds character").

I hope you have a prosperous 2009!

Thanks,

Rand

P.S. Here's the link again, just in case you missed it :) To claim your full month of PRO member services for just $1, visit http://www .seomoz.org/trypro (using SUCCESS09 in the promo code!)

In classic "growth hack" format, we made an offer with limited quantity to leverage scarcity bias, used a massively discounted price that was way below our usual rate (at the time, $79/month), and time-boxed the promotion with an expiration date. If the email sounds a little like one of those "limited-time offer" TV infomercials, that's no coincidence. The same tactics apply to both.

On Wednesday, February 4, we sent out 122,451 emails with the headline: "Try SEOmoz Pro for Just a Dollar" . . . and the reply-to email address was my personal one. (The result was, among other things, a seven-hour email marathon in which Geraldine and I manually replied to more than two thousand messages. My poor wife remains uncompensated for many of the hours she poured into the company; sorry, honey!)

That was an intentional move, designed to improve the delivery rate and to make it a more authentic offer. But it also resulted in thousands of email responses over the first twenty-four hours, most of them asking exactly the same question—"Am I obligated to pay for the subscription after the first month?" As a result, we quickly decided to send a follow-up email with the title "I made a mistake about the $1 offer email," clarifying that no lengthier obligation was required, and subscribers who paid us $1 for the first month wouldn't have to pay anything else in the future.

That email had an even higher engagement rate than the first one, and drove a huge number of visitors and new signups. All combined, the two emails and a blog post the following week drove almost the full five thousand new subscribers we said we'd take, more than doubling Moz's paid membership. By our estimates, the email offer and the resulting signups drove about $1 million in additional revenue for the business.

It wasn't until later that I learned why growth hacks deserve the name "hacks."

They're Called "Hacks" for a Reason

The email offer didn't make our product better; it didn't make our subscription stickier; it didn't help people to do their jobs better. It simply created a short-term boost of attention that led to a lot of complex, long-term problems. Among those:

- The subscribers who signed up via the $1 offer had a much lower retention rate than subscribers who'd signed up via a non-promotional offer. For years after the promotion, the remnants of those five thousand promotional signups would haunt our churn numbers (one of the most important metrics for a SaaS business).
- As a team, we became overly enamored with the impact this email campaign had on our revenue and growth. We spent years trying to replicate it through a series of aggressive discounting and limited-time-offer tactics, with middling success. In retrospect, an addiction

to finding the next great "hack" dissuaded us from the long-term product and marketing investments on which we should have focused.

- Promotional pricing, especially when offered to a very large audience, creates an impression that discounts and special offers are part of a brand's ethos, and that rather than signing up at full price, you, as a potential buyer, should wait until the next promotion launches. We found that a large swath of the SEO community viewed Moz this way after our ongoing offers (usually two to three every year). If you've ever stopped yourself from paying full price for a brand or at a store because you suspect there'll be a sale in the future, you're familiar with the mind-set.

The conversion rate optimization efforts on the landing page for our subscription product, however, were an ongoing success, and something we've continued to invest in with positive long-term returns. The CRO efforts of identifying the right audience, discovering their objections, overcoming those objections with information on your landing pages, and smoothing the checkout/signup processes aren't "hacks"; they're improvements to the fundamental flywheel powering our marketing.

I deeply empathize with the temptation to chase growth hacks. Startup marketing blog posts and presentations are filled with stories of how one great tactic transformed the growth curve of a nascent business and made them leaders in their field. If you've spent any time investigating this realm, you've probably heard the same stories.

Airbnb's hack was to scrape Craigslist's vacation and rental home listings, then contact all of the owners and convince them to also list their properties on Airbnb (or, according to some accounts, do so without even getting permission). Technically, this violated Craigslist's ToS (Terms of Service—the publisher's guidelines for how the website is allowed to be used), but it's now the stuff of legend among growth hackers of the startup world. They point to this story and argue that you can't make a growth omelet without breaking some ToS eggs.

Dropbox's hack was a double-referral system wherein, when a Dropbox user referred someone else to the service, both the referrer and the receiver of the referral got upgraded account benefits. For years, that growth "hack" was featured on marketing event stages and in blog posts across the web. The endless copycatting of this tactic resulted in plenty of frustrations as other businesses failed to capitalize the way Dropbox had. When Drew Houston, Dropbox's founder, presented his "Startup Lessons Learned" in 2010, he wisely noted that "marketing tactics for one market type fail horribly in others." Dropbox itself had tried to replicate the growth hacks of other startups without success. Drew's deck walks through these many failures in paid search, PR, affiliate marketing, and AdWords.

Hotmail's hack was one of the earliest in the web field and wasn't referred to commonly as a growth hack until many years later. If you were on the web during the late 1990s and early 2000s, you'll probably remember it. Hotmail's free email service featured a line at the bottom of every email sent proclaiming that the email had been sent through the free service and inviting anyone who received the email to sign up for their own account. The rapid expansion of the web, and of email itself, led to millions of people taking advantage of this message in an era when many other email services charged a monthly or annual fee.

In 2006, Yelp launched a hack that had an immense benefit to their overall traffic and branding—the website badge strategy. Yelp sent restaurants with four- or five-star ratings from their users a visual "badge" restaurant owners could put on their websites to showcase their positive reviews. The badge linked back to the Yelp page, sending Yelp both traffic and, through the search engines' love of links, high search rankings for restaurant names, categories, cities, and more. That strategy had been tried before, by TripAdvisor and Citysearch, but no one nailed the process more effectively than Yelp, and for years, Yelp rode the wave of SEO returns those badges helped enable.*

These stories aren't atypical. PayPal's $5 signup referral, Uber's many city-by-city hacks (the littering of referral cards, the unpaid posters in bar and restaurant bathrooms on Friday nights, the totally evil practice of faking ride pickups to their competitors so as to hurt their profits and response times), Facebook's college-focused growth tactics (e.g., get the Greek systems on Facebook and everyone else will follow) in the early days, and dozens more are pointed to by startup founders, investors, and pundits as evidence that finding the right, innovative "hack" has replaced classic marketing practices as the way new companies can and should achieve sky-high growth rates.

Like most stories of success, there's a kernel of truth surrounded by a mountain of hyperbole and oversimplification.

Some growth hacks do work. Most don't. Even at the companies just described, the vast majority of individual growth tactics didn't take. Sadly, they don't get the press coverage or focus. The lesson should be: these companies tried dozens of innovative marketing tactics, combined them with strong, constantly improving products and plenty of traditional marketing best practices, and in some cases, a

---

* If it sounds like I'm unusually familiar with this hack, that's because it was my idea. . . . Weird, right? I worked as an SEO consultant for Yelp at the time, and the badges with embedded links back to Yelp's site was a great way to improve their rankings in Google, so I suggested it; they approved and executed. Additional credit to Michelle Broderick, who worked on the project from Yelp's side.

few specific tactics proved particularly effective as part of this mix. Instead, the shiny-object-chasing narrative is the one that earns headlines and lives on in the subculture of technology startups.

But if observing the life cycle and hardships of company formation and growth has taught us anything, it's to look beyond simple explanations for the deeper, more complicated truth. We should do that here, too. Growing your startup's brand, customer reach, conversion rate, retention, engagement, and virality *can* include finding that one great hack, but to do that, you need a broader understanding of the problem you're working to solve.

The Alternative: Sustainable Marketing Flywheels

Great companies are almost universally fed by a powerful, ongoing set of marketing processes that earn attention from the right audiences and bring them to the company's (physical or virtual) doorstep.

I like to describe the complexities of the marketing process as a flywheel. This metaphor refers to a piece of machinery from the industrial revolution that stored up rotational energy from inconsistent sources in the form of inertia. This could then be used to power any number of systems that require a consistent output of that energy. I'll show you how Moz's marketing flywheel works as an example.

Our flywheel is powered by content that audiences in SEO find through a variety of channels: search engines, social media, word of mouth, conferences and events, email subscriptions, referring links on other websites, etc.

The process of creating that content, amplifying it through various channels, reaching new audiences via that amplification, and bringing people back to our website is a powerful, ongoing system that drives millions of visitors and thousands of new software free

MOZ'S MARKETING FLYWHEEL

START

① ②
③

RANK FOR MORE
COMPETITIVE KWS

KEYWORD
RESEARCH &
INDUSTRY INTUITION

KW

PUBLISH

CREATE CONTENT

PUSH TO EMAIL &
RSS SUBSCRIBERS

EARN SEARCH &
REFERRAL TRAFFIC

DA

GROW DOMAIN
AUTHORITY

PROMOTE VIA
SOCIAL CHANNELS

GROW SOCIAL,
EMAIL, RSS, &
WoM FOLLOWERS

EARN LINKS &
AMPLIFICATION

trials each month. But like a flywheel, it took an immense amount of energy to get started, and only after it was rotating smoothly, growing its inertia, did it function in this friction-light fashion.

For the first five years of Moz's existence, I blogged four or five nights a week. I'd take my intuition and my experiences from client work, online forum participation, conversations with other SEO professionals, and news coming out of the search engine world and turn it into content of all kinds. I made written blog posts, illustrated visuals, PowerPoint presentations, live videos filmed against a whiteboard, webinars, statistical surveys, interactive quizzes, and more, and I put them on our website. In those first two years, I was lucky if anything

I created received more than a few dozen visits. In 2006, after the success of the Beginner's Guide to SEO, that trajectory improved and I could regularly reach several hundred folks with new content, then a thousand, then more.

The effects built on one another. The more people were exposed to something we'd created, the better chance it had of being amplified. Those amplifications, often in the form of links and shares, led to better search engine rankings, which drove more traffic and exposure and generally more-qualified visitors (no surprise that searchers, who are actively seeking out a specific answer or resource, engage at higher rates than those who've simply seen something of potential interest in their social, news, RSS, or email streams). This flywheel has powered our marketing efforts for years. It brings to our website high quantities of visitors interested in search engine optimization and web-marketing topics, and through our content, we hope to instill knowledge of and trust in the Moz brand. Later, if and when those same people are seeking out software and tools to help with their SEO efforts, we hope to earn their business and often do.

In fact, an interesting stat about Moz's marketing and customers was uncovered a few years ago as we analyzed our visitor and conversion funnel. These numbers are somewhat older now, and have likely changed somewhat, but retain this characteristic:

Say you visited Moz for the very first time via a Google search for a phrase like "SEO tools," then immediately signed up for a free trial of our software. Chances are good you'd be a Moz customer for less than four months versus the overall global average of about nine months.

But if you visited Moz twelve times or more in a three-month span before signing up for that free trial, chances are you'd stick around for fourteen-plus months as a paying subscriber. Whoa. I know.

Turns out, our best, most loyal customers tend to be those who've spent considerable time on our website, participating in our community, consuming our educational resources, and testing out our free tools. Thus, it's actually in Moz's interest *not* to promote our products or conversions too heavily or too fast, especially to new visitors. The classic funnel optimization promoted by many marketers has this peculiar idea that we must race to turn as many visitors as we can into paid customers and that any missed opportunity represents a flaw in our marketing process. Our metrics show just the opposite. If we want to have the best long-term impact on customer growth and retention, we need patience. We need to wait for our audience to be ready and engaged with us before we nudge them toward our subscription.

I think this foments a beautiful, symbiotic relationship between our values, our content, and our paid subscriptions. We want to help people do better marketing. We want them to learn first and sign up only if our products are right for them. And our business actually prospers most from long-term, low-churn, high-engagement customers—the kind we get from deep investments not just in a visitor's conversion path, but in their professional and educational journey.

Pro Tip: If you have any type of subscription or recurring revenue, make sure you measure LTV (Lifetime Value—the total revenue customers spend during their relationship with your firm) by referral source(s) and by the number of visits prior to conversion. If your stats look like Moz's, you'll probably want to adopt a similar, slow-burn conversion process.

The power of the marketing flywheel is clear to us. But it's not just Moz for whom this works. Of the most successful startups, nearly everyone has a clearly identifiable marketing flywheel that brought awareness and traffic from the right audiences and helped those people convert to a sale or a signup at the right time.

Dollar Shave Club, the famous Los Angeles startup that offers traditional men's razor blades for a few dollars a month (originally one dollar, until their acquisition by Unilever), built a funnel based on humorous, online videos that positioned them against stodgy, expensive shaving product companies. Those videos would earn massive viral views from an audience perfectly poised to help them spread (usually young, heavily online, social-media-savvy men). The videos earned news coverage, which themselves got shared, and all of it combined to create a mass of traffic that Dollar Shave Club then bought remarketing and retargeting ads against (along with earning loads of high rankings for key search terms in Google).

Zillow built a remarkable flywheel on the initial strength of their home price calculator and "Zestimate" (Zillow's patented formula for estimating a home's value), and the traffic, shares, links, stories, and controversies that inevitably followed. Initially, visitors weren't going to the site to buy houses, but once they began associating Zillow with residential real estate data, and once Zillow leveraged the engagement, content, and links to help earn high rankings in the search results, the outcome was inevitable.

WP Engine, the popular WordPress hosting site renowned for its reliability, started by writing about and serving WordPress sites that had been overwhelmed by viral traffic, often to the point of going offline. By associating their brand and technology with the "Reddit Hug of Death" (and other, similar phenomena that overwhelm a site's web servers by sending huge amounts of visitors in a short window), and by appealing specifically to site owners whose domains had received this sort of popularity (as well as the tech-savvy crowds that often influenced them online), WP Engine developed a cult following that led to broader popularity and traffic over time.

While flywheels are critical to build, there is overlap between investing in them and experimenting with growth hacks. My experience has been that the best time to leverage a hack is when it perfectly fits with an area where your flywheel is experiencing friction.

Early on, Moz's flywheel struggled most with how to get in front of bloggers, journalists, website owners, and influencers who might be likely to link to our content. I recall vividly how, in 2005, when a few websites linked to a piece I'd written, I stood up at my desk cheering and bought a bottle of cheap champagne on the way home from work. It might sound silly, but in those days, I knew that links to my posts were what stood between toiling in relative anonymity and earning highly relevant visitors who might become consulting clients. The friction in our flywheel was how to get in front of those who might link to us and how to convince them to create those links.

The solution was to find a hack—the right hack—that could get us noticed by these specific sorts of website owners and bloggers and writers in the search technology and marketing fields. We found our hack with a piece of content we called "The Search Engine Ranking Factors."

To be fair, we were not the first or only website to attempt to list out the elements Google used to determine how sites and pages ranked via their famed algorithm. But we were the first to do it with a community-recruited crowd of influencers. Our approach relied on crafting a survey of all the various potential ranking inputs, then asking notable professional SEOs to take the survey and contribute their opinions. The resulting document aggregated quotes, summed up and averaged numerical rankings, and then ordered them by relative weight. More than a hundred folks with websites and followings of their own gave their input, and each received a personal email from me, thanking them for their participation and asking for their help in spreading the work.

This growth hack produced high value content—the ranking factors document itself—and a long list of people who helped us overcome our biggest challenge: earning links and amplification. Because each influencer had contributed, they were predisposed to help share the content. Our drought of awareness was over, and within months, nearly all of the websites where our respondents posted their own works had referenced ours. Not only that, but those links had the hoped-for impact. Moz (at the time using the SEOmoz.org domain) ranked number one for "SEO ranking factors," "Google ranking factors," "search engine ranking factors," and a host of related keyword phrases that collectively drove thousands of monthly searches.

We identified our flywheel. We found the point of friction. And we applied a growth hack to ease that friction and let the wheel start to spin faster. Today, this tactic of including influencers in the creation of content (often called "roundups") is a staple of the content marketing practice. I'd even say it's massively overdone at this point. But a hundred new, creative opportunities await.

When thinking about how to build a marketing process that's going to work for the long term, that can scale without friction, that can build on itself even as your business grows, consider the flywheel analogy. Each one will be different, and yours should be substantially unique from your competitors, built to take advantage of your particular skills, and targeted to your specific audience.

The "hacks" or marketing tactics you employ should be in service to this funnel, not instead of it. If you've got a great idea for a landing page or a referral program or a way to reach the right customers via a social network in a scalable manner, just make sure you know how to test, track, and apply it inside the funnel you're building. Growth hacks alone can't solve all your marketing problems, but the right ones may add immense value to an already humming marketing flywheel.

CHAPTER 10

REAL VALUES DON'T HELP YOU MAKE MONEY (IN THE SHORT TERM)

Corporate values, usually chosen by senior executives, are adopted to prevailing business circumstances and are not rooted in fundamental philosophical convictions, morality or ethics. In this sense, corporate values are often selected as a strategy to "rally the troops," and therefore, manipulative in nature.

—Ray Williams, 2010

My friend Rob Ousbey once had a brilliant idea for how to make Moz millions of extra dollars each year. So why did I tell him, "Hell no, we're not doing that?" Read on, friends.

In a SaaS business like Moz, churn is perhaps the most important, most studied number. It shows what percent of your customers are canceling their accounts each month (or year). A high churn rate means you need to earn a lot of new customers just to make up for the ones who are leaving your service. A low churn rate means that growth is vastly easier and usually much faster. Investors, in particular, tend to value SaaS businesses like ours with low churn rates at far greater multiples than those with high churn.

In 2011, our churn rate was about 8.5 percent per month and we had about 10,000 subscribers. This meant that, each month, we had to find 850 new subscribers to sign up, just to maintain our revenue. If we wanted to grow, we needed even more.

We were, in fact, signing up far more than 850 new customers each month, which enabled the business to scale quickly despite the high churn rate. But we were scared about the inevitable consequences of such a brief customer engagement. On average, folks stayed with their Moz subscriptions for about eleven months. Based on some research, we estimated there were close to a million potential Moz customers in the English-speaking world, but it's not hard to imagine how, in a few years of thousands of monthly signups, we could work our way through a significant portion of that group and put the long-term future of the business in jeopardy.

We needed to make our subscription stickier and provide value to our customers such that they'd want to stay with us for multiple years. That's where Rob came in.

"Why," he asked, "do you let people cancel with a click right on the website?"

"You think we should make it harder to cancel?" I replied.

"If you change the cancellation process to a phone call," Rob explained, "I'm willing to bet that friction alone will improve your monthly churn rate. Plus, you can then talk to folks as they're canceling and get a much better understanding of who they are and why they're leaving. You could probably save a good number of them, too, or get them back as customers again in the future. Maybe switch some to a cheaper plan or convince them to buy a different product from you."

I'd seen some stats that backed up Rob's guess and told him so.

"You're right. Making the subscription cancelable only by phone can have a real impact on churn rate. But we all hate services that require a phone call to cancel after a purely online signup. They're intentionally making it difficult. It's not empathetic, and that means it's not TAGFEE."

"Fair enough," Rob replied, "but you're leaving a lot of money on the table."

"Well," I answered, "we always say: they're not core values if you're willing to sacrifice them in exchange for money."

Yes, but Is It TAGFEE?

Values may not make you money in the short term, but they're invaluable to any business in the long term. Values are not always easy. They force hard decisions. They can work against short-term growth. They restrict paths that might otherwise be open to pursuit. Establishing and adhering to core values carries great intrinsic and extrinsic benefits. But usually these become evident over the long term, and that can be immensely frustrating for startups struggling simply to stay alive long enough to get to profitability or fundraising. This tension is hard, but my experience and the correlation of values adherence to performance suggest it's worth it. Plus, sticking to values makes it possible to look in the mirror without hating the person staring back.

At Moz, we have six core values, represented by the acronym TAGFEE—Transparency, Authenticity, Generosity, Fun, Empathy, and the Exception. These are the beliefs we prioritize above the success or growth of the business. TAGFEE acts as a litmus test for whether we should or shouldn't take an action, hire or let someone go from the team, or create a process or policy. We use it in everyday discussion about the content we put on our website, the ways we engage with our community, the products we build, and the internal actions we take.

TAGFEE started in 2007, when Moz's first investor, Michelle Goldberg, gave me a copy of *Good to Great*, Jim Collins's classic analysis of the elements that correlated with companies that achieved long-lasting greatness versus those that didn't. In his research, Collins identified seven characteristics highly correlated with companies that have remarkable financial and growth performance over long periods. One of these, which Collins called "First Who ... Then What," posits that great organizations are made up of people who share fundamental core values and use these as their guiding light for decisions big and small.

Everything I've experienced as an entrepreneur, a CEO, an individual contributor, and a student of startups and business culture reinforces this concept: people who share core values and believe those values to be the most important part of their contribution to the world have the greatest potential to accomplish remarkable things together.

And conversely, when individuals in an organization don't align to the same values, every goal, project, and effort is undermined. Success, in any form, is made massively harder or easier depending on the degree to which your team, in the deepest part of their personal beliefs, shares an unwavering commitment to the same values and agrees with the implications of what values mean to an organization. This quote sums it up:

> The core values embodied in our credo might be a competitive advantage, but that is not why we have them. We have them because they define for us what we stand for, and we would hold them even if they became a competitive disadvantage in certain situations.
>
> **—Ralph Larsen, former CEO of Johnson & Johnson**

Moz, in its early days as a software company, latched onto this idea, and I believe we have always been at our best when we embraced and embodied our core values, and were often at our worst when we strayed from them.

Geraldine is TAGFEE's author. That might come as a surprise, but she was a copywriter by background (and is now the published author of *All Over the Place: Adventures in Travel, True Love, and Petty Theft.* You should probably get a couple of copies, in case you want to read it more than once). When we started down the path of identifying Moz's core values, she was an obvious choice to assist. She knew me incredibly well, she was familiar with the company and all eleven of our employees at the time, she was a talented writer, and she didn't charge very much (important to an early-stage startup).

Each of Moz's employees went through a written exercise, listing the traits and qualities we admired most in others and aspired to ourselves. We talked together about what we wanted to be as a company, what we wanted to stand for, and what we regretted from our pasts—personally and professionally. The notes from these exercises and discussions were passed on to Geraldine, who transformed them into a written document that we then shared, edited, commented on, and returned to her for a final version. It begins:

Moz's Guiding Principles

This document represents the rules we have created and ideals we strive towards for all the work we produce as a company. We embrace these as the embodiment of who we are, why we exist, and what we endeavor to achieve in every arena—from software to website content to actions in the workplace and on the road as representatives of Moz.

And the six values themselves are:

- **Transparency**—We believe in sharing what we know, learn, and do with everyone who's interested. We reject secrecy, obscurity, and opacity in all its forms and strive instead to make the worlds of marketing, of SEO, of software startups, and of Moz itself open and accessible to all.
- **Authenticity**—We hate pretending to be people we're not or hiding our true identities, thoughts, or feelings in our work. We despise corporate, inauthentic behavior and the trappings of the business world that hold back our humanity or diversity. We will always work to make Moz a place where all of us can be our real selves.
- **Generosity**—We believe in giving back without asking for anything in return. Our goal, greater even than growth or financial success, is to help make our peers, coworkers, and the world of marketing a better, more nurturing, giving environment.
- **Fun**—The work we do can be challenging and stressful, but we believe work is only work if you make it so. We aim to make our jobs and the jobs of those around us enjoyable, rewarding, and humor filled.
- **Empathy**—Our most important value, empathy, demands that we put ourselves in the shoes of others and see things from their point of view. We endeavor to create products, content, interactions, and environments that are welcoming and respectful to all. We believe the best kind of empathy is that which aims for the most long-term good, not just a short-term veneer of niceness. Our goal is to apply this empathy with the highest priority to our community, audience, and customers, then to ourselves, and finally to our shareholders and investors.

- **The Exception**—If everyone else is doing something one way, we believe there's innate value in finding an alternative path. Moz strives to be unique, innovative, and weird. We cut against the grain and hope to stand out as an exception to the rule.

You can find the original version online in a blog post I published a little more than a year after its original creation.

It's very possible that TAGFEE's values resonate with you personally. But it's also completely okay if they don't. No two organizations should have precisely the same values, and values should not be arbitrarily created and then forced upon a team. Moz's values have worked for us because they come from a deeply personal place inside its founders' and early employees' beliefs, shaped by our experiences as people and professionals. They are not designed to work for everyone or appeal to everyone. Core values have proven their worth to me, as a founder, CEO, and employee, because they provide *three* powerful, unifying organizational forces:

The *first* is a shared commitment among the team. In a company with hundreds of people, there will naturally be tension, disagreement, and occasional discord. But core values help everyone know, from the day they're first interviewed, that unifying beliefs bind us together. Even when we disagree on how to accomplish our goals or on whether we have the right goals, we at least know that our deepest foundation is the same. My in-laws fight constantly about pretty much everything (usually in their native Italian, so I catch only every third or fourth word), but they all agree when it comes to politics, a rare thing in American families. That shared consensus of the most important parts of what's right and wrong for the world and its people can take a Thanksgiving dinner going off the rails and bring everyone back together. The same is true at a company with resonant, shared values.

The *second* is a set of blueprints for decision making. When we're faced with a challenging decision, lots of data, intuition, and analysis will naturally be a part of the process. But these can be powerfully bolstered with our values acting as guardrails we stay inside. As with the example from this chapter's opening of requiring a phone call to cancel, we are able to use our values to help determine how to invest in improving the company, its products, its people, and its growth. I'll share some more examples of this process later in this chapter and in the book.

The *third* is evaluation criteria for retrospection. Most companies do some kind of retrospecting (looking back at previous decisions, projects, and investments to determine whether they were worthwhile), and use inputs like return-on-investment, cost/benefit analysis, and other varieties of metrics depending on the circumstance. The addition of fit-with-core-values to these operations delivers a special kind of insight, and one that both helps reinforce those values and sets up future investments for better success. Consistency and commitment loom large in the human psyche, and when it's perceived by your internal team, external customers, and wider audience that your organization maintains them, your brand benefits.

We Hold These Core Values to Be Self-Evident

Values-driven organizations have proven that even in the early days, there is an unassailable magic that comes from having the right people on the team, and for those people to share a set of common values (alongside a shared mission and vision). The all-too-common problem comes when founders and leaders believe that recruiting can be separated from values alignment.

Collins explains this brilliantly in his essay on aligning action:

In describing the alignment process, I have assumed that your organization's core values are already clearly defined—a big assumption. Let me make a few points about identifying core values, for without this stake firmly in the ground, there can be no effective alignment.

First, you cannot "set" organizational values, you can only discover them. Nor can you "install" new core values into people. Core values are not something people "buy in" to. People must be predisposed to holding them. Executives often ask me, "How do we get people to share our core values?" You don't. Instead, the task is to *find* people who are already predisposed to sharing your core values. You must attract and then retain these people and let those who aren't predisposed to sharing your core values go elsewhere.

—Jim Collins, "Aligning Action and Values"

I don't think there's an easier or more tempting mistake to make than to hire someone who has great ability or a great track record of performance with the recognition that while they're not a match with the current values and culture of the company, over time you believe you can bring them into alignment. I've made this same arrogant move multiple times over my career, and each time it ended in something between disappointment and disaster. The visual on page 148, originally from Moz's investor Brad Feld, sums it up.

In the professional world, we're accustomed to hiring for competence. It's been drilled into us by popular culture and long-held business practices that the goal of hiring is to recruit someone to the team

COMPETENCE
— VS. —
CULTURE FIT

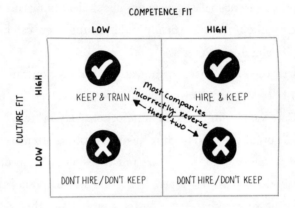

COMPETENCE FIT

	LOW	HIGH
CULTURE FIT — HIGH	✔ KEEP & TRAIN	✔ HIRE & KEEP
CULTURE FIT — LOW	✖ DON'T HIRE / DON'T KEEP	✖ DON'T HIRE / DON'T KEEP

Most companies incorrectly reverse these two

CULTURE FIT = Shared values, ability to work well together, mutual respect & trust, brings positive energy to the team

COMPETENCE FIT = Productivity, quality of work, raw intelligence, ROI of contributions

who has demonstrated skill and experience in a similar role. That's not a terrible thing to include in a hiring process, but if you want extraordinary results, it can't be the only thing you seek out.

Instead, you need a hiring process that considers core values and broad culture fit. Don't arrogantly presume you can transform a person who isn't predisposed to believe in or share your core values into someone who is. Build that screening into your interview process, your onboarding process, and the way in which contributions are judged. Use it to inform how raises, recognition, and promotions are given. That's the only way you'll prove to your team that values are on par with work output.

Values Demand Vigilance

It's oh so tempting to let a few values mismatches and clashes slide because an employee is doing high-quality work or has skills that seem hard to replace. But every time we've done this at Moz, it's backfired. Sometimes it's quick and the damage is minimal, but other times we've kept someone around far past the time they'd proven their values to conflict with our own; it wreaks havoc on morale.

Take Maya Angelou's advice: when someone shows you who they are, believe them the first time.

A few years ago, Moz hired a longtime veteran of a big software company. He came highly recommended with a number of leadership positions on successful products in his past. But early on, he clashed with a number of folks on the team. He played politics well, though, and neither his managers nor the broader Moz leadership felt his transgressions were untenable. Unfortunately, his peers and subordinates at the company, especially those not on his team, came to feel that Moz's commitment to TAGFEE and to upholding core values must be slipping. They assumed, given that we'd recently raised a large round of venture financing, that people like this guy were "the new normal," and it wasn't that leadership didn't know about his cultural mismatch, it was that they just didn't care as much anymore. So long as he performed, they figured, we'd keep him around. In their eyes, Moz lost some of its magic, and its leadership lost some of their credibility, especially on values issues.

I found out only after he left that in addition to these professional conflicts, he'd made sexist remarks and jokes to some of the young women on our team. He'd brought up inappropriate subjects at the office, sent around borderline offensive memes and links, and verbally bullied people who'd since left the company. I was heartbroken. I asked our head of HR why she'd never mentioned any of these things or taken action.

Her response shocked me: "You're the first person I've ever heard this from," she said. "A few people have complained about him, but never with these specifics."

His behavior had gone unreported. I asked a couple of the folks who told me about it why they'd never raised these events with their manager or with HR. Those replies were even more heartbreaking: "I didn't think it would do anything," and worse, "I figured everyone knew but didn't care so long as his projects did well."

Hearing stuff like that was like a knife in my gut. This company I'd built, that I'd worked so hard to make into a place that cared about people and values, had clearly changed. It wasn't because we'd hired dozens of vindictive or evil assholes. It was because letting even a few people (and this example I'm sharing sadly wasn't alone) break our core values repeatedly without visible action from leadership led to the normalization of discordant behavior.

There are *three* common ways values fail at organizations:

First is when they're viewed by the team as merely paper platitudes, hung on a plaque on the wall but not consistently enforced. If you overlook your stated values when they come into conflict with an employee who's performing well (or perceived by managers to be performing well), you're revealing reality—that performance (or perception and politicking) matters more than embraced values.

Second is when those values are created because the founders or executives thought they'd help build the cultlike environments that Silicon Valley culture broadcasts as a "must-have" element of startup recruiting and retention. You've almost certainly seen or heard about companies whose values have become the stuff of parody: values like "hustle," "work hard, play hard," "get shit done," and "always be shipping."

If any values you hold deeply are ones that, even if you found them to be a competitive disadvantage, you'd still uphold despite that conflict, then by all means, keep them. But if your company's values are merely marketing for potential hires, don't call them values. Be honest with yourself and your staff. Make them part of your recruiting materials and your internal lingo if you must, but don't attempt to pull the wool over your own eyes and everyone else's by calling them something they're not.

Real values have costs. They're difficult to embody. A lot of people (but hopefully not the ones you recruit) will disagree with them. People internally and externally should, at least some of the time, view them as a barrier to making a financially beneficial decision.

Real values are truths you hold to be more important than making money. They will come into conflict, and you'll have to make that hard decision and show everyone on your team why you're choosing that path, not just once, but over and over in order to instill the idea that values mean something at your organization. Because, usually, they don't. People who've been in the professional world for even a few years get pretty jaded about "company values." That means you have to go above and beyond to prove that you take them seriously.

If you're not willing to sacrifice and to make money-costing and painful decisions that bias to your values, don't bother having them. Say, instead, that your core values are financial growth and monetary success. You'll attract like-minded people who appreciate your honesty.

When you fail to live up to the expectations you've created with values statements, no amount of pretending can distract the incredibly talented, smart people that startups recruit from the uncomfortable truth that these so-called values can be willfully violated so long as the real goals (financial or otherwise) are met. Real values are proven through hard decisions and reinforced through recognition of times when they've caused real pain and still been "the right call." When your employees go out for drinks and bemoan the loss of revenue or opportunity and say, "Well, I guess they really believe in X more than just making money," that's when you know real core values are a part of your organization.

Third is when values aren't publicized at all and must be discovered over time through trial and error or by watching the reactions of scared employees in meetings with management. Working in environments like this is frustrating, tiring, and off-putting for those who can't quickly learn or keep up with the system. Every company has unspoken rules and idiosyncrasies that take time to learn. But values should be explicit, because they act like the operating system for a person's employment, affecting every action and decision they make. When you force people to figure out a secret, unwritten code for behavior, you are guaranteed to drive away a fair portion of otherwise talented contributors. Worse still, all the benefits you could achieve from recruiting and hiring with explicit values are forfeit. If you can't be bothered to identify, amplify, and reward your beliefs, there's no way for your recruiting process to seek out those shared beliefs in new employees.

A team with shared culture and shared values will, almost always, outperform a team without these elements. Why?

- **Retention**—It's far more difficult to retain team members who fundamentally disagree with how things should be done and why, even if they agree on what work to do. And constantly rebuilding a team through hiring is both exhausting and inefficient—people do their best work a year or two into working together with the same group. They learn one another's intricacies and idiosyncrasies, anticipate needs, establish efficient communication and process patterns, and know what works and doesn't for their teammates. According to Namely's analysis of more than twenty thousand startups in the United States, average employee tenure is only 10.8 months. 10.8 months! If you can improve yours, you'll have a powerful competitive advantage.

- **Motivation**—The difference between working with people you like, trust, and agree with versus working with those whose tactics, style, and ethics you question is immense. The former promotes the assumption of good intent (among the most critical elements for team bonding, productivity, and quality of output). The latter fosters political environments where work quality suffers.

- **Cohesion**—It is massively easier to ask a team to commit to a road map, a project, or a process (even when they disagree) if core values and culture already bind you together. When those elements are lacking, so, too, is the basic structure for what makes a compelling argument or what elements should be part of decision making or which paths are available and worthy of consideration.

Homogeneity Hobbles Innovation

There is one big, fatal flaw that often accompanies the pursuit of shared culture and values: uniformity.

Startups and early-stage ventures need diversity. I mean that both in the sociological sense (i.e., not just young, white men from the same country and background) and in the broader, thought-pattern and experience sense (i.e., everyone in the company thinking the same way and bringing only a single set of professional/personal experiences). These two might seem at odds: diversity versus shared culture. They are not.

In fact, shared culture combined with diversity should be exactly the combination you're seeking in a team. Diversity, culture, and values might sound like a complex, tough combination. I agree it's challenging to build a team with these attributes, especially if your own background lacks exposure to diverse people and/or those who share your values. But real magic happens when these come together.

A major roadblock is the easy-to-make assumption that diversity of employees, especially early on, isn't desirable, because it conflicts with or contradicts the goals of shared culture. When I hear this pushback from founders, it gets my blood boiling. This is a fundamental misinterpretation of what culture, values, and diversity mean. When we talk about diversity in a founding team or an early-stage organization or a larger company, we're talking about recruiting and hiring a wide range of people from different backgrounds, ethnicities, ages, genders, and identities (in all their forms). People with these varied attributes are not fundamentally at odds with your culture or your values. Women of color and disabled veterans and Asian men in their sixties and young people with nonbinary gender identification can all share the same core values and believe the same things about how a company should be structured and how people can work together.

I'm not saying that every randomly assembled group of diverse people (or every randomly assembled group of straight, white, cisgendered men in their thirties from New York) *will* share these beliefs. I'm saying that recruiting diverse people who do share these beliefs is a massive advantage—a cheat code—for your organization.

Diversity is immensely desirable because it improves perspective, empathy, and creativity. A diverse group brings unique life experiences and, as a result, a unique ability to contribute that non-diverse groups can't match. It's often hard to know when you're benefiting from diversity (or when you're being hurt by lack of it) because the input given by people is seldom directly attributable to their background, but I'll give six short examples.

1. When we started recruiting to grow the company, gender diversity made a big difference. My mom was my cofounder. Sarah was my COO. Our board comprised more women than men until 2012. That meant Moz was seen in Seattle as a place where women in the startup world were welcomed and encouraged. I hired a woman (Kate Matsudaira) as our vice president of engineering in 2009. She was a critical hire who seriously upgraded our engineering practices. I suspect I never could have swayed her to join an all-dude company. The same held true for many other folks we brought aboard—junior and senior, technical and not. Imagine excluding 50 percent (or more) of your potential workforce because you recruited only your same-sex drinking buddies. Not a smart move given how hard it is to hire in our world.

2. In developing personas for our products, we started with what can only be called the whitest, most generic naming conventions ever. Thankfully, some more thoughtful and diverse Mozzers noticed this convention, and noted the subtle effects that subtle biases like names and genders, even in fictional characters (like personas) can have on how we perceive the world of our customers and design for them. If a persona is called "College-grad Chad," there's a certain associated gender and background identity for most folks. Our designers assumed Chad could read small text. Our engineers assumed Chad was familiar with advanced query modifiers. Our marketers assumed Chad was active on Twitter and Instagram. By moving to more inclusive persona-naming conventions and descriptions, we brought to the process a more accurate view of the diversity of the customers we were actually designing for,

building more accessible products and marketing them more thoughtfully in the right places and ways.

3. At one of Moz's executive team lunches some years back, someone brought up the City of Seattle's decision to stop using the term "brown bag" to describe lunchtime presentations. I thought it was very odd until our CTO at the time, Anthony, who's black, noted that the phrase was used to segment and classify people based on the color of their skin, and he'd personally been subjected to it as a kid in eastern Washington. We immediately got rid of the term at Moz and switched to "lunch and learn" (which has the added benefit of being much more understandable to our non-American-born employees and guests).

4. At another executive meeting, we were all talking about the various "tribes" at Moz (a term we'd been using to denote groups across teams that work together on projects). Annette, our CMO, whose background is American Indian, wondered if we could choose another word to describe these groups. . . . Cue another head-smacking minute, and a shift in terminology.

5. When Sarah (now our CEO, at the time COO) was pregnant with her son, she noticed the lack of private rooms at Moz where moms and moms-to-be could comfortably take care of themselves or their kids (and that restroom stalls were not an option). That pain and awareness caused us to correct the issue with rooms specifically for that purpose, but if she hadn't been part of the office design team, it's very possible we wouldn't have been sensitive to the issue.

6. Finally, and perhaps most broadly, in a design review of the first version of Moz Analytics, one of our software tools, Sarah, and a number of other women on our teams who looked at the product, took exception to several elements of the design (color, layout, font

usage, and word choices). When we modified these in response to their input, metrics improved. David Mihm (whose company we acquired in 2012, and who is partially color-blind) helped identify which contrast variations he literally couldn't see. Martin York, one of our senior engineers, who has dyslexia, commented on form inputs missing auto-corrections for common mistypings. One of the older members of our team noted that she had difficulty in parsing the text because the lines were too close together (a.k.a. overly tight leading). I couldn't have caught these issues myself and neither could a team of people with my background, gender, age, or abilities. Diversity made our product more accessible, improved engagement, and reduced customer frustration.

This is why diversity is so well correlated with success everywhere from early-stage startups to Fortune 500 boards of directors. Research from McKinsey showed that more gender-diverse companies outperform their less gender diverse peers by 15 percent while more racially diverse teams outperform their peers by 35 percent. PE Hub, *Venture Capital Journal,* and Women VC published a joint report analyzing the returns of investment funds with gender-diverse versus mostly male and all-male investor teams and found the more balanced teams had returns 3.78 times higher than their less-balanced peers. When First Round Capital analyzed the performance of the hundreds of investments in its own portfolio, it found that teams with at least one woman founder performed 63 percent better than all-male founding teams.

If I were founding a new startup today, I'd do almost anything to have a feature that's 63 percent higher correlated with better performance.

Where founders need to seek out shared attributes isn't in what we look like or where we're from; instead, focus on ethical beliefs and the right ways to operate a company. You want a team that has significant overlap in its answers to questions like:

- What traits and behaviors should be rewarded and recognized in our employees?
- Which ones should be discouraged?
- What criteria should be applied to people we hire, those we promote, and those we let go?
- What makes someone a good person versus a bad person?
- How should hard-to-resolve conflicts be handled at our organization?
- What's your preferred form of communication and why?
- What enables you to deliver your best work? What stops you from it?

You've probably seen stories in the tech press about how a startup is asking potential hires about *Star Wars* versus *Star Trek* or which craft beers they prefer or what sports they watch in order to help determine "culture fit." These types of questions are awful not only because they promote homogeneity of thinking ("we're all from the same town and love the same soccer team and the same video games" is *not* the kind of shared culture that will help your organization succeed), but because they, intentionally or not, bias to people with homogeneity of experience, too.

Twentysomething white men from upper-middle-class and wealthy upbringings are the most plentiful founders in the technology world. I fit into this group myself. My dad was an engineer at Boeing. My mom was a designer, a marketer, and an owner of her own small business. They're both ethnically Jewish, but not practicing.* My parents made decent money and were extremely thrifty, enabling them to pay for college for all three of their kids (though only one of us, my sister, actually graduated). We grew up in a rural area outside Seattle. And I get how tempting it is to find someone like me as a cofounder for a new venture. I already know lots of other white and Asian men in the Seattle area who grew up in middle-class families, are in their midthirties, don't have kids, like computer games, and cheer for the Seahawks.

What's wrong with starting a company with friends I already have, whom I know I get along with, and whose interests and passions match my own?

It's not additive.

Together, my peers and I of similar background and identity combine for only a very slight bit of extra perspective. Try as we might, our outlooks and our framing of events will be colored by who we are, where we've lived, what we've experienced—the benefits of diversity will be generally lost to us. And, as a result, our ability to empathize with, design for, market to, and serve broader groups with whatever we make will be limited. Additionally, we'll almost certainly find it harder to recruit diverse early employees, which will have a domino effect on our hiring and team composition for the long term. If you wonder why so many startups are so homogenous, or why so many serve only to address the problems of a very thin slice of the world's populace, look no further. It's usually not intentional, evil,

---

*Interestingly enough, in the 1970s, Jews successfully lobbied the US government to be classified as "white," and have mostly fit under this umbrella since (well . . . at least until the 2016 election).

biased hiring practices, but rather deep-rooted, systemic drivers like the design of interview questions and where job postings are placed and the practice of recruiting through friends and family networks.

Moz itself struggled massively with diversity, especially on the technical side. I think this is because we unintentionally fell prey to all of these inherent biases. We looked for familiar experiences. We sought out many of our early employees through the people we already knew. We made no intentional efforts to create a diverse pool of candidates from which we could hire. Like many companies, we didn't think much about diversity for years until, one day, we did, and it looked awful. In 2012, more than 90 percent of all of Moz's engineering hires were white or Asian men in their twenties and thirties. We could have been the poster child for stereotypical tech monocultures. And this was despite having a woman (Kate) and then a black man (Anthony) serve as CTO.

We didn't just struggle on the diversity front, though; we struggled on shared culture and values, too. We'd hire people for their experience, skills, and ability without a consistent, intentional process to determine whether they supported TAGFEE or agreed with how we did things at Moz.

We addressed both issues in the space of a year. First, we built a new process called the "TAGFEE screen," wherein members of a team not making the hire would spend time with candidates during an interview day and have discussions designed to elicit alignment with our values and our culture. For example, if our Big Data engineering team was interviewing a candidate, that person might go out to lunch with two folks from customer support to talk about values and culture issues. If the customer support interviewers had substantial concerns about the engineer's proclivity toward (or away from) TAGFEE and Moz's people-centric culture, they could veto that hire . . . even if the engineering team thought the candidate was a perfect skills match.

Next, we looked into our practices around diversity. We found, not surprisingly, that a high proportion of our candidates were sourced internally through referrals. And of course, few of those candidates had any diversity of background or experience. They went to the same schools, lived in the same places, had the same sorts of upbringings, etc., as our existing team. We made a number of intentional efforts to change by investing in and supporting local programs aimed at promoting diversity. These included Returnship, a program for parents (usually moms) returning to work after a few years off for childcare; Ada Developers Academy, a program for women learning to code that we hosted at our offices; and TAF Academy, a school program to help get kids from underprivileged backgrounds access to science, technology, engineering, and mathematics education. Our goal was to gain exposure to potential candidates whom we'd otherwise miss.

The results were remarkable. A couple of years after implementing, our engineering organization has improved gender-balance and background diversity, more than tripling the number of people of color and women engineers on the teams (though we still have a long way to go). Other parts of the company—customer success, finance, marketing, product, and facilities—have become more diverse, too. We've discovered places to post jobs we never knew about, language that was holding back diverse candidates from applying, and new networks of people to help us attract broader groups of applicants.

Pro Tip: We use and love Textio (https://textio.com/) to analyze our job postings, about page, and other recruiting-focused content to make sure we're using inclusive, unbiased language. It's worth checking out and has a number of free and low-cost options.

On the shared values and culture front, we've shown similar

improvement. From 2011 to 2013, we hired very fast. This brought a cohort of Moz employees who reported less job satisfaction and had higher voluntary turnover than prior cohorts (i.e., those folks were more likely to leave the company in a shorter period of time). After the implementation of our TAGFEE screens and our more considered focus on culture and values in the interview and hiring process, we improved voluntary retention. We have, in my opinion, also improved the caliber of new employees joining the team. Teams work better together, get more done, and produce higher-quality results than ever before.

If you're building a team from scratch or are in the early stages of recruiting and hiring, I hope you'll learn from our mistakes and from the data. Hire people who share a belief of what deserves a promotion and a raise versus a reprimand or coaching. Hire people who are naturally inclined toward your values and who want a place that's willing to sacrifice short-term growth or financial success in exchange for adherence to them. But don't hire only the people who look like you and see the world through the same set of experiences. Bolster your potential for high performance and for broader customer empathy by intentionally seeking out diversity. These two elements, when combined, forge the underpinnings of a remarkable team.

CHAPTER 11

LIVING THE LIVES OF YOUR CUSTOMERS AND THEIR INFLUENCERS IS A STARTUP CHEAT CODE

A great way to build software is to start out by solving your own problems. You'll be the target audience and you'll know what's important and what's not. That gives you a great head start on delivering a breakout product.

—Jason Fried, March 2006

I thought I had an amazing idea. I thought it was going to change the world of marketing. I thought we were going to build a set of software that every business needed. I thought it would catapult Moz's growth and revenues. I thought wrong.

It was 2011 when Adam Feldstein, then Moz's chief product officer, and I sat down to plan out a project we called "Moz Analytics." The new product stemmed from a theory I had that in the near future, the siloed practices of social media marketing, search engine optimization, content marketing, public relations, and online brand marketing would all merge into a single set of tactics undertaken by the same person or group at an organization. I saw how social media and content marketing worked together to bolster each other. I wrote and talked at conferences about how many PR and brand-building efforts were merging with SEO. I saw how a few organizations had already combined these practices into remarkable flywheels that generated returns greater than the sum of their parts. I knew these practitioners would need tools that worked together to optimize their efforts, track their progress, and compare themselves against the competition.

Notice how I never thought to validate my idea externally? How nearly every sentence in the passage begins with "I"? You can almost picture the train wreck on the horizon.

The Case of the Disappearing Conversions

In November 2013, after more than two years of planning and development, we finally released Moz Analytics. More than ninety thousand people had seen a preview of the product and signed up to get notified of the launch. It was by far our most successful product marketing campaign, and the buzz from our community felt extraordinary. Every day, we found new, speculative discussions about what might be in the product or how it might help with their work. It felt like we were releasing a blockbuster movie rather than a business tool for marketing professionals.

But internally, we were struggling. The delivery date slipped five different times. We'd had to replace our engineering lead on the product. Features were cut, then whole sections of the product were cut. The version we released was buggy and incomplete. But worse than that, it wasn't what our customers wanted. That month, I delivered an all-hands presentation (my last one as CEO) to the Moz team, detailing what had gone wrong and where we stood. This slide was the setup:

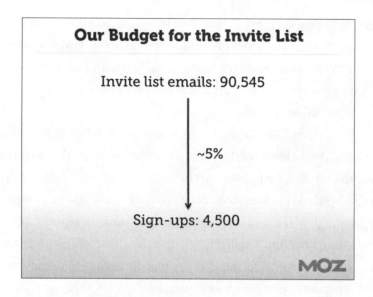

And the next one was the kicker:

Of the 90,545 folks who'd said they were interested in our new product, only 2.3 percent actually paid for at least a month of the service. Worse still, those customers tended to quit the subscription far earlier than customers of our prior product. It was almost a year of additional work before the new product was performing as well for our customers or our bottom line as our previous one.

What did we get wrong?

First, we built software in the worst possible way. Rather than creating a small kernel of the eventual finished product, then iterating and adding until we had a satisfyingly useful and high-quality deliverable, we designed a massive scope of work and asked large groups of engineers (both internal and contracted) to work on separate pieces that would then (supposedly) fit together. Multiple contractor groups failed to deliver what we needed. So, too, did multiple internal engineering groups. Everyone was demoralized. Dates were moved back by months at a time. We had no ability to show off any version of the tool set until just a few weeks before the final launch, costing us invaluable customer feedback and time to make things better or rethink the product.

Second, because of our delays, we felt insurmountable pressure to release as soon as possible. Even though customer testing a few weeks before launch revealed loads of bugs and dissatisfaction, our morale as a company and leadership team was so low that we were desperate for a release. We figured we could launch with a "good-enough" product, then iterate until it was great.

But guess what? People judge by first impressions. When those 26,832 people visited the page announcing Moz Analytics and showing off what it could do, most of them disappeared, never to return. Many who tried the product came away unimpressed. The "word on the street" (or in our case, the web forums, conference halls, and social media discussions) said Moz had a crappy new product that wasn't worth the money. That reputation dogged us for three, long, growth-stunted years.

Third, we spent years building a product based entirely around a theory—one that proved to ultimately be false. Five years after my prediction that social media marketing, SEO, content strategy, PR, and all those other "earned media" practices would combine and be the responsibility of a single person/team, online marketing remains as specialization-heavy as ever. I was so confident in my knowledge of the field and my ability to predict what people needed that I failed to do the real research required to validate those assumptions. Instead of spending time with my customers and potential customers, I spent it with my product designers and engineers, dreaming up wild new things we could build.

It wasn't until October 2013, just a few weeks before we released that doomed product, that I did what I should have done years before: put myself in our customers' shoes.

If you're ever tasked with a large software project, learn from our mistake. Pare back your design until it's the smallest possible element of what you eventually hope to have. Show that to people you trust and get their feedback. Iterate on the fundamentals. Then build it one element at a time. Add functionality, data, features, visual elements, etc., until you've got something new to show your trusted advisers and beta customers. But don't release it broadly until the buzz you're getting from these groups is firmly in the "we love this and can't live without it" camp.

That Time We Reenacted the '80s Classic *Trading Places*

Wil Reynolds is the founder of SEER Interactive, a 150-person web-marketing agency in Philadelphia with a stellar reputation, ten years of steady growth, and a vast array of impressive client work. Wil and

I have been friends for many years, having spent time together at numerous events and finding our way to more than a few dinners and after-hours gatherings. We both have strong opinions, a desire to make the world of marketing a better place, and experience building companies from the ground up.

Somehow, one night in 2012, at a drinking hole in Philadelphia, we'd shared a few whiskies and decided that the following October, we'd each take a week off from our own lives to inhabit the other's. It's the kind of conversation that usually never makes it out of the pub. We'll answer each other's emails! We'll live at each other's houses! We won't just be CEO in name only—we'll have real, decision-making authority! When we woke up and sobered up, it somehow still seemed like a good idea, so we made it a reality.

On Friday, October 4, I flew to Philadelphia with Geraldine. We took a cab to Wil's house in Northern Liberties. I learned how to care for his dog, Coltrane. Wil learned that, because we traveled so much, we'd already killed all our houseplants. We swapped email logins and critical passwords. We walked each other through the major projects and meetings on our schedules. We traded house keys. And on Saturday, Wil flew to Seattle and moved into our Capitol Hill apartment.

That week was indescribably challenging, intense, and rewarding.

Managing another human being's email, by itself, was a massive undertaking. I had to research new people, learn about projects, reach out to Wil's coworkers to ask for help with context, and constantly flex my best judgment muscles. I replied to emails from Wil's mom (with whom, delightfully, I'm still in occasional email contact to this day). I scheduled calls with new potential clients. I responded to team members and existing SEER clients who'd been instructed by Wil to treat his email as though it were any other week.

Wil starts his days early. I'm a night owl. And because of the time zones, Wil's schedule was already three hours ahead of mine. Getting to the office at the equivalent of five a.m. Seattle time took its toll, but I muddled through. Wil's assistant, Stephanie, was both immensely kind and unflinchingly strict. She had me scheduled most of the days, back-to-back, with meetings, events, or one-on-ones of one kind or another. My amazing assistant, Nicci, did the same for Wil. We both still rave about each other's EAs. (*Pro Tip*: If you can afford an exec admin, get to it! You'll boost your productivity threefold, I promise.)

I got mentored by Wil's team members in how they did many of their client projects and how they used software, including Moz's tools and several of our competitors', in their processes. With help from SEER's CFO, Larry Waddell, I dug into how they attracted customers and how they managed the complexities of waxing and waning client demand. I learned about SEER's finances and their management structure, about their promotion criteria and their team's strengths and weaknesses.

I even had an unexpected meeting crop up on Thursday, during which one of Wil's employees turned in her two weeks' notice. Remarkably enough, the same thing happened to Wil in Seattle as one of Moz's senior engineers announced his intention to leave.

We didn't just do each other's jobs; we lived the other's life. Geraldine and I volunteered at the Ronald McDonald House in Philly (a commitment Wil had made months earlier). I attended his monthly meeting with Covenant House, a charity that helps homeless youth get housing and support services. We ate dinners with Wil's wife, Nora (who couldn't participate in the swap due to work). I fed Coltrane and took her to the office. On Monday, everything felt awkward, but by Friday, both of us and our respective teams had reached a surprising level of comfort and normalcy with the swap.

I sat in on meetings with Google's advertising team and pitched

SEER's services to a pair of potential clients (they closed one deal but lost the other). Several SEER employees took me under their wings, showing me the processes they'd built and explaining the ins and outs of their site audits, their keyword research processes, how they managed client ad spend accounts, and more.

I watched SEER's consultants use tools. Sometimes it was Moz's, sometimes our competitors'. Two things stood out.

First, it was clear that every data point needed validation. If Moz's tool said there was a link from site A to site B, or that page X had a particular problem, the consultant would go check, manually, that there was indeed a link from A to B, or that the problem on X was the one we reported. Only after they confirmed the tool reports with spot-checks would they start to trust the results and assume accuracy. And if they found discrepancies, they'd switch to another tool, or worse, to an entirely manual process.

Second, in every case where SEER consultants were using tools, they'd happily switch from one hyper-specialized solution to another. If Moz's keyword data wasn't ideal, they'd use SEMRush or Übersuggest or Google AdWords. If our link data wasn't comprehensive, they'd move to Ahrefs or Majestic. There seemed to be no loyalty between tool providers and no barrier or switching costs from having to change up the UI, log in to a different tool, pay another monthly fee, or get data in another format.

The benefits I thought an all-in-one tool set created were being dismantled before my eyes.

That exposure to Wil's professional life and to SEER's inner workings was transformative. What started as a bit of a gimmick emerged as possibly the most intense, high-speed course in customer empathy imaginable. Instead of merely watching customers use our products or interviewing them about their work, I was living their lives, eating, sleeping, and breathing the challenges of an SEO agency. That week impressed upon me how different reality was from my expectations, and, along with the poor reception of Moz Analytics, made me question everything I'd assumed I knew about the web-marketing industry.

I desperately needed that humbling. I only wish it could have come sooner. It was too late to change the scope of launch and impossible to go back in time to warn my colleagues and myself that we were embarking on a voyage without the necessary compass. But that week in Wil's shoes made me more thoughtful about every plan and product I've committed to since. No longer do I trust solely my own judgment. I validate not just with interviews and testing, but by forcing myself to do the work, by using our competition's products to accomplish those tasks, and by spending time with my industry compatriots, often while on the road for conferences and events, to share side-by-side, working time with them on real projects.

Another big change I made was a return to the consulting world. Though I didn't charge for my assistance, exposure to SEER made me realize how crucial it was that I didn't just theorize and prognosticate, but actually got my hands dirty. Most of the projects I take on now are either nonprofits or via personal and professional friends I'm seeking to help. Often a half-day session with a team of marketers at a startup will uncover a huge blind spot in our tools or in the universe of available tools, and I'll return to Moz with a half-baked idea I can validate over and over before deciding if it was something real, and worthy of pursuit, or just a one-time problem.

If Life Swapping Isn't an Option . . .

Many paths exist to live the lives of your customers, but before you can do any of them, you need to know these people as people, not as "personas" or "sales targets." I've found repeatedly that when our product and engineering teams comb through user interview or review data, we tend to create features and products that are barely better than the already-established processes our customers are using.

I think this happens because of how we've been socialized and trained to use data in professional environments. We see numbers, we analyze them, and we make decisions based on how those numbers lean.

Say you're tasked with making software to help people manage their finances. You survey a large group of people about their spending habits, what they want to track, what information they need to be informed about, and where they have financial analysis pain today. The surveys and interviews reveal the ten most important categories of spending and that the proportion of spending over time and the absolute amount spent are both important. Thus, you create the same app that nearly every major bank and credit card has today to serve this purpose.

But if you knew the people personally, and spent time with them while they did their banking, financial management, and planning tasks, you might find that post-spending analysis isn't nearly as important or helpful as alerts before they spend, tracking progress against goals, or incentivizing healthy spending and saving behavior.*

---

*Yes, I realize that these types of features might dissuade a person from spending as much, running counter to the financial institution's goals of getting them to spend more (and hence won't be popularized in their feature sets).

Facebook had a great example of this several years back. Internal data showed Facebook that many users loved to reminisce by viewing photos from years past. The high engagement rate these photos received prompted the social network to launch a new feature called "your year in review." The feature was beloved by many, but also made headlines in the press because for some users who'd had tragic events, it was an unexpected, heartbreaking, and painful experience. Eric Meyer famously wrote a blog post called "Inadvertent Algorithmic Cruelty" about the experience of losing his daughter, then seeing Facebook push photos and stories of her to him at unexpected times.

The data was clear, but empathy for the real-life experiences of a crucial subset of Facebook's customers was missing. I want to believe that if an engineer on the Facebook year-in-review product had shared experiences like Eric's, or if they'd known people who did, that feature would have launched with some preventative logic built in for those who'd experienced tragedy like his.

How do you get to an empathetic place for product design and development? Create regular customer exposure for your team and yourself.

That exposure can come through extreme efforts like my CEO swap with Wil, or it can come from more subtle actions. There's a few that have worked particularly well for Moz's product folks and for other startups I've worked with, including:

- **Conferences and Events:** I get a lot of marketing value from speaking at events, but equally valuable is the exposure to professionals in our field who need and use the tools we offer. Hallway conversations, session Q&As, coffee meetings, and after-hours hangouts offer a wide range of experiential cases from which you can gain perspective and insight. Just be sure to have a few consistent, open-ended questions that get to the core of your customer-empathy issues.

- **Volunteering/Apprenticeships/Internships:** A handful of startup founders and startup product owners have taken the innovative step of volunteering a day, a week, or even a few months through an apprentice/internship (formally or informally) with their customers in order to learn what their day-to-day work, challenges, and current solutions look like. If you're in the early stages and have the ability to *be* the customer you're going to serve, even for a very limited period of time, I highly recommend it.

- **Paid or Pro Bono Consulting:** This is how Moz got its start. We were consultants first, built software that we ourselves needed, and then opened it up to a broader audience we'd built via our blog. Nowadays, I do this through pro bono consulting, and several of Moz's other product contributors still do some independent paid consulting. It's true that consulting doesn't always provide perfect insight into the issues or work faced by your target customers (unless they, too, are consultants), but it can contribute experiences and build relationships you otherwise couldn't get.

- **Teaching:** Not only does teaching require you to understand a subject or process deeply, it also gives you exposure to a wide range of practitioners or future practitioners of your subject matter. Those relationships bolster empathy as you show folks the what and how behind a process. It's no surprise that so many professors and educators are recruited as startup advisers.

- **Hiring or Contracting:** If you or your current team have no bandwidth or no passion for embedding yourselves into your customer processes, there's no shame in recruiting to help fill this gap. We've done this many times at Moz, hiring SEO professionals who know the field well and have used dozens of tools for years to assist us in building better software for customers like them. The key is identifying those individuals who can translate their own problems into more global solutions and have a product-driven mind-set, rather than focusing exclusively on their own processes. We've done best with this through the worlds of social media and blogging, ID'ing folks whose public contributions to the field clearly show an affinity for holistic, empathetic pattern matching and helping the industry as a whole.

Thankfully, after learning from my mistakes with Moz Analytics, a couple of years later I was given a second chance to build a new product. In this next chapter, I'll walk you through how we did it and try to reverse engineer why it worked so well.

CHAPTER 12
GREAT PRODUCTS ARE RARELY "MINIMALLY VIABLE"

If you are not embarrassed by the first version of your product, you've launched too late.

—**Reid Hoffman, March 2011**

In the past decade, the "lean startup" movement has had, arguably, a greater impact on the approach that product designers, engineers, and entrepreneurs take than any other. The fundamental concept is undeniably compelling: craft a version of your product (and company) that requires the least amount of time and effort to validate whether the problem you're solving is an important one that real customers will pay for or use. This "minimum viable product" will help you learn faster, iterate faster, and survive longer on less money. It's a powerful way to overcome many of the problems that plague (and often prematurely kill) young companies and new product efforts.

But it also leads people to create a lot of crappy, barely useful products.

We'll Learn a Lot Once the MVP's Out

In late 2014 and early 2015, I worked with Moz's big data and data science teams designing a minimum viable product (MVP) to help people identify websites that Google might consider to be spam.

We started with a few assumptions about the field of web spam and SEO that we then validated through research and customer interviews:

- Getting links from spam sites can potentially harm rankings and visibility in Google.
- Knowing which sites are spam is hard because Google won't label them (if they did, spammers could easily see what passes Google's filters and what doesn't).
- If you take the time to perform searches in Google related to a website, and see that it doesn't rank for any terms and phrases that it obviously should (e.g., if Moz.com didn't rank on the first page in Google for "Moz" or "Moz com," we'd know something was wrong), there's a good chance Google's penalized or banned that site for spam.
- If spam does link to you, Google recommends using the "disavow tool" system in Google Search Console, but you must be incredibly cautious, because disavowing non-spam links to your site can result in massive traffic losses. (Cyrus Shepard, Moz's head of SEO at the time, tested this by disavowing all the links to a site he owned, and it plummeted in the rankings . . . lesson learned).*

---

* You can see more about this humorously fatal experiment here: https://moz.com/blog /google-disavow-tool.

• Many of our interview subjects said that fear of Google penalties and the constant need to identify and validate spam versus non-spam links was driving them up the wall and consuming a lot of their SEO work time.

Based on these learnings (and others I've excluded for brevity), we decided to build a "Spam Score" into our web index. This score would help indicate the degree to which a site might be perceived as spam by Google, and thus a potentially risky place from which to get or have links.

The MVP process used a clever bit of research from our head of data science Matt Peters. Long story short, Matt and I dreamed up nearly a hundred potential factors that might be correlated with sites Google had penalized or banned. We then generated a large list of websites that didn't rank for their own brand or domain name (indicating they had been flagged by Google) and looked at the relative connections between all those hundred factors and the penalized or banned websites. In the end, we found seventeen factors that were relatively good predictors of whether a site had drawn Google's ire.

We called them "spam flags" and saw in our research that the more flags a website had, the more likely it was to be penalized in Google's rankings. The flags included things like the length of the domain name (turns out spammers often have very long domain names) or the presence of many external links with very little content. Having a few flags wasn't a particularly bad thing—most websites triggered at least two or three. But if a website triggered eight or more of the seventeen flags, it was more likely than not to be penalized.

The great part about Spam Score, at least for us at Moz, was that it required a relatively small amount of additional work (all in, about three months of effort from five people, though it spread out across almost a year due to overlapping priorities) to include in our data sets and to publish in our tools. We knew that initially it would receive some fair and justified criticism, and we expected folks to have concerns like:

- Moz's web index wasn't large enough (at the time) to cover all of the domains that may be spam, and thus couldn't provide a comprehensive list of sites to disavow with Google.
- The percent-risk model can be confusing. Many people would prefer a model that simply showed whether or not a domain was penalized by Google (rather than a percent-chance tied to a count of features), but we didn't have the bandwidth to make that happen.
- Spam flags could be misconstrued as a potential problem for one's own website rather than a filter system for reviewing links from other spammy websites.
- The scores of five through eleven (out of seventeen) could be particularly vexing because they indicate a higher risk of penalization, but could also be totally innocuous.
- The flags weren't actually the spam signals Google uses (we don't know what those are because Google doesn't disclose them). They're simply well correlated with sites that have drawn penalties in the search engine.

At launch, we figured, despite these issues, our MVP would still help a lot of people and, like all good MVPs, it would help us learn more about our customers and what they wanted from a spam-identifying product long term.

But here's the kicker: Our research had already revealed what customers wanted. They wanted a web index that included all the sites Google crawled and indexed, so it would be comprehensive enough to spot all the potential risky links. They wanted a score that would definitively say whether a site had been penalized by Google. And they wanted an easy way of knowing which of those spammy sites linked to them (or any other site on the web) so they could easily take that list and either avoid links from it or export and upload it to Google Search Console through a disavow file to prevent Google from penalizing them.

That would be an *exceptional* product.

But we didn't have the focus or the bandwidth to build the exceptional product, so we launched an MVP, hoping to learn and iterate. We figured that something to help our customers and community was better than nothing.

I think that's my biggest lesson from the many times I've launched MVPs over my career. Sometimes, something is better than nothing. Surprisingly often, it's not.

Spam Score launched on March 30, 2015, and while we did receive a good bit of positive feedback, we also got a lot of criticism, confusion, and questions. The score's design was suboptimal. The way the flags aligned to a percentage risk model wasn't intuitive. Many users focused on the flag count for their own website rather than the flags of the incoming links to their sites. These were things we knew would happen in the design and construction phase but pushed to the back burner in favor of a faster release.

Marie Haynes, one of the world's foremost experts in the field of web spam and Google penalty issues, left a comment in the launch blog post that summed up a lot of the sentiment around the release:

> *I wanted to like this tool, but I am really concerned that it*
> *could do more harm than good. Perhaps I have misunderstood*

its purpose. If used as an adjunct to a manual link audit, it could be helpful. But to me, it came across as an all in one solution to link problems. I think that other people are going to assume this as well.

We'd talked to Marie during the development of the metric. We knew her concerns. We knew she was massively influential in the space and that her approval and support (and others like her) were a great barometer for our success at solving the problem, but we chose to launch while we were still "embarrassed" by our first version of the product, rather than waiting until we could develop something better. Perfect is the enemy of done, right?

Six months after launch, while looking at our product performance metrics, we noted that spam score had become mildly popular with a small group of our customers (about 5 percent of the folks who regularly used Open Site Explorer visited the spam score section), but it had no observable impact on free trials, on vesting rate, on retention, or on growth of the Moz Pro subscription overall. In other words, we'd probably have seen exactly the same performance in our customer base and growth rate if we'd never launched Spam Score.

Great use of (at least) $500,000 in data collection, research, and engineering time, eh? Thank god I'm the founder . . . otherwise I might have been shown the door.

Do MVPs Have to Be So Minimally Viable?

The problem with MVPs, and with the "something > nothing" model, is that if you launch to a large customer base or a broad community, you build brand association with that first version. To expect your initial users (who are often the most influential, early-adopter types you'll attract—the same ones who'll amplify the message about what you've put out to everyone else in your field) to perceive an MVP as an MVP is unrealistic.

In my experience, our customers (and potential customers) don't see new things and think: "Oh, this must be their initial stab, and while it's not exactly what I want or need, I can see that it's a product I should pay attention to and help support, because eventually I can imagine it getting to the place where it really is useful and helpful to me."

Instead, they (usually) see new things and think: "Is this interesting? Does it do what I need? Is it way better than what I already use? Is it worth the hassle of learning something new and switching away from what I've always done?" and if the answer to those questions is a "no," or even "Well, maybe, but I'm not quite sure," your product is unlikely to have substantive impact.

Worse, I've found that when we launch MVPs, the broad community of marketers and SEOs who follow Moz perceive our quality to be shoddy and our products to be inferior. I've termed this brand reputation that follows an initially incomplete, minimally viable product's launch the "MVP hangover." It seems to follow the product and even the broader brand around for years, long after we've iterated and improved to make the product truly exceptional and best-in-class.

My theory about MVPs applies differently to different stages of your organization, based mostly on reach:

For an early-stage company with little risk of brand damage and a relatively small following and low expectations, the MVP model can work wonderfully. You launch something as early as possible, you test your assumptions, you learn from your small but passionate audience, and then you iterate until you've got something extraordinary. Along the way, your (tiny) organization is associated with an ever-improving product, and by the time large groups of influencers and potential customers hear about you, you're in great shape to be perceived as a leader and innovator.

Conversely, if you already have a big following with high expectations, publicly launching a traditional MVP (one that leans more to the "minimum" side of the acronym than the "viable" side) can be disastrous. If you've reached a certain scale (which could vary depending on the reach of your organization versus the size of your field), perception and reputation are huge parts of your current and future success. A not-up-to-par product launch can hurt that reputation in the market and be perceived as a reason to avoid your company/product by potential customers. It can carry an MVP hangover for years, even if you do improve that product. And it can even drag down perception of your historic or currently existing products by association.

Tesla's a great example of an early-stage company that could not afford to launch an MVP. Prior to producing its first mass-market-available vehicle (the Tesla S in 2008), its reputation and reach was already so vast by virtue of Elon Musk's fame and the media surrounding the formation, growth, and, later, government loans to the company that anything less than extraordinary would have sundered its public perception and perhaps shuttered the organization.

Or take Slack, one of the darlings of the SaaS and tech world over the last few years. Had it become publicly associated with its initial MVP group chat product (which wasn't nearly as good, as feature-rich, or as compelling in user experience as HipChat or Yammer), it's likely that it never would have achieved the great success it did. But because Slack started small, with an internal-only product that slowly spread until it was truly exceptional and ready to earn broad adoption and reach, the model of iterating internally on a minimum viable product but waiting until that product was exceptional before launching worked wonders.

When Google launched in 1999, it could afford to be just like Slack—a slightly different and sometimes better version of what other search engines like Yahoo! and AltaVista were at the time. But today, if you wanted to compete with Google, your search engine would have to be immensely, obviously better in order to have even an iota of a shot against it. Microsoft's Bing, when it launched in 2009, sadly wasn't massively superior and thus, despite being an impressive effort, was generally perceived as a poor also-ran. Bing's gotten much better since then, and is now as good as or better than Google on most queries, but that MVP hangover has stuck with the brand for years and, in my opinion, continues to dampen the prospects of what should be a very decent option for web searchers.

The Alternative: An Exceptional Viable Product

My proposal is that we embrace the reality that MVPs are ideal for some circumstances but harmful in others, and that organizations of all sizes consider their market, their competition, and their reach before deciding what is *viable* to launch. I believe it's often the right choice to bias to the EVP, the "exceptional viable product," for your initial, public release.

It is absolutely the right move to first *build* an MVP. Developing every feature to perfection before you have anything people can test in the real world can be devastating. But as we saw in chapter 11, depending on your brand's size and reach, and on the customers and potential customers you'll influence with a launch, I'd urge you to consider whether a private launch of that MVP, with lots of testing,

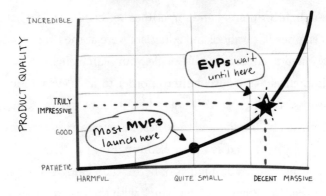

THE VALUE OF LAUNCHING AN EVP VS. AN MVP

PRODUCT QUALITY

INCREDIBLE

TRULY IMPRESSIVE

GOOD

PATHETIC

EVPs wait until here

Most MVPs launch here

HARMFUL   QUITE SMALL   DECENT   MASSIVE

ATTENTION, CUSTOMERS,
AND EVANGELISM

EVP = Exceptional Viable Product
MVP = Minimal Viable Product

learning, and iteration to a smaller audience that knows they're beta testing, could be the best path. For Moz, it's worked out remarkably well in several of our product efforts. I'll share an example that highlights how that process can work.

After the disastrous launch of Moz Analytics and the mediocre reception of Spam Score, I vowed not to make the MVP mistake again. In early 2015, I pitched Moz's executive team on a plan to build a new keyword research tool. Despite my last few product challenges, I got approval to work with a small team of five engineers on my proposal, with the caveat that those folks would have to continue their regular work maintaining the infrastructure, upgrades, and operations of another product. I talked to the team, and they agreed they could simultaneously support our existing workload and take on this new project.

I knew that if I messed this up, it would likely be my last shot at having product ownership responsibilities at Moz. I can even recall the exact words my CEO had with me as I was embarking on it. I asked if she trusted me to do a good job on these new keyword research tools, and she replied: "I think you're good at seeing what's wrong with a product, but I don't think you're a good product designer." Those words became my mantra and my motivation over the next year. I was determined to prove to her, to my team, and to myself that I'd learned my lessons and could still make something remarkable.

And yes, I realize that proving other people wrong is not an emotionally healthy form of motivation, but for me, it's always been an effective one.

The new product I wanted to build would eventually be called "Keyword Explorer." The goal was to help people determine what their customers and audiences were searching for online, craft lists of keyword terms and phrases to target on their websites, and prioritize those lists so they could logically know what to work on first. For example, if you're starting up a new Italian foods website, and you want to help your visitors choose the best brands of fresh and dried pasta, you need to know what people type into Google when they're looking for that type of content. You also want to know which words and phrases are used more commonly than others—do more people search for "fresh pasta" or "dried pasta"? More for "best pasta brands" or "best pasta makers"? And which of those search queries are harder versus easier to appear in (usually determined by which other sites are already ranking in the results and how popular/important/well-linked-to they are).

My first step was to create a slide deck in which I "pitched" the concept of a keyword research tool to the Moz team. I shared this first with my executive team and then with the entire company. I made three primary claims about why we should invest in solving the problem of keyword research:

1. The keyword research tools space was far less competitive at the time than other areas in which Moz had invested product and engineering resources (like links, rankings, and website crawling).
2. Keyword research was (and still is) the most commonly performed task in the SEO world, mostly because it's important to do every time you produce new content.
3. I believed that Moz had access to unique data and the ability to combine that data in ways that no other company in the world could.

My research process for the pitch and the product design involved a lot of requests to my friends and colleagues in the SEO community. I asked a few dozen folks for detailed information about how they did keyword research currently and what tools and processes they applied. I sent out a pair of surveys via Twitter and BCC email blasts to get a sense of what was already popular in the field (and wrote a blog post about it). Those surveys showed me which tools people were most familiar with and which ones people paid for. That gave us a huge head start in knowing what naming conventions and design layouts and existing structures our audience was already familiar with.

And, finally, I sat down, face-to-face, with a handful of SEO practitioners as they showed me exactly how they did keyword research for their websites or clients.

Those surveys, interviews, and email conversations confirmed a few big truths:

• Almost everyone who did SEO professionally used a very similar methodology for keyword research. First, they gathered a bunch of potential terms and phrases from lots of different online tools. Next, they put them all in a spreadsheet (Excel or Google Spreadsheets) and, often manually, gathered metrics about the search popularity, relative ranking difficulty, and traffic potential. Finally, they used some version of a formula to combine the metrics and prioritize the list.

- No existing tool performed this work automatically. Everyone had to use multiple tools and data sources alongside a manual process to build their lists.

- A strong majority of professionals were paying for one or more keyword research tools.

- The accuracy (or rather, gross inaccuracy) of keyword volume data was perceived as the biggest challenge and frustration among people I surveyed and talked to.

My one fear coming out of this process was that I hadn't learned much, if anything new. All the data I'd collected and all the interviews I did merely confirmed my preexisting suspicions. I worried that I'd somehow biased my product research—it couldn't be that my intuition was perfectly matched with reality, right?

Well, maybe. In this case, I wasn't just a product designer, I was also technically my own customer. I create lots of content for the web, and I'd been doing keyword research myself for more than a decade. Like a lot of the folks I spoke to and surveyed, I, too, used many tools, created spreadsheets, and built my own prioritization calculations. I went to conferences and events, read blog posts, and watched industry insiders and newcomers write about, talk about, tweet about, and share their processes. I lived and breathed the life of my customers, and, I think because of that, my empathy radar was especially well tuned to this problem set. I'm still very, very glad I did the research, though, because I needed it to prove to my team what was necessary for a release-worthy tool.

We started building Keyword Explorer in May 2015, initially hoping to launch by the end of the year. That slipped into January, at which point we had a workable version that included the basics. Input a word or phrase and it would analyze Google's search results, suggest related search queries, return volume estimates, and enable you to easily build a list for export or analysis. I was pretty excited about the tool and went about showing it off to many of my SEO colleagues. I stayed over at Wil Reynolds's house (my CEO swap friend) in January and walked him through the tool. I shared it with colleagues from Distilled, another consulting company to whom Moz has had long-time close ties. But I think the experience that triggered my change of heart came most saliently from a demo I gave to Dan Shure.

Dan's an SEO consultant and well-regarded podcast host (of *Experts on the Wire*) based in Worcester, Massachusetts. He has a sizable following in the SEO community and is particularly passionate about keyword research. Dan and I were scheduled to be at a conference together in Orlando, Florida, at the end of January, just before Keyword Explorer was scheduled to launch.

When I opened my laptop and showed Dan our application, I was nervous. I desperately wanted him to like what we'd built, and I knew that if he didn't, we'd have serious work ahead. I typed in a few keywords, showed him the basics, and invited him to try some of his own searches.

In the good news column, the interface was intuitive. Dan picked it up right away and started building a list of keywords for one of his recent clients. He had a lot of questions about our data sources and whether he could trust the numbers we provided. He seemed mostly satisfied by my explanations but said he'd need to double-check them against his own data and the Google search advertising campaigns his client was running.

In the bad news column, Dan was underwhelmed by a number of missing features, a lack of clarity around the sources of some of the data, and the inability to filter, sort by, and view metrics he deemed critical to his keyword selection process. I showed him some of the behind-the-scenes data sources (essentially command-line-style interfaces that could surface some of the filters and information he wanted), and his eyes got wide with excitement.

That night, I wrote up a lengthy email sharing the notes from my review session with Dan. I told the development team, and in a later email my executive team, that based on Dan's feedback (and several others'), I wanted to delay the launch until we had released five more features I felt were critical to earning the reception and adoption we wanted. Frustratingly, those features would take an additional four months of development! We were going to be nearly six months late delivering the product launch.

Thankfully, because Moz had so many other bets placed for 2016, and because our small team and the Keyword Explorer tool was considered a side project less central to the company's growth plan for the year, we were granted the reprieve. From January to May, we worked tirelessly to upgrade and improve the tool. When we finally launched, it was with a product of which we could be truly proud.

Those first two days after launch, we had just over seventy thousand visits to Keyword Explorer from more than sixteen thousand unique visitors. Keyword Explorer was the second-most up-voted product on Product Hunt the day it launched and made news on more than a dozen industry publications in the SEO and web-marketing fields. Hundreds of people commented on the launch post and on social media sites, nearly all of them in an overwhelmingly positive fashion.

My favorite came from Dan Shure himself, whose endorsement I wasn't sure we'd earn given his critiques back in January:

> *Incredibly excited to see @Moz's new Keyword Tool launched. It's a "must-use" for all my keyword/topic research now.*
>
> **—Dan Shure's tweet on the day of Keyword Explorer's public launch**

Over the next year, Keyword Explorer would become the most lauded, positively reviewed, and fastest-growing new feature (by use) in Moz's subscription. Our customer success team shifted much of their onboarding efforts to showcase the product, and our metrics showed that its use by customers had a strong correlation with subscribers who stuck around as paying customers versus those who quit.

It wasn't an unmitigated success, though. We offered access to Keyword Explorer two ways: through the traditional month-to-month Moz subscription (at $149/month) or as a stand-alone product (which could only be purchased with an up-front payment of $600 or a higher-tier at $1,800). The month-to-month subscriptions were significantly bolstered by the launch and the product's success, but the stand-alone subscriptions had almost no adoption at all. Don't underestimate the power of packaging and pricing.

For me, the lesson about MVPs versus EVPs was a powerful one. In the future, I don't think I'd ever willingly publicly release a product that leans minimum rather than exceptional (at least, not with a brand that has any substantial reach). The impact of reputation and word of mouth on potential success versus the risks of MVP hangover is too important to ignore.

CHAPTER 13

SHOULD YOU SELL
YOUR STARTUP EARLY?
YES, PROBABLY

An anti-IPO, pro-acquisition mentality plagues the tech industry
and prohibits companies from hitting the long ball.

—Bill Gurley, May 2013

Investors. Media. Employees. Fellow entrepreneurs. Startup enclaves. They push us to "go big or go home." Entrepreneurship culture broadly and the technology world in particular glorify founders who've stayed independent, turned down the big acquisition offers, and built "world-changing" companies as a result.

Mark Zuckerberg turned down all those offers to buy Facebook. Larry and Sergey rejected early offers to buy Google. Snapchat famously said no to billions. Netflix rebuffed Amazon's millions. Slack has turned down a reported "eight to ten acquisition offers." These stories form the popular mythos of what it means to be a founder, one that pervades the mentality of the rest of us. Getting out early with a nice payday is viewed as a fine lifestyle choice, but it's not a path to become a celebrated, legendary entrepreneur.

Infuriatingly, there's an ugly flip side of the much-venerated choice to stay independent. Scorn and criticism are heaped upon founders who reject acquisition offers only to see their companies plateau or decline. Groupon, Foursquare, Path, Dropbox, Yahoo!, Zynga, and more have all been the subject of numerous headlines excoriating them for turning down big payouts.

So here we are as founders, stuck in the middle. Take an early exit and be branded a sellout who couldn't hack it and went for the easy money. Reject that same offer only to struggle in the years ahead and you're an overambitious fool who recklessly turned down a sure thing. Play for the IPO path and you face interminable struggles and the stark reality that less than 5 percent of VC-backed companies ever make it.

What's a founder to do?

Not That I Don't Love Our Fifteen-Year-Old Kia, but Being a Millionaire Might Have Been Fun

In our thirteen-year history, Moz received only one serious acquisition offer. It came over the course of twenty-four fateful, freezing cold hours in Washington, DC.

In 2009, as Moz was just establishing itself as a software company, I had formed a personal and professional friendship with Dharmesh Shah, a successful entrepreneur (who'd previously founded and sold a company), angel investor, blogger, and cofounder of HubSpot, a Boston-based marketing software company. HubSpot and Moz were semi-competitive at the time (less so today, as they've moved away from SEO to focus on other things), but that only strengthened our relationships.

Shared struggles make for fast friends, and Dharmesh and I certainly had those. We spent late nights chatting on the phone about raising money from VCs, product innovations, what was happening with Google, how to choose a good board member, and, of course, personal stuff, too. Geraldine and Kirsten (Dharmesh's wife) came up often in our chats, and when we found ourselves in the same city, the four of us would regularly go out for long, vegetarian dinners at fancy restaurants with multicourse meals and ludicrous wine pairings. We'd spend hours talking about family, politics, books, TV shows, travel, and, of course, startup life. The bill at the end was the kind that rivaled our rent payments. I think Dharmesh let us pay only once; his generosity is unbridled. I've often wondered how it is that we found ourselves lucky enough to have Dharmesh and Kirsten in our lives.

As HubSpot and Moz grew, and as Dharmesh and I grew closer, it struck both of us that overlaps and opportunities for collaboration between our businesses were becoming more apparent. HubSpot became a customer of Moz's data via our API. We regularly promoted and linked to each other's content. Dharmesh spoke at Mozcon, our annual customer conference in Seattle. I teased him that Moz might one day buy HubSpot, knowing that theirs was the faster-growth trajectory. On one of our late-night calls, in January 2011, he told me that HubSpot's leadership team had decided to try some acquisitions, and that Moz might be in consideration.

Dharmesh introduced me to Brian Halligan, his cofounder and HubSpot's CEO. We were both scheduled to speak at a conference in DC on January 24, so Brian and I made plans to have coffee together at the event.

The weather outside was so cold that the building's heat could barely keep up. I remember walking into a deserted, cavernous cafeteria, ordering a drip coffee, and waiting for Brian with my coat on.

I wasn't sure how serious the discussion would be. Was this mostly a theoretical conversation about combining forces? An exploratory chat? A purely social chance to get some time together before going further?

Nope. It was a straightforward, right-down-to-business, formal-offer conversation.

Within minutes of Brian shaking my hand and sitting down, he laid out his plan. HubSpot was making a formal, cash and stock offer to buy Moz. They wanted me to work on products with Dharmesh. They wanted to merge our teams. They were ready to have a Seattle presence. I'd probably have to travel to Boston a lot (or maybe move there). But before we got into those details, Brian wanted to make sure the financial side of the offer would work.

In 2009, Moz did $3.1 million in revenue, but almost $900,000 of that was consulting, which we closed down as a business unit to focus on software. In 2010, revenue was $5.7 million, almost all of which was from the software subscription (and a little from Mozcon ticket sales). We were aiming to double again in 2011, to about $10 million.

Brian opened the financial discussion by saying HubSpot expected to spend in the range of twenty to thirty million dollars.

Let's take a minute to appreciate that this was an extraordinary amount of money. The startup world can make you into a highly irrational thinker with its constant news of hundreds of millions and billions of dollars changing hands and of kids in their early twenties walking away from a company after only a few years with payouts that put them easily in the top 0.1 percent of wealth owners. These outliers dominate the media and seem to the rest of us like the status quo. The infamous line from *The Social Network* should be taken as hyperbolic satire, but in Silicon Valley, it's treated almost like a mantra: "A million dollars isn't cool. You know what's cool? . . . A billion dollars."

That's fucking insane. A million dollars is plenty cool. A million dollars would have meant an incredible lot to my family and me, and Geraldine's, if we'd had it anytime in the past decade. And that's the case for more than 80 percent of American families. Phew. Sorry. Rant over.

Considering all that, I'm ashamed to tell you about the series of events that followed.

I called Michelle Goldberg (of Ignition Partners) and Kelly Smith (of Curious Office), the investors from our first (and at the time, only) round of funding. I called my mom. I called my COO, Sarah. I talked to each of them only briefly, because I had to give my presentation at the conference. Then I called them all again after. We talked through valuation scenarios and expected outcomes. We talked about the relative value of HubSpot's stock and what it might be worth in the future. At the time, HubSpot was a private company, but they were targeting an eventual public offering. We weighed the risks and the benefits, or at least we thought we did.

Our logic went along these lines:

- Software-as-a-Service companies like Moz and HubSpot were getting valued in private markets and recent deals in the 4–10X revenue range (i.e., a company doing $1 million in revenue might be bought for between $4 million and $10 million).
- While the deal would be lucrative for Moz's founders (my mom and I each owned 32.5 percent of the company at the time) and early employees (twelve folks each owned between 0.5 percent and 3 percent), it wasn't meaningful for our investors, who'd make back only three to four times their initial $1.1 million investment.
- Moz was growing relatively fast, around 100 percent year-over-year, and had a strong net margin on our revenue (about 80 percent,

meaning that our costs for each subscriber was only about 20 percent of what they paid us each month).

- We were unique in our market position, were already considered a leader (if not *the* leader) in the field of SEO software, and thus should command a premium in an acquisition.
- Given our $5.7 million in revenue in 2010, trending to $10 million in 2011, an offer like Brian's was in the 4–5X revenue range, and we felt we should push for a higher, 6–8X multiplier.

Late that afternoon, I talked to Brian again. I told him we were excited about HubSpot and interested in the deal, but the money felt too low. My position was that at $40-plus million, we should keep the conversation going, but below that, we weren't interested.

He sent back this email the next morning:

Subject line: I don't think we can really afford you

Brian Halligan <   >   1/25/11

to Rand

Hi Rand,

You folks just might be too expensive for us . . . eyes bigger than our stomachs. We could probably afford $25 million for y'all. If that's worth discussing, let's continue the dialog. If not, perhaps we could have the conversation again down the road.

It was great hanging out with you in DC.

Rand Fishkin < ██████████ >

to Brian

Thanks Brian—I think we're not in the ballpark, but really appreciate you thinking of us.

Congrats on the raise and good luck with whomever you buy!

I've probably pulled up that email thread fifty times in the last six years.

Twenty-five million dollars.

Thirty-two point five percent of $25 million is $8.125 million. And in 2014, HubSpot had one of the most successful IPOs of any SaaS company. Their stock has soared to great multiples since. That $25 million would have turned into a lot more. I've tried hard not to estimate it, but it's probably double that number. Maybe more.

Every time I talk to my grandparents about their financial situation and how they have to sell their house and stretch their budget to afford a nonideal retirement community, I think about that offer. Every time I visit Geraldine's mom, who has to rent out rooms in her house to make ends meet, I think about that offer. Every time my in-laws or our friends ask us why we're still renting and haven't bought a home, I think about that offer. Every time we make a charitable donation of fifty dollars to a cause that deserves five hundred, I think about that offer. Every time Moz struggles, every time we face heartrendingly hard decisions about the business, every time we miss our budget or have to scale back our ambitions, I think about that offer. In late 2011, when that New York investor pulled out of our signed term sheet for a Series B.

In 2014, when, during a bout with depression, I stepped down as CEO. In 2016, when we laid off more than a quarter of our staff.

Geraldine and I are not poor. Our income puts us in the top 20 percent of American earners. We can afford meals out and fun vacations. We've been able to help out family when they're struggling. We can pay for a nice apartment even in Seattle's ridiculously expensive rental market. Geraldine sold a book to a major publisher. We're almost 75 percent of the way to what we'd need for a down payment on a home in the city.

But $8 million is a life-changing amount of money. And unless extraordinary things happen with Moz in the future, it's likely to be a considerable amount more than we'll make even in a successful long-term scenario because of how startup equity works.

The Peculiar Reality of Founder Equity

Moz in 2016 made $42 million, 7.5 times as much money as we did in 2010. But today, thanks to two follow-on rounds of investment (which we were, at the time, thrilled to raise), Geraldine and I own about 23 percent of the company versus the 32.5 percent we owned in early 2011. It's probable that in years ahead, we'll own even less as the employee option pool (the percentage of stock that's distributed to folks we hire and keep at the company) increases, and as dilution from future fundraising rounds (the average "successful" startup raises about $42 million and we've done $29.1 million so far) hits. Moz's investors also have what's called a liquidity preference of 1X (thankfully, a very founder- and employee-friendly number), meaning that upon a sale or IPO, the investors receive their money back first (the $29.1 million), and then the remaining value is split up between the remaining equity shareholders.

Let's imagine that in 2020, Moz has a successful exit for $250 million, ten times the price offered by HubSpot in 2011. Depending on dilution and ownership at the time and on investor liquidation preference, and based on the established history that HubSpot's stock skyrocketed in value between 2011 and their 2014 IPO, it's probable that our financial return, while substantial, will not reach what that 2011 offer would have.

Even that success is by no means probable. It's statistically just as likely that the company will be sold for much less, maybe only enough to cover our investors' preference. And there's a reasonable possibility of a mediocre outcome in the $75 million to $150 million range (just writing those numbers alongside the adjective "mediocre" makes me feel ridiculous, but such is our environment) that makes some money for everyone but likely wouldn't be much more than the delta between my salary the last twelve years and what I'd have made at a Google, Microsoft, or Amazon during that same period.

It's fair criticism to ask why I've focused on my personal, financial gain from Moz. I do so here because so few people are willing to be transparent about real numbers or honest that a big part of the motivation for founding a startup is in the hopes of an extraordinary payday. We don't talk about money because it's uncomfortable, but that silence excludes important stories and important statistics. It hides the truth about a significant startup motivation behind a facade of "changing the world" and "building something from scratch." Those motivations exist, too! They're important. They deserve recognition. But real transparency is talking about the uncomfortable parts of entrepreneurship and startups.

Let's focus next on an equally critical player in this equation: Moz's employees.

In 2011, if you'd been at Moz for two or three years, it was likely that you held between 0.5 percent and 3 percent of the company's stock. A sale of $25 million at the time would have netted you somewhere between $125,000 and $750,000 (not accounting for HubSpot's eventual IPO, which would likely have made you considerably wealthier). Due to the incredibly low option strike price, a Mozzer who started in 2008 or 2009 would have paid next to nothing to execute their options (that price is based on something called a "409a valuation," in which an external auditor like Deloitte determines a "fair market value" for the company and its employee stock options), meaning you would realize almost the full price per share as cash. In addition, acquisition offers almost always come with signing and/or retention bonuses, which can be particularly lucrative for key employees the acquirer is hoping to keep on staff. Moz was still quite small in early 2011 (about thirty-three people), and most of the team was paid a less-than-market-rate salary, which would have been bumped up to HubSpot's relatively generous, generally higher-than-market rates.

In 2020, the financial picture for an employee who's been at Moz two to three years looks dramatically different. On the plus side, your salary and benefits have been competitive with all but the highest-paying employers in the city. Because Moz regularly fights with Facebook, Google, Amazon, and Microsoft for talent, our salary offers and benefits for the last few years have been nearly comparable to those big players. The downside is that stock options are both lower in size (0.05 percent to 0.1 percent of the company's stock is now on the high end of the employee grant spectrum) and higher in strike price (an early 2017 409a put the gross, common stock value at about $65 million) meaning you'd only realize gains in the delta between that number and the acquisition price. Lucrative signing and retention offers would still be a possibility for more senior and critical roles (these are usually engineering-centric), but probably wouldn't be offered at meaningful levels for most other folks.

This is the fundamental trade-off of startup finances: earlier stage usually means lower salary, fewer benefits, more risk, but more potential reward if things go amazingly well. Later stage usually means competitive salaries and benefits, less risk, but only a small reward even in exceptional outcomes.

All that said, money isn't everything. Ego, pride, reputation, and notoriety are also big players in how startup founders (myself included) and employees think about their companies and any eventual exit. Startup culture creates a notable distinction between "aspiring entrepreneur" and "successful entrepreneur." In the first category, people are still trying to accomplish their end goal, and in the second, they've achieved it at least once.

Those goals could be any number of things. It could be building a business that's profitable and enables you to live the way you want, as Maciej Cegłowski famously has with the "artisanal SaaS" model of Pinboard. It could be the creation of a new trend, say, popularizing high-quality ramen noodles in the United States (which Sun Noodle of Hawaii actually did in the early 2000s). Or, most commonly in the tech startup world, it could be delivering on the promised return for your investors, as Moz strives to do.

The Founder's Gambit

Once your venture has taken outside capital, your goal necessarily shifts to returning a multiple of that capital through a sale or public offering. The criteria for "success" is much more limited. Moz may have popularized SEO software, we may have built a solidly growing, profitable business, we may have made the world of marketing better, or created a great work culture, or accomplished any number of milestones, but those can no longer be defined as demarcation lines between striving for success and achieving it.

In November 2007, when we raised our first round of investment, a promise was made: we will work to return five to ten times that amount of money through growth and a liquidity event. As we raised subsequent rounds, that promise hardened.

For many founders, this clear line of separation between aspiring entrepreneur and successful entrepreneur is a fixed, psychological obsession. I find myself jealously reading Techmeme (a website that aggregates technology and startup news), seeing the dozens of companies each month that sell for millions, closing my eyes, shaking my head, and closing the browser window before returning to work.

It's not just the financial side—many founders I know didn't make out particularly well in their exits, but so long as they returned a multiple to their investors and achieved that liquidity event, they can forever have the moniker of "successful entrepreneur" in their biography. You might think this is hyperbolic bullshit, that a small exit from a tiny startup doesn't equate to "success" or that building a $40 million-plus/year business like Moz from the ground up is absolutely "success." But I've done the legwork on this one. It's a pervasive frame of mind in the startup ecosystem.

I've talked to dozens if not hundreds of founders about this exact phenomenon. Everyone who's had an exit agrees that it brings with it an almost mystical sense of closure and accomplishment. And everyone who hasn't yet confirms that same sense of striving and hopefulness and desperate desire to cross that mentally dominating finish line. Startup entrepreneurs know how the press writes about and future investors think about those who've had "a win," even if it was only a "base hit" (yes, this the language of my peers, and yes, we've become a parody of ourselves) versus those who haven't. That culture's ingrained in how founders see and judge one another and themselves.

The association goes beyond founders, though. A startup employee who's part of a successful exit gains a hard-to-describe level of credibility and an aura of immense perceived value in the startup world. The ability to say "I started at XYZ corp and was part of the acquisition by . . ." carries weight among the subculture of technologists, entrepreneurs, and investors who inhabit Silicon Valley (both geographically and mentally). The bigger the acquisition, the more impressive the acquiring company (Google and Facebook top the list, of course), and the earlier you joined the acquired team, the more your status benefits.

As CEO, once a quarter for seven years, I'd stand in front of my team and repeat our mission, vision, and values, along with important news and updates about the company. As part of that, in the later years I almost always went over an answer to the constantly implied question: "Why are we here?" This is what I told the Moz team:

- We have a chance to accomplish something useful and worthwhile: to make the world of SEO and web marketing accessible, to remove the opacity and secrecy from these practices so that anyone can leverage great marketing.
- We've built a remarkable team and culture, a special bond and feeling that doesn't usually exist in a workplace, and that comes from our values and our commitment to one another.
- We are the arbiters of our own future: if we succeed, through a remarkable sale or an IPO, Moz will be forever held up as an example of how our values, our culture, and our approach can create extraordinary results. But if we fail, those values and that culture will likely recede into obscurity.

- Stock options will help you participate in and realize gains from a successful liquidity event, but they are not the only benefit. If Moz has an exceptional outcome, our CVs will carry a reputation and weight that can open doors everywhere.

At venture-backed companies, promises like these (implicit or explicit) pervade the culture. We all realize the stakes: become one of the "successful" 5 percent of companies that deliver extraordinary returns and reap rewards both reputational and financial, or found/ join a company that fails to meet that high bar and misses out on these accolades.

Startups are punishingly hard slogs for everyone involved— founders, employees, spouses and families, and often customers and investors, too. The model most institutional investors have doesn't work well with "small exits"; thus, Silicon Valley startup culture has crafted a shared narrative in which it's considered "selling out" and not building a "real company" to *only* sell for millions or tens of millions of dollars.

If you're a founder, an early employee, or someone who cares about and talks to these folks, I urge you to wholly reject these biased, investor-serving ways of thinking. Craft your own path and encourage other founders to do the same. Just as a great startup rejects the status quo in its market in order to build something better, so, too, should you put aside any indoctrinated notion that an IPO or a billion-dollar sale should be pursued at the cost of any smaller outcome. The odds are against you, your team, your investors, and your ego. Be realistic about your chances, and do what feels right to you and your team. Your investors will, I promise, be just fine.

CHAPTER 14

IF MANAGEMENT IS THE ONLY WAY UP, WE'RE ALL F'D

In a hierarchy every employee tends to rise to his level of incompetence.

—Laurence J. Peter, 1969

In May 2012, Moz raised $18 million in a Series B round, and something strange happened: everyone suddenly wanted to be a manager.

After the cash injection, we went a little overboard trying to grow the team with the false belief that more people meant we could build more and better stuff faster. As anyone who's worked in software will tell you, a team of ten engineers, rather than five, working on the same project is more likely to double the time it takes to finish rather than halve it. But we hadn't yet learned this lesson, and so, believing that staff size was holding us back, invested relentlessly in recruiting.

We had job ads everywhere. We participated in and hosted dozens of local events, hoping to boost Moz's profile. We launched a ludicrous hiring bonus program wherein anyone who referred a software engineer whom we eventually hired would earn a $12,000 cash bonus (and that engineer would get another $12,000 hiring bonus themselves).* We hired full-time recruiters to work on nothing but hiring. And we devoted a great deal of our existing employees' time to screening résumés and interviewing candidates.

Alongside all these new hires came an unprecedented swell of requests from many of our longtime best and brightest engineers, marketers, help team members, ops personnel, and product folks to build their own teams. Of Moz's existing forty(ish) nonmanagement employees from prior to the fundraising round, no fewer than twenty-five made requests to join the management ranks and to start hiring their own subordinates.

Saying yes to everyone was not an option, and most of our staff understood that. But saying no to any one person was perceived as an affront to their skills and accomplishments. For months, this played out in a suddenly political environment that had never previously existed (or at least, never been so visible). There was no malice or bad behavior, no malignant players or intentional attempts to inhibit progress. But as you can imagine, progress on many teams and many projects slowed to a crawl while efforts around hiring and anxiety around team structures distracted many of us from the real work of building products our customers needed.

---

*Quick aside: this was a terrible idea, as it encouraged a lot of purely financially motivated referrals and applicants and created the perception internally that engineers were the only employees we valued. Cue loads of strife and bad feelings between teams, and a huge amount of wasted time following up on referrals and interviewing people who weren't good matches.

Managing Is a Skill, Not a Prize

You've almost certainly heard of *The Peter Principle*, a 1969 book by Laurence Peter and Raymond Hull, which popularized the quote at this chapter's start. The theory behind it is that each employee is judged for their next promotion based on their performance at the current one, rather than their potential aptitude for the new work required in that higher-up role. Hence, people advance at an organization until they are no longer competent in their positions, and the company is left with more and more incompetence at senior levels. It's inevitable that this ugly scenario will occur if employees stop being promoted only after they can no longer perform effectively.

Knowing this theory is one thing. Finding a way to combat it, another.

Here's the challenge in a nutshell: Say you want to grow your product design team. For the past two and a half years, you've had an effective product designer who's built great stuff and earned the trust and respect of the people around them. But the designer's proven value comes from the work they do—understanding customers, crafting user experiences that serve those audiences, and managing communication with the engineers who build the product, the marketers who promote it, and the end customers who use it. This designer is clearly effective but doesn't have management experience and hasn't displayed the skills or passion for the demands of management.

The designer comes to you and asks to manage this new team of designers. You were planning to hire only one new designer, and it's awkward to have a manager with only a single report, but you figure maybe the team will get bigger if the company maintains its growth. You also want to reward the great work this designer has done and the loyalty they've displayed sticking with the company. On the flip side, you hate to lose the designer's high-quality work as an individual contributor, and in the last few years they've shown increasing effectiveness and quality as they've gelled with the people around and built strong product intuition.

You're between a rock and a hard place. Do you tell your designer to stick with what they're good at and risk losing them to a company that will promote them to the management role they believe they've earned and deserve? Or do you promote the designer to manager, and then hire or contract extra help to make up for the work they used to do, hope that they'll eventually learn and excel at those managerial skills, and sacrifice the direct application of their learned expertise?

Underlying this problem is a belief that anyone can be a people manager, and that unlike any other specialized role (e.g., accounting, marketing, engineering, design, or sales), all it takes is the will to manage and an understanding of the problem space. This is bullshit.

One of the hardest, most frustrating conversations I consistently have with team members is the one about what managers do versus what individual contributors (ICs) do. Many ICs believe that management is just telling people what to do and making sure they do it. They assume (falsely, in my experience) that only managers who've previously done the work themselves can be effective. They make an inherent assumption, often based on real, personal experiences (which are impossibly hard to argue against), that the best managers are the people who used to be the best ICs, thus proving their worthiness as leaders. A mediocre engineer will make for a poor engineering manager. A great customer service manager could never be an effective engineering manager. These myths are so easy to believe and so tied up in standard business protocols that unraveling them is like pulling teeth every time.

Thankfully, I've got the evidence, after a decade of growing teams and shrinking them, of observing great people doing awful work and seeing previously poor performers excel to say that the line between being great at the work yourself and being a great manager of the people doing that work is largely disconnected. I will absolutely concede that much of the time, great people managers were good at, or at least performed, the jobs of their reports at one time or another. But that, my friends, is correlation, not causation. Just because most managers apply for and are promoted into their role by virtue of their IC work in that same arena does not mean that IC work is necessarily connected to effective management.

Moz's own history may be too small a sample size, but thankfully, I have help. Google, one of the most admired companies in the tech world, has spent years analyzing the most and least effective teams at their company and trying to identify what consistently separates high performers from low. In their research on what makes for managers through the re:Work program, Google started from a novel premise: assume managers don't make teams better. They attempted to prove this hypothesis by identifying high- versus low-performing teams and looking for any correlation with the managing individual. Was it the case that "great" or "terrible" managers could be identified—folks who moved from team to team and consistently brought up (or down) the performance of their groups? Indeed it was. Unsurprisingly, Google found that managers did make a difference after all, and that teams with great managers were happier and more productive.

What might be surprising, though, is what Google found to be the eight behaviors consistent across strong people managers. Here they are, in order:

1. Is a good coach
2. Empowers team and does not micromanage

3. Expresses interest/concern for team members' success and well-being
4. Is productive and results oriented
5. Is a good communicator
6. Helps with career development
7. Has a clear vision/strategy for the team
8. Has important technical skills that help him/her advise the team

Number eight. Dead last on the list. That's where the quality of technical work the managers themselves are capable of comes into play. It's not that it doesn't matter at all, but of managerial qualities, it sits behind every other crucial skill.

On the great teams I've observed in which the manager did not possess technical skills, there was often a surprising benefit: the team members themselves upgraded one another's skills, mentored one another, and more often, took greater responsibility for the output of the work. I suspect that's because in teams with managers who possess their own strong technical skills, the work gets done their way, and the improvement in skills tends to be clustered around the managers' specific strengths. It also strikes me that because of the reliance on these highly skilled managers, there's less individual effort given by the team's members to explore and expand on their own. This isn't always the case—sometimes a great IC will make for a great people manager who encourages broader education from the team and who encourages dissent on how to do things rather than enforcing his own tried-and-true methods. But both my own lived experiences and the research suggest that people management and IC work are two fundamentally different things whose overlap is neither obvious nor consistent.

Given this, how do we proceed with the problem of a talented IC wanting to become a people manager?

Don't Make Management the Only Ladder Employees Can Climb

There is a deeply held misconception in business culture that people management is (a) the only way to lead and (b) the only way to advance one's career. If we address both of those, dismantle them, and create clear, obvious paths to prove that this isn't true in our organizations, we can build better teams composed of the right people properly suited to the work (management and IC).

At Moz, we addressed this by creating a new, dual-tracked career pathing system.

We modeled these paths on how engineering roles work at big companies like Microsoft and Google. In those structures, a junior engineer starts out as a lower-level individual contributor, but as they gain skills and prove their effectiveness, they can move up the ladder of promotions, salaries, benefits, stock options, and influence *without* ever becoming a people manager. Those progressions enable these firms to retain high-quality talent, groom them to serve in consultative roles involving important technical projects and discussions, and benefit from their expertise without demanding that they get good at people-management skills, which may not interest them or fit with their talents.

Like most tech companies, we had something similar for many years, but only for engineers. The surge of requests from ICs to become managers in 2012 caused us to rethink and broaden our approach. We realized the following:

- We had to do more to recognize and reward ICs (or it would never be perceived as a viable, prestigious path).
- We had to formalize the influence of ICs (or else their contributions would be interpreted differently by different people and create hot spots in the organization where ICs were more versus less respected/influential/involved).
- We had to expand the IC path from purely engineering to every role and team.

Thus, we made this chart:

INDIVIDUAL CONTRIBUTOR TRACK

PEOPLE MANAGER TRACK

AT EACH LEVEL INDIVIDUALS IN THESE ROLES HOLD:
- EQUIVALENT PAY & STOCK
- SIMILAR LEVELS OF INFLUENCE
- EQUIVALENT LEVELS OF EXPECTATIONS

ARCHITECT ROLE
(e.g., product owner, engineering architect)

C-LEVEL EXECUTIVE
(e.g., chief product officer)

SENIOR ROLE
(e.g., senior designer, senior engineer)

VP LEVEL
(e.g., VP of sales)

ADVANCED ROLE
(e.g., mid-level engineer)

DIRECTOR LEVEL
(e.g., director of paid marketing)

MID-LEVEL ROLE
(e.g., tenured help team, entry-level engineer)

MID-LEVEL MANAGER
(e.g., help team manager)

EARLY-LEVEL ROLE
(e.g., entry-level marketer)

NEW MANAGER
(e.g., marketer w/ one direct report)

JR. ROLE
(e.g., entry-level help team)

N/A
(may not exist)

Moz's dual-track career progression operates on a simple principle: individual contributors should be able to grow their skills, their influence, their titles, and their paychecks just like people managers.

In theory, and as a new element of Moz's structure, this change was appreciated and celebrated, and it garnered no contention. In practice, it required a tremendous amount of work and discipline, because the status quo's inertia was (and still is) constantly pulling people to the default belief (and the accompanying behaviors) that managers alone have the real power. This "real power" supposedly comes from the ability to hire, fire, and give performance reviews, career-affecting decisions that supposedly inspire or inhibit quality work.

You need only dig an inch below the surface to see why, in most modern workplaces, and especially in the technology and startup worlds, that's not the case. Projects in our fields succeed because enough people on the team were dedicated, diligent, and thoughtful, because the project was well designed and potential pitfalls were identified early, because the processes helped guide the team to the right solutions, and because individual contributors effectively completed the work to which they'd committed. The threat of a poor review or of being fired is barely applicable because, for the last couple of decades and probably the next few, workers with jobs like software developer, product designer, and web marketer have vastly more marketplace leverage over their companies than those companies have over them (at least in most major US cities).

Individual Contributors Don't Deserve to Be Second-Class Citizens

We hoped that Moz's ICs would see this new path to grow their careers and embrace it. But we quickly discovered that without visible, reinforcing pillars, the path would be viewed as mere lip service rather than an equal alternative. Those pillars included:

- Prominent role models along that IC track had to be regularly called out by leadership during all-hands meetings, strategic presentations, external public communications (like blog posts), and in status report emails.
- Regular interfacing needed to happen between high-level ICs and the rest of the Moz staff, so every employee had facetime and access to them.
- Influence had to be granted to ICs to guide initiatives, to advise on process, to be included in key decision making, and to have final say over project areas.

Only once these pillars existed could we credibly make the claim that the IC path received similar levels of respect and a prominent voice inside the company. Yet even after we made these efforts, skepticism and bias to the management track persisted.

I think that's because, initially, when ICs and people managers are given similar influence, the default is still for managers to have final authority. You must choose how equal you really want the two paths to be, and where to assign accountability. Be wary—accountability without the means to control it is a recipe for frustration and disaster. Those who are held to account must also be given the freedom to own (as much as possible) the inputs that can affect their success. That's harder with ICs than managers because ICs are usually not perceived as having final accountability, nor are they able to hire and fire, which many believe (falsely, in my opinion) to be where the power comes from in a project.

We tackled this in different ways with different people and teams.

The most prominent was a role we created called "Product Architect." It's a role Moz gave me a few months into my post-CEO tenure, and one I think can be very successful if done right. The idea is to have an individual who is responsible for a project's or product's success, has a team to work with, and is given the means to direct that work, meaning he determines what's to be created, has final say over product design decisions, and works with a people manager to evaluate the work and contributions of the ICs building it.

But it wasn't just product architects. We also crafted a role called "Subject Matter Expert," which folks like Dr. Peter Meyers (better known in the search and online world as "Dr. Pete"), a marketing scientist and renowned tracker of Google's ranking changes and algorithm updates, assumed. Pete's responsible for advising numerous teams on key changes Google makes to their search results and on making the call about how Moz should respond in its products and with its metrics. He works with folks on the marketing team to create content (blog posts, presentations, long-form documents, and interactive tools like Mozcast, which makes Google's daily shifts transparent through a "temperature" metric that shows the degree of change across thousands of rankings). Pete's one of our highest-level ICs, and his influence, responsibility, stock options, and pay are all on par with VP-level people managers.

Every company is different, and unlike people managers, which have a tried-and-true "box" into which they fit and historic associations that are familiar to most, IC roles should be crafted to your unique culture and needs. Not every company needs a marketing scientist like Dr. Pete or a product architect like me. But I've never seen an organization where a deeply skilled, experienced expert in an area of core competence for the business couldn't provide massive benefits. If you've been pushing great ICs to become managers so they can use their powerful technical skills to help others grow, my advice is to remove the false construct that you have to be the person doing the hiring and firing, giving the performance reviews, handling the interpersonal conflicts, and/or running the communication processes in order to have that influence.

A path for ICs to progress means you get the best people in the right roles with the ability to advance their careers and their pay. Forcing management to be the only way up will cost you talent in places you need it, and worse, install the wrong people in those roles, harming everyone on the team.

CHAPTER 15
VULNERABILITY ≠ WEAKNESS

In Silicon Valley, admitting mistakes and showing your vulnerable side is one of the biggest social faux pas that I'm tired of trying to follow.

—**Maren Kate, May 2016**

I met my wife, Geraldine, on a bus coming back from a Weezer concert in November 2001. I gave her my email address, which she thought was a brush-off (back in the early 2000s, the whole "I never got your email" line was actually pretty believable). Two weeks later, we had our first date (I maintain that it seemed like a lifetime before she contacted me), and a year after that, we moved in together. Lucky break for me. My paychecks quickly dwindled from paltry to nonexistent, my credit card debt skyrocketed, and only her steady jobs kept the lights on and the rent paid. I proposed in 2007. We got married in

2008, and, ever since, we've had as close to a storybook romance as Fezzik and Inigo's in *The Princess Bride*.*

But in 2012, I thought we were doomed.

That June, Geraldine went to see her primary care physician about worsening migraines she'd been having the past couple of years. Her doctor ordered an MRI, noting that it was extremely unlikely to reveal anything but was worthwhile to rule out some potential causes. Cue ominous music.

I didn't accompany Geraldine for that first scan. She went alone on a Thursday, lay down in a giant tube while some magnets and cameras rotated around her head, and waited for the results. The next morning, she received a call from her doctor who said they found a brain tumor on the scan, attached to her hypothalamus (the bit right in the middle of everything).

They nevertheless tried to sound reassuring.

"We won't worry until we know there's something to worry about."

Geraldine and I were unconvinced. The clinic also sent out an email with a link to the automated results in her online health account. We logged in together and looked at the scans but couldn't really understand what we were seeing. What we did understand was the radiologist's note, left helpfully next to the images that read "1cm mass on hypothalamus; worrisome for glioma."

In the era before search engines, we'd have spent the weekend nervously worried about what "glioma" meant but generally waiting until Geraldine's doctor appointment the following Tuesday. But de-

---

*That's right, Fezzik and Inigo. Not Westley and Buttercup—those two had a messed-up disaster of a relationship characterized by noncommunication and a martyr/victim complex bordering on the absurd. Rewatch the 1987 classic and you'll see what I mean. Then check out Geraldine's and my Halloween costumes from 2015 here: http://www.everywhereist.com/halloween-2015-the-princess-bride-of-course/.

spite Geraldine's suggestion that I not google the phrase "glioma," we spent Friday reading about how average life expectancy from discovery was three to seven years (and not very pleasant ones) with survival rates under 20 percent. I broke down. I tried not to say anything. But I've never had much of a poker face. She asked me to be honest. I told her I was scared she was going to die.

In fact, I'd sort of convinced myself of it. Geraldine and I had always had a storybook kind of love filled with humor and happiness, partnership and kindness. After the diagnosis, my brain went to a dark place, convinced that the price to pay for a romance like ours was a tragic end. I was so scared to spend the rest of my life without her.

I spent Saturday and Sunday in states of alternating sadness and shock. Then, needing to make sense of it all, I asked Geraldine what she wanted to do over the next few years. It seemed like an important question, particularly if these were going to be our last ones together.

That weekend was heartbreaking and hard, but it also gave me perspective I'd never before had. When there's a potential end in sight, everything that's not important quickly gives way to the stuff that really does matter. We talked in ways we probably never otherwise would have about what we wanted from the years ahead, what we didn't want, who we needed to see and didn't. We made phone calls to some friends. We ate every meal together. We stayed mostly off our computers and phones. We drove around our favorite Seattle neighborhoods. I bought a ukulele and taught myself a couple of songs. I played them only for Geraldine.

On Monday, I went into work.

We'd agreed over the weekend that until we knew for sure, we should treat the radiologist's concern with skepticism and not give in to irrational, potentially unwarranted fear. But I was a mess. Nothing to do with Moz seemed to matter. I couldn't focus or contribute in meaningful ways. The discomfort of having to pretend that every-thing was normal drove me mad. I kept up the facade for about two hours. After lunch, I called an impromptu all-hands meeting in the lobby, at the time the only space big enough (just barely) to hold us all.

I didn't say much. I could barely make it through a few short sentences. I just told everyone that the prior week, Geraldine had been diagnosed with a brain tumor and that we'd find out more soon, and that until we did, I was going to be a wreck. I told them I needed their help to make it through, and Moz did, too.

Then Jess, my assistant at the time, asked if they could all hug me. I sobbingly agreed, and we shared a giant group hug. I went back to work after that with a powerful sense of relief, of support, of camaraderie. I experienced an amazing pride for Moz and the people there with me. I don't think I've ever had a more professionally affirming experience in my career. I cried in front of everyone in my company and not for a second did I think anyone thought worse of me for it. I felt safe.

A month later, Geraldine had brain surgery to biopsy her tumor. The doctors told us it was a pilocytic astrocytoma, a very mild form of tumor that posed almost no long-term risk. After a long recovery, she's in great health, and yearly scans have shown the tumor remains non-impactful. Thank you science and modern medicine (and Obamacare, which saved her from having a "preexisting condition" that would have invalidated our insurance).

The Myth of the Strong Leader

Growing up in the United States in the 1980s and '90s gave me a very particular impression of what leadership was supposed to look like. Leaders were strong, resilient, unflinching. They were masculine in the way tough guys from TV and film were—loud and brash about their accomplishments, silent and impenetrable about their feelings. The only acceptable emotions for a leader were anger, envy, pride, and courage. Anything else was meant to be felt on the inside, never outwardly betrayed.

Think of how Mark Zuckerberg, Steve Jobs, or Elon Musk are portrayed in media and film—recalcitrant geniuses who have no life outside their work and no end to their drive, but likewise are utterly useless when it comes to caring about people. The company is all that matters. Projecting strength and achieving success; that's what a real leader does.

Repression as a means of handling emotion has a long history in American masculinity and in our culture of leadership. It's often blamed for the glass ceiling (because women leaders are asked to walk an impossible tightrope between strength and caring, with poisoned invective awaiting a slip to either side). It's often associated with self-medicating behaviors like alcohol, drugs, gambling, and other addictions. It's likely a big part of why so many executives suffer from impostor syndrome, anxiety, and depression.

The qualities stereotyped by the "strong, silent type" may make for good TV, but they make for awful leaders. In the past, I've foolishly hired and worked with people like this, and I've seen the distrust that comes from a leader who puts process ahead of people, who shuts down personal conversations or social banter, who manages politically and eschews any semblance of humanity. When that's happened, I've watched good people quit, mercenary types get hired, and work go from something people want to do to something they only do because it's required.

Ironically enough, vulnerability, when exposed openly, has vastly more positive effects on a team. In researching the most successful groups of people in technical and nontechnical professions, on technical and nontechnical tasks, over long periods or just a few hours, university studies and private company research has found that one attribute predicted performance better than any other: psychological safety.

If People Have to Cry in the Bathroom, You're Fucking Up

When teams felt safe expressing personal issues, sharing mistakes, and speaking up without the risk of harsh criticism or judgment, they dramatically outperformed their peers. This, above all other attributes researchers have been able to identify or measure, correlates with strong team output and work quality. Emotional comfort with one's colleagues was a better predictor than IQ, than years of experience, than the strength of previous work, than literally any and everything else researchers had hypothesized about.

Project Aristotle, an internal Google research project, looked at thousands of teams at the company with years of empirical data on performance and concluded that empathy between team members and a group norm of emotional support was **the best, most consistent predictor of a team's success.** A 2012 North Dakota State University study found that social sensitivity, "the ability to perceive, understand, and respect the feelings and viewpoints of others," was strongly correlated with high-performing teams. A 2008 Carnegie Mellon University study uncovered much the same in their analysis of 699 individuals broken into small groups for five-hour-long projects. The *New York Times* wrote about its results:

> What interested the researchers most, however, was that teams that did well on one assignment usually did well on all the

others. Conversely, teams that failed at one thing seemed to fail at everything. The researchers eventually concluded that what distinguished the "good" teams from the dysfunctional groups was how teammates treated one another. The right norms, in other words, could raise a group's collective intelligence, whereas the wrong norms could hobble a team, even if, individually, all the members were exceptionally bright.

I've seen this phenomenon play out on dozens of teams over the years both at Moz and in other professional settings. When we show care and trust with the people around us, and believe that they care for and trust us, too, something remarkable happens. Our collective work becomes more than the sum of its parts. We're able to achieve better results while peculiarly feeling less like the work we're doing is . . . work. Parallel to the concept of "flow" for an individual (when you get into the groove of your work, and time seems to melt away as you make rapid, high-quality progress) is this idea of group cohesion that lets multiple people function as a single unit, stronger together than they are apart. To get into that group flow, each member has to feel safe.

Psychological safety was first described by MIT researcher Amy Edmondson, who noted its difference from group cohesion (which, research observed, could cause a lack of healthy conflict and lead to groupthink). She wrote:

> The term is meant to suggest neither a careless sense of permissiveness, nor an unrelentingly positive affect but, rather, a sense of confidence that the team will not embarrass, reject, or punish someone for speaking up. This confidence stems from mutual respect and trust among team members.

Neither Edmondson nor Google nor the researchers at Carnegie Mellon proffered a theory as to why psychological safety is so predictive of a group's performance, but I'll take my own stab.

The common threads I've seen separating successful teams and projects from unsuccessful ones generally have the following elements:

- Clarity and shared understanding of goals (i.e., everyone gives the same answer to the question "Why are we building this and what do we hope to achieve with it?").
- Unity around the specific work required and how each person will contribute to it (i.e., everyone can give an answer to the question "What am I supposed to be doing and how does that fit with what each other person on the team is doing?").
- Confidence in the people around them to contribute equitably (i.e., everyone believes the statement "If I contribute my portion, everyone else will contribute theirs and we'll be successful").
- Belief that should things go wrong, they/we will have the ability to catch it, fix it, and survive it (i.e., everyone agrees with the statement "If this doesn't work, it won't mean the end for my project/team/company/career").
- A powerful sense of camaraderie and kinship, such that everyone on the team/project cares about the people around them and takes joy in the shared experience of working together (i.e., everyone would say "I want good things for all of the people on my team, and I'd be happy to make sacrifices for them and believe they'd do the same for me").

My hypotheses are that (a) psychological safety in oneself and social sensitivity in those around you nudge all of these essential elements in the right direction and (b), perhaps more impactful, a lack of feeling safe and supported pushes all of them in the wrong direction.

I've been around teams where, perhaps due to a lack of feeling safe, there was deep suspicion about the strategic approach, the long-term goals, and the connection between work and results, but no one said it aloud. I've sat in those meetings where skepticism and resignation were the underlying emotions—you could read it on people's faces. Nine times out of ten when I or another project/team leader has had to pull the "we're doing this because I'm in charge" card, it's a signal that the project (or the team) is doomed unless we can turn those prevailing attitudes around.

Recently, Geraldine and I had dinner (well, mostly drinks) with one of Moz's developers, Kenny Martin, a longtime employee and a friend. Kenny started on Moz's help team, but learned front-end web development while at the company, trained under some of our senior folks, and over the last couple of years has turned into one of our most talented contributors. We talked about everything from his father's passing away to his dating life to Moz's plans for the future. When he told me that he'd heard the strategic plan for his team's next year and felt it wasn't well thought through, a red flag went up in my head.

We spent the rest of the night socializing (and ended up at a dive bar with a surf rock band playing Christmas music, as you do), but the next day, I sent Kenny an invite to meet for an hour and talk through the product plans together. We walked through the big-picture goals, the specific work items tied to each, and how the elements fit together. Kenny asked questions, caught some blind spots I'd had, and got excited. We both did. The conflict that started as "I don't think we have a good, workable plan for next year" turned into an immensely positive experience for both of us, for the project itself, and for the company more broadly.

It's this ability to have creative, transparent, healthy conflict that drives better plans and better sentiment. When Kenny and I feel good about the plans, we can help others get on board. When everyone on the team has that same positive excitement and hopefulness, and when they know it's okay to be openly skeptical or critical, that they don't have to hide those feelings or risk their standing with their peers or managers by expressing them, the plans and the quality of work both improve.

Pro Tip: Digging into this skepticism in group settings can be hard and uncomfortable, particularly for more introverted folks or those who don't have experience working with a team. I've had far better luck taking the time to get folks in a room one-on-one, walking through the plans, and asking for their feedback, their questions, and their concerns. Yes, it's much more time-consuming, but it also means that when you get into a room all together or buckle down to do the work, the big conflicts have already been thought through and worked through. This isn't just for the sake of project contributors; it's for leaders and managers, too. It is deeply uncomfortable to defend your ideas and plans in front of a group, and even harder to admit mistakes or gaps, or to make on-the-fly changes in a group setting. But it's vastly more comfortable to do it one-on-one with team members and to know everyone's concerns before you present or start work on a final plan.

Elizabeth Schmidt, a Seattle-based consultant who works with many startups, offered a related theory from the world of biology, noting that being stressed out works against emotional intelligence. If the output of a group working together on a complex technical problem is based not on raw intelligence or perseverance (which correlate well for individuals but fail in group settings) but rather on creativity and shared understanding, it would make sense that a lack of feeling safe and trusted would inhibit successful outcomes.

What's interesting is the nuance of psychological safety—it's not about being, as Edmondson put it, "unrelentingly positive," but rather about feeling comfortable speaking up, contradicting, questioning, and expressing criticism or nervousness.

I've certainly had the experience of working alongside people I perceived to be cold, distant, or not empathetic toward me or their fellow team members. But until I discovered and processed this research, I never reflected on how detrimental it was to the quality of output we collectively produced. Looking back, I can remember meetings that felt frustrating and unnecessarily combative, but, at least consciously, I can't recall feeling a diminished capacity to contribute or having my work quality suffer as a result.

On the other hand, when I think back to the groups that have produced the most meaningful, high-impact, high-quality results in my career, my memories of camaraderie and friendship, of caring and affection for one another is clear. Sometimes our relationships started as friendships, sometimes as acquaintances, and plenty of times, of course, as total strangers. But in each case, I can recall getting to know the people, not just the work. I remember stories from their lives outside the office, warm conversations having nothing to do with work, invitations to coffee or drinks or meals absent any particular agenda. I think there's something almost akin to a chemical reaction that occurs as people form personal bonds that go beyond their professional work. We build up tolerances to criticism, acceptance of faults, appreciation for idiosyncrasies. It's like a long-simmering sauce. At first, the flavors don't work together and things taste off, but after a couple of hours together on a hot stove, there's a mellowing and blending that works an almost-indescribable magic.

What Safe Looks Like (and Doesn't)

That day I shared my fears and sadness about Geraldine's tumor with the Moz team never seemed to me to be connected to our work or our effectiveness as an organization, but the two were likely coupled. In a less psychologically safe environment, I probably wouldn't have felt comfortable disclosing such personal news. And at a less helpful, caring place, my peers almost certainly wouldn't have rallied around me in such an affirming way.

Thankfully, Moz has had many other amazing examples of this deep, personal comfort among team members.

Years ago, we started a lunch-and-learn program, where individuals from across the company would give a presentation on topics of all kinds (from technical talks to motivational issues to vacations, hobbies, and more). Around the time I announced Geraldine's tumor, one of Moz's engineers, Maura Hubbell, gave a lunch and learn about her gender transition. She created a PowerPoint presentation that walked through elements of the emotional, medical, financial, and familial parts of becoming a woman. She stood up in front of dozens of Mozzers in attendance that day and explained this incredibly personal, life-changing decision and process. She took questions with grace and aplomb.

In possibly my favorite slide from the deck (okay, maybe my favorite slide ever), Maura had a still image of the fairy godmother from *Cinderella* with the title "The Magic Day, June 3rd, 2008." An arrow on the slide pointed to the godmother and read "Steve Ballmer." And a second arrow pointed to her magical wand with the caption "Microsoft sex reassignment surgery benefit." Maura explained that, as president of Microsoft during her tenure there, Ballmer worked to include gender transition surgery and hormone therapy as a covered part of the company's medical plan. Amazing.

Maura was only the second person I'd spent significant time with who'd been through this experience. I'm both ashamed and proud to admit that her transparency made me more accepting, more progressive, and vastly more knowledgeable about the subject. It was inspirational and deeply rewarding to know Moz was a place where people felt comfortable sharing in this way.

A couple of years later, Marc Mims, an engineer we'd hired as part of an acquisition, stood in front of the company at another lunch and learn to share the story of his son's coming-out. Marc's from Spokane, Washington, a deeply conservative and religious part of the state, and explained that many of his family members were not at all accepting of his son, Chris, after learning that he was openly gay. Marc himself struggled with it, and his reflections on the shame he feels now for the fear and discomfort he experienced at the time gave the presentation a depth and resonance that's stuck with me. At the end of the talk, Marc surprised us all by thanking Chris, who'd helped build the presentation and was sitting in the audience, unbeknownst to the crowd of Mozzers. I got to shake Chris's hand, and to hug Marc, my eyes still wet with tears.

Conversely, during one of the company's most stressful and poor-performance years, an incident fit almost too perfectly into the dysfunctional category.

You'll recall from chapter 10 the sexist manager we'd hired who was promoted several times but whose behavior was deeply poisonous and political. He was casually (but carefully) harassing young women who worked with or near him. And tragically, it was only after his tenure that I found out about the disparaging and inappropriate comments he'd made to these folks. When I separately asked two women who'd been on the receiving end of this behavior why they'd never brought it up with his managers or with HR, the answer was "Because I didn't think anyone would care, and he's clearly getting promoted anyway."

These women didn't feel safe pushing back against this manager. And they didn't feel safe bringing up the issue with the Moz HR team. So instead the issue festered, with results that likely went far beyond those two recipients of his shitty behavior. Without the transparency of people who struggled with this guy's harmful speech or actions, his negativity spread like a cancer, amplified by the reactions and inter- nalizations of people affected, hurting motivation and trust in hard- to-track-down ways.

It's hard to make logical connections between these personal, emotional experiences and the output or quality of work at the com- pany. Could it really be true that sharing stories of brain tumors and gender transitions, or accepting our children's sexuality, impacts the value our software delivers or the success of our marketing? Or that discomfort in sharing personal conflict or fear of retribution for speaking up about harassment could have negative impacts on those same outcomes? According to both the research and the anecdotal experiences, yes.

When people work together, our performance is governed not by individual genius or singular, outstanding contributions, but through complex interplay between the members of the group. Vulnerability and transparency in sharing our conflicts and concerns about work, about our teammates, and about our personal lives yields high- functioning, highly successful teams. When opacity, secrecy, dis- comfort, and fear exist, they can overwhelm even the smartest, most talented groups.

CHAPTER 16

SELF-AWARENESS IS A SUPERPOWER

People LOVE change (when it's about changing others). People HATE change (when it's about changing themselves).

—Richie Norton, 2016

I don't waste time being depressed. If you're unhappy, you should change what you're doing.

—Marc Andreessen, April 1998

In September 2014, Brad Feld, our investor from the 2012 round, asked me to run Foundry Group's annual CEO Summit in Denver, Colorado. I had stepped down as Moz's CEO seven months earlier, but had, apparently, done a good job running the summit the year prior and so they asked me again. I surveyed the portfolio CEOs about topics that warranted discussion, selected moderators and topics, created a schedule, and worked with Foundry's staff on the logistics. The discussions were wide-ranging, from sales compensation to marketing tactics, engineering best practices, partnership opportunities, M&A, fundraising, and more.

At the end of the day, all the CEOs were together in a large meeting room underneath the Renaissance Hotel, seated in a semicircle around Brad, who moderated the final session, titled "Being the CEO: Personal Struggles, Work/Life Balance, & Emotional Health."

Near the start of the session, Brad asked all the CEOs in the room to raise their hand if they had experienced severe anxiety, depression, or other emotional or mental disorders during their tenure as CEO. Every hand in the room went up, save two.

At that moment, a sense of relief washed over me, so powerful I almost cried in my chair. I thought I was alone, a frail, former CEO who'd lost his job because he couldn't handle the stress and pressure and caved in to depression. But those hands in the air made me realize I was far from alone—I was, in fact, part of an overwhelming majority, at least among this group. That mental transition from loneliness and shame to a peer among equals forever changed the way I thought about depression and the stigma around mental disorders.

I am not alone. Neither are you.

For me, pinpointing the start of my depression is hard to do. I didn't know the signs or what to be aware of. I know that I exhibited at least some of the associated traits and tendencies as early as May 2013 but only came to recognize and call these symptoms "depression" (with the help of a therapist and coach) in the summer of 2014.

My natural disposition is lightly introverted and introspective, but I function well in social settings and form friendships easily. If we met prior to 2013, you might use words like "friendly," "humorous," "approachable," maybe even "optimistic" to describe me. But if we spent significant time together during my episode with depression, a very different picture would emerge.

Most noticeably, I became an argumentative pessimist about work, convinced that nothing in my professional life or with Moz would or could go right. I berated my executive team, employees, investors, partners, and even customers about how badly we'd screwed up, how disappointed I was in everyone around me for letting us down, how any sign of positive progress was false and would soon be proven so.

I'd speak at conferences about SEO or web marketing, as I have for many years, and at the end of my talk, there was often a line of people, just off the stage, waiting to get questions answered or chat about some aspect of my presentation. My negativity ran so deep then that when folks would say kind things about Moz and tell me they'd been a subscriber for months or years, I'd spend a few minutes working to convince them that they should really switch to one of our competitors, because our product was so shamefully behind this other tool due to some missing feature or inferior data set.

Depressed Rand is arrogant. He's convinced that his dark view of the world is correct, and nothing anyone can say or do will change his mind. He's self-pitying, believing that the past decisions and mistakes he's made have created forces beyond his control that prevent any future progress or change. He wallows in misery, taking actual pleasure and happiness when things go wrong because it proves his predictions right.

In perhaps the darkest twist of depression's grasp on my intellectual reasoning, I pointed those who'd question my negativity to research on "Depressive Realism." Rachel Adelson described it in an article for the American Psychological Association's Science Watch like this:

> Psychologists have thought for decades that depressed people tend to distort the facts and view their lives more negatively than do nondepressed people. Yet, psychological studies have consistently revealed a peculiar exception to that pattern: Depressed people, studies indicated, judge their control of events more accurately than do nondepressed people.

I cited this phenomenon to my coworkers, my board, even my wife. "See," I'd say, "I'm the one who can see things clearly, and I know that everything is unrecoverably awful."

Depression affected me physically, too. I've had a herniated disc in my spine for many years. Seeing it on X-rays is particularly unnerving (no pun intended), as it makes my spinal column look like someone's taken a hammer and chisel to a crucial point near the base. That disc presses on the sciatic nerve that runs down my left leg. If I'm not religious about doing physical therapy exercises and using lumbar support when I sit down (I almost always carry a scarf to help with this, even on hot summer days), my leg will spasm and contract, causing sharp physical pain and trouble walking. During my depression, my leg/sciatica/back issues were the worst they've ever been. I'd experience shooting pains, my ankle and calf locking up as every part of the muscle tensed uncontrollably.

And sleep. Anyone who tells you it's a badge of honor to sacrifice sleep for work is full of it (the data's crystal clear—less than 1 percent of human beings function effectively on less than six hours/night and most of us need at least seven). I remember weeks on end where I was the most tired, worn-out, poorly functioning version of myself I'd ever been, barely able to keep my eyes open during meetings, tense, overcaffeinated, and quick to irrational anger. But when I'd climb into bed, "the loop" would begin—an awful circle of thoughts fixated on how much I'd messed up and how it could never be fixed and all the opportunities and wonderful things I and all the people around me would miss out on as a result.

In the midst of that emotional anguish, I had conversations with Sarah Bird (my longtime chief operating officer) about her taking over as CEO someday. Sarah joined Moz in 2007, just after we'd raised our first funding round, ostensibly as chief counsel. We were much too small to need a full-time attorney on staff, but Sarah proved her value in all areas of the company. She is smart, flexible, and willing to work as hard as need be to get projects finished, and she always puts the best interests of the organization above her own. Her clear, calm rationality balanced my own more manic and emotional approach to the business, and within a few months, we'd promoted her to director of operations, later to COO, and then in 2013 to COO and president. When my mom, Gillian, stepped off the board of directors after the 2012 funding round, we asked Sarah to take her place.

I believed that Sarah could be a great operational CEO, and that Moz needed less of the vision and industry-influencer-driven skill set I'd brought as we matured in our market. In November 2013 I had a phone call with Brad Feld and we decided, together, to ask Sarah to step into the CEO role. I think Brad recognized that in my current state, I was not reflecting the qualities of leadership Moz needed. My depression had taken a toll on the team's morale, and my decisions and failures with Moz Analytics had led to our first growth-rate slowdown in seven years.

Sarah accepted the position with humility, grace, and passion. In February 2014, she formally took over as Moz's CEO. I stepped into my current role as an individual contributor, working with product, engineering, and marketing teams in a consulting role.

My depression continued, and although stepping down as CEO lessened some of the pressures and demands on my time, I quickly filled the gap with more conferences, content projects, and external work (helping a number of nonprofits and some of our fellow Foundry portfolio companies with pro bono SEO advice).

That Valentine's Day, I (somewhat unintentionally) got very, very high. Seattle had recently legalized recreational marijuana, and some friends brought by a set of chocolate, pot-laced truffles. I ate one. It was tiny. I didn't feel much of anything, so I ate another. For the next six hours I was mind-meltingly nervous and embarrassed. I couldn't talk to my friends or even to Geraldine. I didn't want to move from my chair in our living room. I was incredibly thirsty but so worried I'd spill water on myself and that everyone would laugh at me that I just stayed put, parched, staring at the clock and wondering why the minutes were taking so long to pass.

The social event was less than ideal, but that night, I slept like the dead. I slept until one p.m. the next day. And the next two nights, I slept wonderfully again. My leg didn't hurt. My brain was quiet. I wasn't cycling on the loop of frustration and work problems. I felt free.

The loop and the leg pain returned later that week, as I reverted to my depressed state, but it was a looser hold than before. I now had an inkling that my obsession with problems at work, my sciatica, my lack of sleep, and that feeling of being trapped in the loop were all connected. If I could stop cycling on Moz's failures, on my failures, I could sleep, which would help my leg pain, which would make me feel better, which could lift my spirits and give me a more positive outlook for the future.

That summer, I got progressively better. Moz did, too. Under Sarah's leadership, we stopped the bleeding of subscribers from the dismal Moz Analytics launch, and the company began to grow again. A new product, Moz Local, launched and had success. We were hiring again. Things felt a little more stable, and I stepped back a bit more, refocusing on the things I was good at—blogging, speaking, making presentations and videos, contributing to product strategy. I slept a bit better, my leg hurt a bit less, my negativity softened.

Lifting the heaviest folds from my curtain of depression required something else: the catharsis of writing about it. The night before the Foundry CEO Summit in Denver, I authored a blog post titled "A Long, Ugly Year of Depression That's Finally Fading." Writing that post, and looking around the room filled with powerful, successful, venture-funded CEOs who openly admitted to their own emotional turmoil the next day, was the tail end of an awful, soul-crushing journey that I hope never to revisit.

I cannot tell you the cure for depression. Nor do I have some secret formula for how to turn around a company spinning out of control.

But I can tell you that we're not alone. And I can tell you that the path that worked for me, a path of self-awareness and active management of my mental health, has worked for others. It might work for you, too.

What's helped Moz and me, again and again, to find greater hope and a way forward is a process that doesn't attempt to reach a specific goal or have a finite end point. It's an ongoing journey, an investment, with steps repeated over and over again, all in the direction of self-awareness.

Depression was a catalyst for me to seek professional therapy and professional coaching, something I hadn't done previously in my career. Brad referred me to Jerry Colonna, a coach who is well-known in the startup world and had a prior career as a venture capital partner. He knows better than most the particular pressures and pains of entrepreneurship, and he's deeply empathetic to those whose emotional health affects others (as CEOs' and founders' almost always do).

Jerry and I worked together for a little more than a year, scheduling once-a-month phone conversations to discuss work, personal life, and my fragile emotional state. From him, I learned a tremendous amount about managing one's own psychology and the reality of self-awareness.

First and foremost: no one is self-aware. And equally, no founder is fully company-aware.

Some of us are more self-knowledgeable than others. We understand a lot of what has impacted our emotional state in the past, what's driving our actions and our goals, why we hold the convictions and core beliefs we do, how our past, our upbringing, our experiences have shaped us, and what patterns (healthy and unhealthy) we fall into. Knowledge of these is on a spectrum. At the far end is my dad, an emotionally unstable man who can be deeply loving one minute and unhinged with anger the next with no understanding of why or any conscious effort made to rein in his outbursts or seek help. On the other end is Jerry, deeply aware of what drives him, making time each day to analyze his actions and reactions, a researcher studying himself as he studies others, always in pursuit of the next level but never unsatisfied by a long journey to get there.

To make progress on this spectrum, we have to be willing to accept that what we believe we know about ourselves may not be true, have the courage to question our beliefs, and start from a place without preexisting assumptions. I like how Dr. Jonathan Koomey phrases it in his blog post on intellectual honesty:

> Someone who is intellectually honest follows the facts where ever they may lead, and does so in spite of discomfort, inconvenience, or self-interest.

Self-examination is rife with opportunities and incentives for bias. We want to believe the best about ourselves, and we know that many times, attacking pillars of our self-worth or our core beliefs sets off a vast minefield of psychological defenses. These are impediments we have to overcome. Easier said than done.

The same applies when understanding the strengths and weaknesses of your entrepreneurial venture. You have hypotheses about why one tactic worked and another didn't. You blame some combination of market forces or poor strategy or too-slow execution, but nine times out of ten, you do it based on instinct and supposition, using those same biases that drive your blindness to self-knowledge.

I know because I've been there. I started down the path of exploration with Jerry confident that I was already self-aware. I started down the path of unraveling the lessons learned from Moz for our future, and for this book, and for my own sanity with that same confidence. I knew what I wanted (a successful outcome for Moz via a large sale or IPO) and why (recognition, influence, wealth, the ability to "give back"), but when I stripped away my assumptions, and the stories I've told myself all of my adult life, and was truly intellectually honest, new stories emerged.

Can I tell you something?

I want Moz to have an exit. One that everyone talks about.

There are lots of reasons, but what's most important to me? What would make me refuse to sell, even if every other condition were met?

Secrecy. It's a highly unrealistic possibility, but if Moz had an amazing sale at a spectacular price, but one that no one could know about, that I could never write about, that no press outlet would cover or any blog post discuss, I'd resent that opacity so much, I might vote against the sale. I don't have high self-esteem. I have a serious case of impostor syndrome. I believe, deep down, that my career and my company might just be the result of accidental, undeserved success. I'm scared that I'll never be able to repeat it, and that's a big part of why I'm so scared to quit and start something new, despite all the opportunity and ideas and potential funders. Despite remarkable people who said they'd love to join whatever company I build next. What if I can't build anything else because I didn't really know how to build this one? That's why the public praise and the financial freedom and the check mark in the "created a successful company and took it to the finish line" box matter so much.

It's embarrassing to admit. I'm almost scared to let this book go to press with that paragraph in it.

When you find a real truth about yourself, or a truth about your company, it's going to have that same feeling. The truths we hide about ourselves and our creations stay secret because we bury them in layers of guilt and shame, of fear and self-loathing.

But when you dig them up, reveal them, hold up the mirror, and, scariest of all, when you admit them to the people they impact (your team, your family, your partner) or do so publicly, their shackles weaken and sometimes break altogether. The moment I admitted to myself that fear of being a fraud, fear of only having this one lucky, accidental venture in me, were responsible for my biases, I was free. Today, I'd be okay with a secret exit I couldn't talk about. I think I'll be ready to start my next company, too. Proving that I can do it matters to me. I'm the one who doubts myself. No one else's perception of Moz's outcome really matters, at least not along that vector.

Pro Tip: When you invest in behaviors based on your newfound knowledge, don't try to control the outcome, just the behavior. This holds equally true for your startup as for your emotional health.

Because, as much as we wish we could, we never have full control over outcomes. We own our behavior, and some of the time (hopefully often), the right behaviors lead to the outcomes we want. Recognizing this is crucial, because many people and organizations reward outcomes rather than behavior. That can lead to punishing good behaviors if the outcome isn't the desired one, even if the forces were outside our control. And it can lead to reinforcing bad behaviors simply because they led to a good outcome (again, even if the outcome was largely disconnected from the behavior).

When I was depressed, I tried dozens of tactics in search of a solution. I tried exercising. I went to acupuncture. I did massage therapy. I tried craniosacral massage (it's kinda weird). I tried Chinese herbal medicines (at the suggestion of my acupuncturist). I went to therapy. I took vacations. I took a night off each week from my computer (Friday night, in a recurring calendar event that still reads "Anti-work night"). I did physical therapy. And meditation. And mindfulness apps.

Every time I tried one of these and it didn't work (i.e., I wasn't fully and immediately back to my old self within a few months), I'd give it up, assume it wasn't right for me, and try something else. I guarantee you've done the same thing, maybe in your attempts to lose weight, or in your dating life, or when you had to finish a big project, or help a loved one through a tough time, or build a company.

Remember how "growth hacks" are almost always inferior to consistent investments in the right marketing channels and tactics for your strengths and your audience? The same principle applies to your life. It's almost never the case that you'll transform your personal psychology and manage your emotional and mental health long term with a single or even a handful of hacks. The "I was depressed but then I installed this great mindfulness app and now I'm teaching my therapist how to live a happy life" story goes right up there with "I was hooked on In-N-Out burgers and Pixy Stix; couldn't program my way out of a Raspberry Pi. But I switched all my meals to Soylent and now I'm a lean, mean, code-crushin' machine."

When you invest in a behavior, invest in *just* the behavior. Assess it based on its strengths and weaknesses, its costs and returns. Anti-work night didn't solve my depression, so I stopped doing it for more than six months. But when I had the revelation that behaviors trump outcomes, I brought it back. I did the same with physical therapy and exercise. I skipped the mindfulness app, the meditation, the acupuncture, and the herbal medicines.

Likewise, at Moz, we've invested in behaviors we believe are healthy, even when they don't have consistently positive outcomes. Our approach to launching internal MVPs and iterating until they're earning praise and accolades from industry influencers has had great results for some projects, and mediocre results for others, but we're investing in the behavior. Conversely, we found performance reviews to be a behavior that wasn't working for us, even though they could sometimes be connected to positive outcomes.

What makes a behavior worthwhile is different for each person and each company, but almost all follow a few patterns:

- The behavior is, in and of itself, apart from any connected outcomes, rewarding and fulfilling.
- The behavior fits with your core values.
- The behavior can turn into a habit and (at least slowly) scales with decreasing friction (i.e., it's easier to engage in the thirtieth time than the second).

- The behavior has a positive, measurable, causal impact. Even if it's small.
- There is no clear causality between the behavior and a consistently negative outcome.

The last key to behavioral investments is to reward the behavior, not the outcome.

When I was fighting consciously against depression with the help of my therapist or my wife or my friends, it was the opposite of helpful to hear about a "solution" that would fix my issues. Why? Because every time I tried one of those solutions, and it failed, I'd write it off, lose hope, and sink further into my malaise.

In weight loss programs, this phenomenon is a constant problem. Diet and exercise work for a while, for some people, then they seem to stop working as the body fights tooth and nail against giving up any additional weight. Fat cells don't work the same way for everyone, and the more weight a person gains, the more their body resists normal caloric burn functions. Personal trainers and diet specialists and doctors and, worst, friends and family blame a lack of willpower but have no idea of the physical and mental struggle that constant, overwhelming hunger inflicts.

In these cases, feelings of shame and failure are entirely counterproductive, as are goal-driven versus behavior-driven tracking. Rewarding weight loss or fat-to-muscle ratio is far less successful in long-term studies than recognizing and rewarding behavior. When we make it about the work rather than the goal, we find that outcomes improve. The field of behavioral science has all sorts of data on what happens when rewards are connected to outcomes rather than behaviors (namely, people cheat, break rules, game systems, and ignore the safety of themselves and those around them).

There is beauty and clarity in this truth. When we're freed from the mythology that we control outcomes and asked instead to concentrate on behaviors, we have a powerful tool to fight against negativity and anxiety. It's a gift.

For me, it means freedom from the burden of fear I long associated with the potential return of my depression. For more than a year after my depression lifted, I was filled with dread that it could return. That fear stemmed from a lack of feeling in control. I didn't have a clear solution that worked instantly, just a random event (the pot truffles) and a slow progression through trial and error that seemed to help. I felt vulnerable and insecure about my rediscovered mental health.

But focusing on behaviors gives me clarity and control. It lifts my burden from things I can't perfectly influence (the reality that someday I might have depression again) to things I can: diet, exercise, physical therapy, investment in self-awareness as an ongoing process, breaks from work, self-forgiveness.

This is where the power to combat negativity resides. When we understand ourselves, and our creations, we understand what influences decisions, behaviors, and outcomes. We then make the conscious choice to put effort into learning from our past decisions, not letting our biases control us, and investing in better behaviors. Simultaneously, we choose not to reward outcomes but rather to use them only as part of our analytics and decisions about where and whether to reward or discard a behavior.

We have the power to change the ways we react and the way things make us feel. As my cousin-in-law Yvonne, a therapist, likes to say: "Feelings are not facts." The same goes for strategy, even for vision. These are malleable things, within our control.

CHAPTER 17
FOCUS

I knew that if I failed I wouldn't regret that, but I knew the one thing
I might regret is not trying.

—Jeff Bezos, 2016

The most awful day Moz ever experienced was, without question, August 17, 2016. That morning, our CEO, Sarah, stood onstage in front of the company and announced that we'd lay off 59 of our 210 full-time employees, shut down two fledgling products, and cease pursuit of the strategy we'd followed for the prior two and a half years. There were tears and anger; nasty write-ups about the company on blogs, review sites, and social media; lost friendships; lost trust; and lost reputation.

Worst of all was that this news came as a complete surprise to most of our team. Of all the missteps and poor decisions, the one I regret most is the lack of transparency our leadership team, myself among them, showed in the months leading up to that event.

What happened? How did Moz go from 100 percent year-over-year growth for seven years in a row to repeated missteps and missed budgets resulting in eventual layoffs? How did we go from announcing (and believing) that everything was fine just three months prior to those layoffs to determining that they were critical to the company's survival? How did we miss the mounting evidence of structural weaknesses in a part of our business until such a late hour? I believe the answer to all of these was a lack of focus.

One of the many foolish beliefs I held after raising capital (especially our $18 million round in 2012) was that we were now obligated to spend that money quickly to find additional growth. This is one of the worst, most pervasive myths in the startup world, and sometimes your investors reinforce it or even heavily lobby for it. Mine didn't. Brad and Michelle both felt that Moz was doing wonderfully well (Brad told me in a 2013 email that Moz was "one of the best performing companies in Foundry's portfolio"). But they supported my vision of going broader and accelerating Moz's already-strong growth rate.

To achieve that growth, I thought I had to try everything. A broader product suite, a range of acquisitions, some totally new products and markets, all sorts of new internal programs. I believed we had infinite capacity and the only limit was our imaginations and drive (well, that and the money in the bank, but if we spent it, there'd always be more VC so long as we found more growth). But this is magical thinking. What I really did was divert attention away from the few things that kept the lights on. Big mistake.

The (SEO) World Is Not Enough

Back in 2011, while CEO, I'd shifted Moz from our focus on exclusively SEO software that helped marketers with rankings and traffic from search engines to a broader set of tools that would assist with other, interconnected channels like social media, press and public relations, and content marketing. Moz Analytics had tried to tackle all these different channels with tragic results. Thankfully, we still had plenty of cash in the bank, and with the exception of a few months in early 2014, we continued to grow revenue, albeit at a slower pace.

But we also maintained course on that broader suite of functions, rather than focusing back on SEO.

The new strategy we implemented when Sarah took over the CEO role was an attempt to follow in the footsteps of companies like 37signals* (makers of Basecamp, Campfire, and Highrise, three separate products serving various unique project and process management functions), Atlassian (makers of numerous software tools including HipChat, Jira, Confluence, Statuspage, and more), and Microsoft. These companies had successfully expanded from their core product into multiproduct suites that served different, but overlapping audiences—and we thought we could do the same.

Together with our board of directors, Sarah and I worried that investing exclusively in SEO could limit the company's potential for growth. We were nervous that if something happened to the field of SEO and we couldn't react quickly or well enough, we could be in big trouble. We felt that the overlap in marketing practices meant that many people who knew of, visited, and trusted Moz were strong customer targets for us, no matter their actual roles. We had perhaps too much confidence in our ability to build and launch new products in new fields, and even more overconfidence in our brand and marketing

---

*Ironically, 37signals, one of the models for our multiproduct strategy, closed down all but one of their products in 2014 in order to focus; founder Jason Fried wrote about it on Inc.: http://www.inc.com/magazine/201403/jason-fried/basecamp-focus-one-product-only .html.

abilities, sure that the Moz name plus any semi-decent product reaching our millions of monthly website visitors would sell.

All of these hypotheses sound compelling at face value. Fear that growth in a product line may have tapped out isn't unusual. Companies worried about putting all their eggs in one basket isn't, either. Confidence in your strengths based on past performance sounds reasonable, too. I don't think any of these were foolhardy, unprecedented, amateur concerns or decision-making criteria. It's just that none of them could (or should) overwhelm the drawbacks that multiple investments in different products, markets, and audiences have.

For us, the multiproduct strategy started with a product called Moz Local, which helps small, local businesses and large companies with many hundreds or thousands of physical locations to get their location data easily and accurately into all of the many directories and networks that people and search engines used. Moz Local started as the brainchild of David Mihm, under the name GetListed. David's company was one of our early acquisitions after the 2012 funding round, and together with a small team of ex-Google engineers, they designed and built a remarkably useful tool.

If, for example, you owned a gelato shop and wanted to earn visibility on the web, you had to figure out (a) What are all the search engines, websites, and apps that potential consumers might use?, (b) What sources power all of those?, (c) Who do I have to pay, how often, and how much to get that information correctly included?, and (d) What do I do if the information needs updating?

David had worked with local business owners for a decade, helping them through these challenging processes. Those owners knew that wrong hours on Google Maps, not being listed in Yelp, not ranking in search engine results, or appearing in the wrong category on

TripAdvisor could cost them customers. And in the local business world, just a few customers a month can mean the difference between survival and bankruptcy.

With Moz Local, you could put your hours, website, address, phone number, and other important details into the tool once and have it propagate that data to consumer sites like Foursquare, Yelp, TripAdvisor, Yellow Pages, Bing Maps, and Google Maps as well as listing aggregators such as Acxiom, Infogroup, Factual, and Localeze (whom Google, Bing, Apple, and others use to validate/verify local information). Moz built relationships with all the various providers so that customers could pay us once ($99/year) and we'd pay all those third parties on their behalf when submitting the data (our raw costs were around half that amount, thanks to buying large deals up front in bulk). As the gelato shop owner, not only did you get correct data on all these sites and listing sources, but you'd also usually see higher rankings in local searches on Google and Bing due to how those search engines give benefit to listing consistency and coverage.

In 2014, we had two primary products: Moz Pro (our longtime tool set for professional marketers doing SEO) and Moz Local (for local/physical businesses to add/update their location information across the web), as well as two secondary products: Mozcon (our annual customer conference in Seattle) and the Moz API (where developers and tool makers could buy large-scale access to our raw data).

The next addition to our suite was a Twitter analytics tool called Followerwonk. Like Moz Local, we'd acquired the company back in 2012. Based in Portland, Followerwonk was a tool for searching the biographies of Twitter accounts and analyzing activity, engagement, and followers. We'd heard about it from numerous influencers in the SEO world who used the tool to help build relationships, better understand their audiences, and optimize their Twitter activity to help grow their followings. When we bought the company, we wrapped the product into the Moz Pro suite such that you had to buy Moz Pro to get access to Followerwonk. We grandfathered in the handful of historic customers and hoped that the combination of the SEO and social media functions would help marketers in both camps.

Unfortunately, we discovered that despite the recommendations and endorsements from prominent SEOs, the overlap between marketers doing SEO work and those who also worked on social media marketing via Twitter was, in practice, very small. Less than 5 percent of the more than twenty-five thousand Moz Pro subscribers used Followerwonk in a given month, and a similarly small percentage of Followerwonk customers and those who signed up for the product via Moz Pro used any part of our SEO tools. Thus, in 2015, three years after we'd integrated the products, we broke Followerwonk back out into its own subscription. Customers could, once again, purchase Followerwonk independently.

Next, we added Moz Content, a product based on a section of the Moz Analytics tool suite we'd never finished, designed to serve content marketers. Our goal was to help websites regularly publishing content to attract visitors and turn them into customers understand which pieces of content were working best, suggest potential topics, conduct a content audit of their sites, and give them metrics to compare themselves to the competition. Moz Content took a little more than a year to design, build, test, and launch. It had a private beta in November 2015 and became publicly available the following January.

Last was Keyword Explorer, a keyword research tool (the one I described at the end of chapter 12) and part of the Moz Pro suite but also available separately via its own subscription.

As of mid-2016, Moz had four primary products: Moz Pro, Moz Local, Followerwonk, and Moz Content. We had two conferences: Mozcon and Mozcon Local (launched in 2015 to support the Local product's unique and growing audience). And we had two secondary products: the separately available Keyword Explorer and the Moz API.

It turns out, selling eight different things to people visiting your website is vastly more challenging than selling two or three. It's nightmarishly harder than selling one. And, perhaps obviously, it's much harder to structure teams within a company to support eight unique products. Even with a much larger staff, we were spread thin—every product and engineering team expressed the anger and frustration of being understaffed. Marketing was overwhelmed trying to keep up with competing requests for promotional space on the site, emails to our audience, social media promotions, etc. Infrastructure teams like design, finance, operations, legal, and HR all struggled to keep up with the demands of these multiple teams with unique products, all vying for attention and support. Every team wanted to hire, and for most of 2014 and 2015, our budget was crafted to enable significant headcount growth. We went from about 125 people at the start of 2014 to more than 220 two years later.

In June 2016, I had a scheduled lunch with Moz's CFO, Glenn. It was a beautiful Seattle summer day, so we walked a dozen blocks to a Neapolitan-style pizzeria south of Moz's offices. On that walk, Glenn asked me, in his hallmark, non-sequitur way, whether Moz had ever done layoffs in the past.

"No," I replied. "We've never even had to consider it."

Despite being a venture-backed business, where risk taking is encouraged and scaling up and down is the norm, Moz had historically been run profitably or close-to-breakeven with two exceptions: the first following our 2012 fundraising, when we acquired three companies, opened a second office in Portland, built out our own private data center to move off Amazon's cloud services, and grew staff significantly, and late-2014 to mid-2016, when we chose to invest in the multiproduct strategy.

Glenn and I spent that lunch talking almost exclusively about his concerns with our declining growth rate and burgeoning budget. Unfortunately, Glenn was preaching to the already converted. I was obsessed with returning to profitability and had been since late 2013. That November, I'd made a poorly timed proposition to my team—I would grow my mustache out until the company returned to being cash-flow breakeven or better. When I stepped down as CEO three months later, I no longer controlled that decision, and Sarah both liked the mustache (I maintain she didn't have to worry about waxing it or how ridiculous it looked on blustery, high-humidity days) and believed that Moz should forgo profits and, as most VC-backed companies do, spend more to get faster growth.

Careful to avoid getting cheese and pizza sauce in my now-ridiculous facial hair (seriously, it curled in giant loops up to my nostrils), I explained my position to Glenn, though he'd heard it plenty of times before. I think he was conveying to me that I had a new ally on my side, and that he, too, felt it was wise for Moz to scale back its spending.

Understanding revenue and expenses effectively was much harder in the new, more complex, more diverse world of eight revenue sources. Those products had different models, different cash-flow issues (Moz Local, for example, paid out its listing costs as soon as a transaction was made, but then recognized revenue over a year, while Moz Pro collected and recognized most transactions monthly). Each product was growing in revenue, but none of them was meeting the projections submitted in December of the prior year for the official board-approved budget. Over the next month, Glenn and Sarah worked with the leadership of each of the Moz products to revise their budgets and understand the cash-flow implications.

When that process was completed, and when June's numbers were put into the projection models, we knew there was a reckoning ahead. Sarah had booked a two-day executive team off-site retreat August 1 and 2. She and Glenn presented slides showing that our financial position was weakening, and that because we'd invested so heavily in personnel to support the multiproduct efforts, we'd need to accelerate revenue growth dramatically to avoid burning through our remaining cash reserves.

We talked briefly about what had gone wrong to bring us to this dark place, but the answer was both simple and unsatisfying: we'd risk-modeled the possibilities that several of our products might miss projections but were caught wholly by surprise when *every* product missed. Looking back over the last few years of product growth rates, there was an uncanny correlation—as if each new product we added to the mix subtracted a little from the growth of every other product we offered. On reflection and after analysis, I believe this was no coincidence.

It was clear that major change was required. We needed a sizable injection of cash, a dramatic reduction in costs, or a huge improvement in growth rate to avoid burning more cash than we could afford. The projections showed that on the current course, we had about twelve months of operating cash remaining. That was an unacceptable level of risk to all of us. Cutting staff seemed unavoidable, but Sarah and Glenn needed time to draw up plans and evaluate scenarios.

At the end of the day, Sarah listed a few ideas on an easel pad—possible product futures for Moz. They included options like:

- Turn the Pro subscription into a cash cow (meaning we eliminate much of its staff and marketing and let its profitability fund other parts of the business).
- Combine Moz Content and Followerwonk into a single product for influencer marketing.
- Sell the Pro business and use the proceeds to fund other products.
- Shut down all products except Pro.
- Shut down all products except Pro and Local.
- Shut down Moz Content, sell Followerwonk, focus on Pro and Local.
- Focus only on self-service Pro and Local; eliminate Enterprise, Wonk, and Content.

Each option would mean significant staff cuts in order to extend our runway or reach profitability. The executives around the table knew it. Several of them volunteered to be laid off, myself included. My offer was declined, but our CMO and two other executives were let go in the RIF (reduction in force) that followed.

The downside of high-margin software businesses like ours is that when you need to save money, people are often the only resource to cut. An average Moz employee costs the company about $145,000 per year (that includes salary, benefits, taxes, insurance, etc.). Cutting back on expensed software subscriptions, office expenses, travel and entertainment budgets, conferences, sponsorships, and hardware would all be part of the equation, but none of them could impact the bottom line to the necessary degree. We would need to do the company's first-ever round of major layoffs.

Layoffs are every founder's worst nightmare. Not only are they a demoralizing, soul-crushing experience (doubly so for those laid off), they often precipitate the beginning of the end. It's a rare startup indeed that can come back from layoffs with the same leadership team and turn the business into a success story. The odds aren't hopeless, but they're certainly not in your favor.

The Seven-Hour Board Meeting

The following Wednesday, August 10, we'd scheduled three hours for Moz's board of directors to meet. The meeting ended up going seven hours. One of our directors had to rebook his flight. Everyone missed their dinner plans. The atmosphere of that meeting was intense, but it was direct, honest, and collegial (well, up until the end). We all knew that everyone in the room had made mistakes. We'd accepted overly optimistic projections, built budgets that didn't account for potential missteps, and made prideful assumptions about what the business could accomplish despite being spread so thin across so many projects and products.

Moz's board comprises:

- Rand—author of this book you're reading, founder, ex-CEO, individual contributor at Moz, board chairperson
- Sarah Bird—Moz's CEO
- Michelle Goldberg—Moz's first investor from Ignition Partners
- Seth Levine—partner at Foundry Group; Seth took over Brad Feld's board seat in January 2016, a rotation that's pretty typical for Foundry's partners (though I was immensely sad to lose Brad, with whom I'd always had a special bond—thankfully, in 2017, he and Seth swapped again)

- Matt Blumberg—independent board member, founder and CEO of ReturnPath
- Julie Sandler—principal at Madrona Venture Group at the time, observer (Madrona bought some secondary shares from Gillian, my mom and Moz's cofounder, and we love Julie's input, so we ask her to attend whenever possible)
- Kelly Smith—investor with Curious Office in Moz's 2007 funding round, observer (Kelly wasn't in attendance, but contributed some thoughts via email)

A typical board meeting for us also includes time with the members of Moz's executive team, but this time, given the sensitivity of topics and need for focused discussion, Sarah opted to make it board members only.

The board's discussion covered these five items, in order:

1. What product mix is right for Moz going forward?
2. What does the market look like for M&A, private equity, and/or additional venture funding?
3. What cuts do we have to make—how deep is deep enough?
4. Should we work to sell off any of our products, or simply shut them down?
5. How should we approach and manage a RIF process?

We spent a lot of time discussing the market and exit scenarios. Our investors, as patient as they are and have been, have time horizons to meet. Their LPs expect returns within about ten years, and Moz will likely be at the outer limit of that range. Hence, the big question we had to ask was: What mix of products and strategy did we believe would give Moz the best chance to be IPO-ready in the next three to four years? It's not that we didn't or wouldn't consider an acquisition, but rather that we had the shared belief that aiming for IPO is the best way to maximize the opportunity for an acquisition, whereas intentionally targeting a particular company or set of companies who'd hopefully buy Moz is both riskier and vastly less motivating for our team.

The answer we eventually agreed upon was a refocus on SEO—helping organizations of all sizes get found in the nonpaid results of search engines. I challenged everyone very specifically on this topic, asking whether our board members really believed

- that SEO was a protocol, like email or social or content, and would garner ongoing investment from businesses for years to come;
- that the market was still underserved and held great potential for growth; and
- that the right product, packaging, and marketing could get us back to a strong growth rate.

Michelle, Seth, and Matt all confirmed their belief in the market. Julie seemed a bit more hesitant but went along. Sarah was skeptical about whether self-service alone could get us to the growth rate and size we needed. Her position shifted the discussion to whether, when, and how Moz could approach the enterprise SEO market. It was at this point that Matt Blumberg made what I felt was one of the strongest points of the meeting. He said:

You can, sometimes, teach a cat to walk on its hind legs. You might even be able to teach it to bark. But that doesn't make it a dog. I'm skeptical that Moz could, on its own, build the DNA to become an enterprise software company. If we need to add enterprise, we should partner or acquire.

That comment garnered vigorous agreement from around the table. We discussed several potential partnership and acquisition opportunities that could get Moz into enterprise SEO, then moved on to talk about funding and M&A.

That conversation was short and brutal. The board confirmed to us that, given Moz's current growth rate (about 10 percent) and cash burn rate, we would all be very disappointed in any kind of acquisition offer. Private equity was likely off the table as well, at least until we improved our financial fundamentals. And additional capital, from insiders or outsiders, was also unlikely until and unless we got our house in order and improved our growth rate. That left us in the clear position of needing to cut costs dramatically and quickly. The only question was what to cut, when, how, and how deeply.

What we didn't do, either as an executive team or a board, was dig into the past or retrospect on the core decisions and missteps that led to layoffs. I think the topic was too painful, too recent, the parties present only too aware that emotion would corrupt the discussion.

The latter half of that board meeting dealt with the painfully sensitive topics that accompany layoffs. I've never been part of one before, and hope never to be again, but I can say that those last couple of hours were heart-poundingly tense.

Glenn put together an assessment of where and how we could reduce costs to reach profitability.

As you can see from the chart, 75 percent of the savings ($8.8 million of $12.81 million) had to come from employees. For us, that meant fifty-nine people who'd no longer work here.

To get to cash flow positive, we must spend less.
Our target is $12mm savings.

Type of Spend	Current Annual Spend	Opportunity for Annualized Savings	Percent	Notes
People	$33.24mm	$8.8mm	26%	People spend is our largest expense. There was no way to get to where we want to be without hitting this hard.
Paid Marketing	$2.6mm	$1.8mm	70%	The trick is to scale this down without hitting our topline revenue growth too much. This is a dial we will be tuning.
Marketing Sponsorships	$400k	$300k	75%	We'll keep obligations we've made so far, but decline future sponsorships.
Conferences	$144k	$144k	100%	Unless speaking, we'll suspend conference attendance.
Travel and Entertainment	$940k	$760k	81%	Reduced for sales and critical travel only.
Recruiting	$60k	$48k	80%	Greatly reduced.
Portland Office	$60k	$60k	100%	Closing in September.
Office Food	$500k	$400k	80%	$51/person per month. Keep snacks. Reduce hot meals.
Expensed Software	$1.7mm	$500k	30%	This account needs to be scrubbed. We assume there is a lot of software we're not actually using. And that we'll get some savings from fewer seats.
Total		**$12.81mm**		We have a little wiggle room here, in case doing 100 percent of all these things is not possible.

We had, of course, let people go at Moz in the past, but those terminations were always driven by performance or culture-fit issues, not by costs or poor decisions. This was different, and far more painful. I let my emotions get the better of me at the end.

Don't Let Aaron Sorkin Write Your Script

Five minutes. That's all it took to cost myself years of goodwill, strong relationships, and the benefit of the doubt with my board of directors. In my defense, I was pissed off. No. Those are the wrong words. I was . . . infuriated. Angry not in a spur-of-the-moment way, but because I felt that the people around me, who'd committed to a set of core values, were now ready to sacrifice those values when it was most critical to uphold them.

The fight was over severance.

Several of our board members believed that spending so much on severance at a time when the company was in tough financial straits was an awful mistake. I was arguing for more. Sarah was, too. The other board members were various degrees of skeptical and opposed.

As the discussion became more and more tense, I raised my voice.

"Six weeks of severance for people who've been here four years is not acceptable."

The response was measured. I forget who said it.

"Six weeks is very generous. In most layoffs I've seen, that's the top end of the range."

Enter Poor-Judgment Rand. Poor-Judgment Rand is a special kind of dumb. He's so sure he's right, and so convinced that morality is on his side, that he doesn't consider the feelings of others or how his statements and actions will affect the future (not even his own). Just watch as he digs himself a hole from which there may be no escape:

"Okay. Question: Seth [it might have been Matt or Michelle I started with, I can't recall precisely]. Have you ever been laid off?"

"No."

Poor-Judgment Rand keeps digging.

"Michelle, have you ever been laid off?"

At this point, one of my board members tried to save me from myself.

"Is this really necess—"

I cut them off.

"Oh, we're doing this. Please answer my question." (I might not have said "please.")

"No. I've never been laid off."

I went around the room. I pointed insultingly with my finger while asking. And at the end, after every answer was negative, I lit a match and burned those bridges.

"Great. So a bunch of fucking millionaires are sitting here deciding whether people who make a tenth of what they do *really need* two or three extra weeks of severance pay after losing their jobs."

I think it was Seth who suggested we take a recess and that Sarah should work with our CFO to present a few scenarios over email, and we'd decide from there. To Sarah's immense credit, she got creative and fought to make sure that six weeks was the minimum, rather than the maximum severance.

Since that exchange, things haven't been the same between me and our board members. There's a coldness in rooms we share that wasn't there before, and a marked shift in our once collegial relationship. I overreacted. I became accusatory. And it was totally unnecessary. Sarah would have found the right scenarios, presented them, and we would have had the same, well-reasoned email exchange deciding on a generous outcome regardless of my outburst. It might make for good TV, but it's an awful way to reinforce relationships critical to one's career. And ultimately, I paid a steep relationship price for my outburst.

The Aftermath

Following the board meeting, Sarah met with our executive team and managers to determine who would be let go (and while they made some personnel decisions I lobbied vehemently against, they also had an immensely difficult job with no win/win outcome possible). The day Sarah announced the layoffs, I was out of the country, speaking at a conference (one I'd canceled on the year prior and couldn't back out of twice). Thus I watched Sarah's presentation to the company from an Airbnb bedroom on my laptop.

When I came home, it was to fewer friends (many of my former coworkers still haven't forgiven or forgotten), angry messages (public and private) across social media, a new crop of awful Glassdoor and Yelp and Google reviews for the company I'd created, and a tense, fearful management team.

The hangover of layoffs lasted for at least six months and even then only lessened in intensity but never fully faded. Into December, Mozzers who stayed talked daily about their friends and former colleagues whom the business had let down. Every week in the executive team lunch, we brought up who'd been rehired, who might still need help, who was still so angry they wouldn't reply to our emails. Comments on blog posts, threads on forums, and social media updates all referenced our layoffs, and those laid off, for months. Each time, it was a reminder to me that we'd let these people down.

You might reasonably argue that employment in the United States is at-will, and that businesses, especially those with investment backing, are supposed to take risks to seek out growth. When those risks don't pay off, people lose their jobs, the business retools, experiments, and (hopefully) grows again. Far better that way than a model where risk taking is prohibited and layoffs are made impossible, or a scenario in which leadership refuses to invest for fear that someone may someday lose their job. After all, skills are highly transferrable, especially in our field, and being laid off carries much less of a negative connotation than being fired.

Those arguments are all true in the abstract and at the macro level. But to an individual who's been laid off, or to their friends and colleagues, it comes across as nothing more than heartless excuses, devoid of empathy. A leadership team that's trying to rebuild trust and relationships across their company can't use "Hey, it's better than getting fired" or "This is how business works" to defend their actions. And with Moz, our culture has always been one of transparency and empathy—if we'd really intended to invest in these multiple products knowing that we might need to lay off a substantial portion of the team, we should have said so up front. If we knew that layoffs were potentially a few months away, we should have made it clear so that those concerned for their jobs could seek out other options.

I believe the biggest damage done by our layoffs came because we didn't live up to our core values in the way we should have. We weren't as transparent as we should have been, partially because our leadership was afraid of the impact that transparency could have (would all our best people have found new jobs if we'd told folks layoffs could be three months away in May?) and partially because we weren't responsibly on top of our numbers. When trust is lost like that, it's incredibly hard to win back.

There was, in the board and leadership discussions, one crucial area where I'm proud to say we lived up to our values of empathy and generosity: financially supporting folks we let go.

The United States has no severance pay requirements. In a situation like ours, Moz could have legally terminated all fifty-nine folks on August 17 without paying any additional compensation. That said, it's traditional to offer a minimum of two weeks, and in the tech field, where interview cycles are often long and where reputations spread far and wide, many companies have done three to six weeks of pay. Moz opted for more. We believed that our severance should reflect the relative difficulty folks would have finding new jobs, and that it should also recognize and reward tenure at the company. Sarah elected to offer, at minimum, six weeks of severance to everyone, even if they'd been at the company only a month or two, and then give an extra week of severance for each year of tenure with no cap. We paid this out in a lump sum, despite the large cash hit to Moz's balance sheet, because it meant that laid-off folks could also apply for unemployment (if we'd paid out the severance over time, federal unemployment benefits wouldn't kick in until after all the payouts were complete).

That severance decision cost Moz $1.4 million in payouts, about 20 percent of our remaining cash at the time. It was a hard-fought number, with plenty of skepticism from board members worried that we put ourselves in jeopardy spending so much on outgoing team members at a precarious time. My counterargument was that every remaining Mozzer would gladly, willingly work at a company with less cash on the balance sheet and more inherent risk rather than know that their former colleagues were struggling to make ends meet while they kept their jobs. I threatened to quit over the issue (twice actually, once in the meeting and again over email). But in the end, the board unanimously supported the severance proposal Sarah crafted.

Undoubtedly the worst part of the process was choosing who would go and who would stay. Sarah and the executive department/ product heads worked with each of their teams' managers to make those determinations. I had access to a spreadsheet where I could see those decisions as they were being made, and it felt like a punch to the gut with every update. I fought particularly hard to change managers' minds about a handful of team members, but ended up only success- fully saving one (and even then, that person being "saved" meant some- one else was let go).

At least three times, I was with Geraldine when a new update came in. I'd show her, and we'd shake our heads in anger, sadness, and frustration. Ever since Geraldine's own layoff from Seattle board- game-maker Cranium, in 2008, she'd been passionate that Moz should never make the same mistakes Cranium did. Namely, over- investing in speculative growth and having to let people go as a result. I'd joined her at a bar after Cranium's first round of layoffs and remember vividly the fear, the anger, the uncertainty of futures from so many people we cared about. I vowed not to repeat that, but here we were, in much the same boat.

There were some positive and unexpected effects from the layoffs. One was the rallying cry generated from the event. In numerous one-on-ones and group meetings thereafter, I'd hear people say (and would, myself, say) things like "We're not gonna let that happen again" or "Let's do this right so we never have to experience that again." Another was the shocking efficiency the business achieved in the months that followed. The best example comes from our marketing efforts, where, despite a team cut almost in half (down from twenty-five to fourteen people) and a budget cut by two-thirds, we actually improved our total traffic, our new free trials to Moz Pro, and our Moz Local signups on the site. A smaller team, with far fewer dollars, achieved significantly better results. This happened in other parts of the company, too, notably engineering, finance, and tech ops.

Publicly, the layoffs were news in the Seattle startup tech field and the SEO world for a few weeks, but the attention died down more quickly than I'd expected. The impact to our customers (apart from Moz Content, whose roughly one hundred paid subscribers had to find alternatives) seemed minimal. Financially, we did slightly better than our budget and in November 2016 had our first cash-flow-positive month in four years.

The layoffs were painful. I keep looking back at how they could have been avoided, which is a fool's errand. Instead, I try to focus on this one truth: if they hadn't happened, Moz might not have survived, and far more people would have lost their jobs. I believe layoffs were the right thing to do, but the financial and strategic decisions we made that put us on that path were absolutely wrong.

And the Takeaway Is . . .

What did we learn from all this? What's the big lesson? (Besides the obvious "layoffs suck" and that the people who are often responsible for the layoffs rarely lose their jobs.)

For me, it was this: we lost our focus.

How? To answer that, we need to see Moz's history of growth, investment, and spending:

YEAR	CASH SAVED/ BURNED	DEBT RAISED/ PAID BACK	VC RAISED	END OF YEAR CASH IN BANK	TOTAL REVENUE
2007	$0	$0	$1,100,000	$1,100,000	$800,000
2008	–$800,000	$0	$0	$300,000	$1,400,000
2009	+$200,000	$0	$0	$500,000	$3,100,000
2010	+$500,000	$0	$0	$1,000,000	$5,700,000
2011	+$1,000,000	$0	$0	$2,000,000	$11,400,000
2012	–$5,000,000	$0	$18,000,000	$15,100,000	$21,900,000
2013	–$12,000,000	+$3,000,000	$0	$5,800,000	$29,300,000
2014	–$1,500,000	$0	$0	$4,300,000	$31,300,000
2015	–$4,600,000	+$8,000,000	$0	$7,700,000	$37,900,000
2016	–$8,100,000	–$6,000,000	$10,000,000	$3,500,000	$42,000,000
2017	+$1,500,000	–$2,200,000	$0	$4,000,000	$47,400,000

Looking at these numbers, my eyes are drawn to the post-2013 period, when growth slowed considerably despite massive spending.

From 2012 to 2016, Moz consumed more than $35 million in venture capital and debt, alongside the tens of millions in revenue we earned, but grew at a vastly slower rate than the five prior years. We added more than $10 million in revenue between 2011 and 2012 and $8 million from 2012 to 2013, but then we plateaued.

In my estimation, there were five key principles driving the growth-rate deceleration. If I had understood each of them in 2012, I believe I'd have been a much better CEO, board member, and contributor.

#1: Subscriber Retention versus Customer Acquisition

There are three ways you can grow a software-subscription business:

1. Acquire more customers

2. Increase the subscription tenure of customers

3. Up-sell existing customers to higher-priced subscriptions/packages

In 2011, the average Moz Pro customer subscribed to our product for 8.5 months. In 2016, the average Moz Pro customer subscribed for 11 months.

In 2011, we signed up approximately 1,000 new free trials each month. In 2016, we signed up about 4,500 new free trials each month.

I'd argue we invested foolishly in marketing and reach when we should have been investing in product and retention. Why? Because of how subscription-based businesses work. You're basically filling a leaky bucket, and eventually, if you grow enough, you'll churn through your entire potential audience of customers, while only retaining a small portion of them.

We knew that millions of organizations and marketers were

interested in using SEO software, but we'd never done enough to make our product into a long-term habit and an essential part of those organizations' operations. Compare, for example, Moz's average eleven-month subscription tenure with a company with Salesforce, perhaps the best-known and most-respected company in the SaaS world. Salesforce's average customer tenure is 120 months, more than ten times that of Moz's.

This means that Salesforce has to acquire only 10 percent of its current customer base each year to maintain the same revenue. Any additional new customers, or any up-sell on current customers, means growth. At Moz, we need to add thousands of new customers each month just to keep up our existing revenue.

Here's where focus comes into play. Because we're so dependent on new customer acquisition in order to stave off shrinking revenue, we have to substantially split the company's priorities between product development that can attract new customers versus investments that improve retention of existing customers. Now multiply that by four different products and you can see how the organization struggled just to keep its head above water. Customer retention versus customer acquisition is a long-running debate in the subscription world, but if I were doing things over again, I'd limit any investment in marketing (of staff, expenses, or leadership attention) until we found a path to consistently grow subscription tenure.

Ironically, that path was something we finally discovered in 2016. We tested a customer success program, whereby trained Moz staff members held phone calls with subscribers in their first month of use, walked them through the features of the product, proactively answered questions, and helped people learn how to solve their problems and goals using the tools. The effect was dramatic. Subscribers who talked to a customer success representative for thirty to forty-five minutes stayed with the product for 30 percent longer than those who didn't. Even our least-experienced customers (those very new to the practice of SEO) stuck around and made better use of the subscription.

Customer success surely isn't the only way we can improve retention, but with the business so dependent on new customer acquisition, and the leadership team spread so thin worrying about multiple products, we were a combination of unwilling and unable to consistently experiment and invest in this crucial element.

#2: Multiple Products Dilute Your Brand

Say you buy a new vehicle made by Honda and experience a lot of problems. You'd probably shy away from buying Hondas in the future, and you'd likely tell your friends not to buy them, either. You might complain publicly via your influential social media accounts, and leave online reviews that express your concerns with Honda, too. You'd almost certainly avoid the Honda brand on other products—lawn mowers or motorcycles or heavy machinery (if you were involved in those sorts of purchases at your job).

But the reverse isn't usually as true. If you loved your Honda vehicle, you might be slightly more tempted to buy a Honda lawn mower, but if you're like most consumers, you wouldn't just assume it's good; you'd do your research. Same story with the heavy machinery or the motorcycle.

Negative experiences with brands tend to overwhelm every other data point (no one thinks "the team making the lawn mowers probably isn't the same one that makes the cars; maybe I should give them a chance"). But positive experiences don't have nearly the same strength of association. Human beings are wired to remember and internalize negative experiences with vastly greater force than positive ones, hence the much greater likelihood that you'll leave a bad review than a good one.

It's not just the potential for negative experiences that carry over from product to product, though. The mere existence of multiple products from a brand causes cognitive strain and a weakening of memory and relevant associations.

A company that makes only a single product is vastly easier to recall, amplify, and evaluate. Think Google, which, for a decade, was nothing but a search engine, versus Yahoo!, which was a directory and a search engine and a publisher and a media business and eventually became best known as a company with lots of divisions, lots of revenue, but no direction. Or Bose, which started in audio of all kinds, but became best-known and most successful based on their award-winning noise-canceling headphones.

Plenty of companies buck this model with multiple products, but the successful ones do so only when their initial products have enough momentum, viability, and traction to stand alone. P&G didn't start with thousands of consumer brands. They made Ivory soap. They sold a lot of it. Then they made other products. Amazon started as an online bookseller, and only once they became known and loved did they brand into broader online retail. Honda themselves started in motorcycles and only expanded to other vehicles after fifteen years of growth, during which they became the world leader in motorcycle sales.

At Moz, we tried to expand into multiple products, selling to audiences outside our core, long before we had the momentum, viability, or traction on our initial product, Moz Pro. Our churn rates were the clearest indication of a still-immature product, but we foolishly took our focus and investments off that product to buy, build, launch, and support others, hoping the brand association and reach would enable faster growth with new products.

#3: The Inherent Complexity of Numerous Priorities

Companies are made up of people. People are relatively good at doing one thing well. We're terrible at multitasking (despite what many of us might like to believe), and we're generally awful at handling complex interplay between distinct, competing requests.

David Strayer, professor at the University of Utah and coauthor of "Who Multi-Tasks and Why?," puts it nicely:

> The people who multitask the most tend to be impulsive, sensation-seeking, overconfident of their multitasking abilities, and they tend to be less capable of multitasking.

I'd apply that same statement to organizations, especially in the startup stage.

When you're building a company from the ground up, for the first time, in a new field, with a new team, you need all the simplicity you can get. Everything is going to be uniquely challenging because you and your team haven't seen it or done it before, and because market forces are inherently structured to benefit incumbents. The great strength startups usually have is that they can uniquely focus all their energy on just one thing, whereas their incumbent competitors have diverse efforts and responsibilities that impede progress.

Losing focus and asking your small team(s) to take on more tasks rather than do one thing better costs you this critical advantage.

Doing just one thing means you can:

- try more experiments in pursuit of success, meaning you learn and iterate faster;

- keep communications overhead lean by hiring fewer people and keeping the task list short;
- get your most senior leaders personally involved in projects, reducing power distance and minimizing the time required to make crucial decisions;
- recruit, train, and hone the skills of the best people for the tasks needed;
- identify and reduce waste (of time, materials, people, or investments) fast, because it's easier to see said waste when you have less to concentrate on; and
- budget time, expenses, and people more accurately with less variation.

For many companies, "do one thing" is unrealistically reductive advice. But it pays to know that adding more priorities scales exponentially, not linearly. At Moz, I found it vastly less complexifying to add one additional product (e.g., Moz Local) to the company's charter than to add a third or a fourth. Each new product and priority cost vastly more resources and created more time dilution than the previous one.

When we removed these products and priorities, and simplified, the results spoke for themselves. Fewer people, more focused on just a few things, could do more than a much larger team pulled in myriad directions.

#4: Competition

Try to name a company that's the best in the world at everything they do. I can name only a few. I think Serious Eats is the best in the world at researching and sharing scientific-method style recipes.

FiveThirtyEight is probably the best in the online world at data-science-driven publishing in sports, pop culture, and politics. Tesla almost certainly makes the best purely electric cars in the world. Fitbit makes the most popular and, by many metrics, the best fitness tracker on the market.

Each of these organizations is deeply focused. But I couldn't find a single company that has multiple business units and is the undeniable best or clear market leader in every space it occupies. Apple makes, arguably, the best mobile phones, but its laptop division is less market leading and its software lies somewhere between serviceable and frustration inducing. Virgin America has some of the best-rated traveler experiences, but of the four hundred brands under the company's umbrella, fewer than a half dozen are as well-rated, and even the airline is nowhere near market leading. Google makes far and away the world's best and most popular search engine, but Google+, the company's social network, isn't even in the top ten of its category. 3M comes close, with market-leading and best-in-class products in a great number of its product lines, but competitors like Gore-Tex (in weather-resistant fabric) or Band-Aid (in medical adhesives) cut against that. 3M even has a goal to turn over a significant portion of its product lines (through divestiture or sale) every few years.

It would seem that many companies can be the best in the world at one or a few things, some can be best in the world at a handful of products in its portfolio, but almost no one can accomplish this feat with consistency across a broad spectrum.

We learned this lesson hard at Moz. In 2011, you could reasonably say that Moz's software was the best in the world (or at least a close number two) at five of the six key functions* of SEO software: rank

---

* We didn't have a true keyword research feature until Keyword Explorer launched in 2016.

tracking, site crawl, on-page optimization, link analysis, and reporting. Over the next four years, at least one company obviously surpassed us in every one of those but two (on-page and reporting).

If I were asked in 2014 which software provider offered the best link data, the best rank-tracking abilities, the best website crawler, or the best keyword research tools, I couldn't honestly say it was us. We'd become too diversified, with too many projects, data sources, tools, and features. In SEO, that was particularly dangerous because of how the field operates. This was another lesson I painfully learned at SEER's offices during our CEO swap.

Say you're an SEO professional helping your company's website reach top rankings in Google. You know that the number one–ranking position gets the lion's share of the clicks (usually between 20 and 50 percent, depending on the search query), position number two gets about half that, position number three gets a third, and the remaining positions on page one get even fewer. Less than 5 percent of searchers ever visit page two of the results. Thus, any slight advantage you can get that helps you move up even one position is hugely worthwhile. If one tool shows you link sources you could acquire that another tool missed, or one finds problems with your site that the other ignored, it could mean the difference between ranking number one and number two (i.e., the difference between hundreds or thousands of additional, high-value visitors each month).

Switching costs in software is usually a big challenge for startups versus incumbents. If you become the default tool in a field or for a particular type of user, you can often maintain market leadership even if your competition produces a technically superior product. It's why in order to compete, startups often need to be a vastly better choice along multiple dimensions (ease of use, features, data quality, price, etc.) than their entrenched competitors.

But in SEO, where a one-position difference on a few keyword phrases can have a huge impact on your bottom line, or on whether your client keeps paying for your services, almost any incremental advantage is worth the additional cost in dollars, time to learn the new product, and the pain of switching over your tracking and reporting systems. We found this out the hard way, bleeding customers to our startup competitors who wisely focused on just a single aspect of the features our suite provided.

#5: Law of Large Numbers

Despite being familiar with the concept that as you grow larger it becomes increasingly difficult to maintain a similar rate of growth due to the math of scaling, I failed to appreciate what it would mean to Moz's business to hit plateauing growth rates, particularly among investors, potential acquirers, and startup-metric-savvy employees.

When, in 2010, we added $2.6 million in additional revenue over the prior year, we were ecstatic. But in 2016, when we added $4.1 million in additional revenue, we were immensely disappointed. That's because 2010's additional revenue nearly doubled 2009's total, while 2016's was only 11 percent higher than the prior year's. Percentage rate of growth, not raw dollars added, is the metric by which venture-backed startups measure themselves and are, from the outside, judged. Growing at 30 percent year-over-year at our stage is considered the minimum level for an "interesting" business in the venture world (one that could reasonably raise additional capital or where equity overall would be a desirable commodity).

I foolishly turned down additional funding in our 2012 round when other investors wanted to participate in our Series B. I turned down offers to sell my personal equity in the company. I turned down that remarkable offer from HubSpot to sell the company at an outstanding price. Had I grasped the mental models outsiders (and some employees and potential employees) used to think about Moz's "success" and the degree to which growth, more so than any other set of considerations, dominates the thinking about a company's prospects, I'd have reversed those decisions.

Granted, other issues can inhibit growth as well, most commonly market size, cost of customer acquisition, and product scalability. Moz didn't face these issues as acutely due to our audience, structure, and strengths (i.e., the SEO field, thanks mostly to Google, continued to grow at a far more rapid clip than our own). Our costs to acquire customers have always been extremely low due to our self-service funnel and high organic traffic, and our software product was engineered to handle many times the volume of customers we've onboarded and kept.

What Makes Focus So Hard?

During those years I was CEO, expanding our products and capabilities seemed to me the logical path. Growing our marketing and reach instead of hunkering down on our product's retention seemed like a rational decision, too. Entering new fields of marketing with tools for multiple audiences resonated as the right way to go.

Why did I ignore the pain these multiple directions caused? How did I miss the benefits of focus for so long?

The answer lies in what I thought I was supposed to be doing versus what I actually should have been doing. It's something that regularly plagues startup founders and leadership teams. It certainly plagued my successor. It adversely affected companies as broad as

37signals (whose aforementioned multiproduct strategy was shut down in favor of focus on Basecamp), Netflix (whose ill-fated split of Flixster nearly bankrupted the company), Microsoft (whose desire to do everything cost them market leadership in division after division), and Cranium (whose failed efforts to expand from games into media and toys cost my wife and all her coworkers a career there).

When you're an early-stage startup founder, your job is clear—find "product:market fit" (Silicon Valley–speak for "a product that a significant portion of customers in your market love, use, and will pay for"), then scale. Beyond that, things get murkier. Once you have "fit" and are scaling, your job is to find growth through any means possible. Greater growth means higher valuations, the ability to attract better talent, the envy of your peers, the coveted press and prestige, the possibility to sell your company or your stock and become wealthy; all of it is dependent on growth as measured by the percentage of year-over-year revenue addition (at least, in the case of companies with revenue).

That bias rapidly leads to thinking along lines like "Our core product is growing, but I bet we could grow even faster if we . . ." Filling in that blank is dangerous, because it's almost always occupied by something that adds complexity and removes focus. Maybe it's new features you believe could get you more growth, or a whole new product line, or the acquisition of another company, or a few R&D projects that could yield the next big thing.

Silicon Valley startup culture embeds founders with the false belief that because growth is what matters most, we should pursue any and all strategies that could lead us there. Far wiser, and much more difficult because of the discipline and patience required, is ignoring those potential off-course avenues in favor of applying the experimentation, learning, and iteration process to the one thing in which you can be best at in the world, and letting those other strategies for growth wait until you've got truly massive scale.

The benefits of focus are too great to ignore, hidden only by the resolve needed to stay on target.

AFTERWORD
CHEAT CODES FOR NEXT TIME

Silicon Valley has become not just a place, but a culture and a
state of mind.

—Vinod Khosla, 2000

I have good news and bad news.

The bad news is, by the time you read this, I'll have left Moz. Like many founders at VC-backed companies, my departure wasn't under great circumstances (but since that story's still being written, I'll save a full breakdown for some future blog post). The challenges beyond $50 million/year in revenue, and scaling past a few hundred employees to a possible (fingers crossed) IPO or acquisition, won't be ones I'll experience, at least from the inside. I remain on the board, and my wife and I are, jointly, still Moz's single largest shareholder. So I'll continue to be involved at least somewhat (and will, I promise, share what learnings I can as the journey progresses).

The good news: I'm gonna try it again. I'm starting another company.

After all the struggles and hardship, the sixteen years of mostly awful, only sometimes awesome experiences, even I think there must be a volatile mix of masochism and insanity pumping through my veins. But here's the thing: I love the journey, and if you've made it this far, perhaps you do (or will), too.

Not all of it. Hell no. But there's something undeniably special in the sense of accomplishment that comes from making payroll at the end of a month you started with no idea how you'd do it. Or the immense feeling of joy that comes from solving problems the way you want, rather than the way someone else prescribes. Or the camaraderie of late nights before a successful launch. Founders have these one-of-a-kind circumstances that become great stories and earn powerful shared experiences that resonate for years to come.

If that journey calls to you, welcome. Welcome to this strange club of hard work and "everything's riding on this" gambles. To the loneliness, the bittersweetness, the high-stakes, low-odds, brave new world you build yourself. Many of us who've chosen this path are cheering for you, supporting you, and hoping that what you learn will be shared openly for the benefit of those who follow.

As I embark on this next project, I want to do a little bit more of that last piece—sharing, and hopefully helping.

This second go-around feels very different, even in the early stages. I'm more confident. I know this path better. I've got cheat codes handy for many of the steps ahead. In the spirit of transparency, here's a handful I'm applying:

Branding: Last time, I started with "SEOmoz.org" and eventually bought "Moz.com" (for six figures) in order to give the company a more pronounceable, less restrictive name. This time, I'm choosing a brand name that:

1. has no obvious associations with a specific product or space, and thus is open for expansion (like Amazon, Google, Uber, Zillow, etc.);

2. has the .com domain extension available—outside of the tech world, branding a non-.com web address is still a huge barrier, and an available .com also makes it more likely that the brand's social media profiles on places like Twitter, Facebook, Instagram, and the rest are capturable;

3. is easy to say and hard to confuse once heard. Years of dealing with ess-ee-oh-moz and all its mispronounced variants taught me the importance of having a name that, once heard, can be recalled and transmitted. There's even research showing that more pronounceable brands and ticker symbols tend to do better in the stock market than their less pronounceable peers (and they say stock markets are "efficient"); and

4. has very few results in a Google search, so that tracking its progress on the web is easy and potential confusion between the brand and anything that already exists is minimal. With Moz, we struggled for years differentiating from DMOZ and, later, the Mozilla Foundation. I plan to be more intentionally unique this go-around.

Funding: Today, there are vastly more funding options to those building a new tech-enabled business. Venture capital comes in more variety than in the past, particularly with the rise of "micro-VCs," who raise smaller funds, invest smaller amounts, and also require less massive exits to meet their LPs' expectations. A fund that raises

$40 million instead of $400 million can be successful with portfolio companies selling for far more achievable (though still rare and amazing) acquisitions of $25 or $50 million.

There are creative forms of debt from firms like Lighter Capital and Indie.vc, who don't (necessarily) take an equity stake in the company but can be paid back like a high-interest bank loan without the ticking clock. There are funds like Backstage Capital (which Geraldine and I invested in) and Black & Brown Founders that offer funding exclusively to underrepresented folks building a company. Nearly every region of the planet has some form of startup accelerator (like Techstars and Y Combinator), which offer networking connections, alongside mentorship, a small amount of funding, and (usually) the opportunity to present directly to angel, venture, and corporate investors upon the program's completion. There're angel investors, now easier to access than ever before through platforms like AngelList and angel collectives in many cities (e.g., Seattle's Alliance of Angels). And last, but not least, there's crowdfunding, available in equity and debt formats (via platforms like Crowdfunder and Wefunder) as well as rewards-based formats (like Kickstarter and IndieGoGo—the latter also offers equity crowdfunding for some business types).

Here's how the options compare, situationally, for my next adventure:

1. Venture capital is, for me, too restrictive, even at the micro-VC level. It forces that binary outcome—either succeed spectacularly (a true rarity) or collapse (far more common). It's absolutely the right call for those seeking to go truly big, but I want the freedom to choose a path of slow, profitable growth, perhaps never selling at all and simply building a business that yields profits for employees and a reliable, high-quality product for customers.

2. Angel investment is a tricky one. There's the ideal outcome—my investors are completely aligned with whatever path the business pursues and comfortable if we change direction from pursuing profitability to aiming for an exit or even choosing to raise VC. But if I raise angel money, there are options that become more difficult: handing over the company to its employees, choosing to have the profits benefit a cause, deciding to stay small rather than pursue growth. Angel investors may not have the technical rights to stop these options, but I've seen what happens when angels and founders clash; grudges are held, reputations are lost, and angels leverage their relationship clout to harm (or to limit help).

3. Debt has some benefits—namely, you can pay it back and be completely free of any external obligation. But that comes at a high monetary price. Debt offerings on crowdfunding platforms require a payback of 1.5 to 3 times the amount within a few years, and it's even more expensive to use some of the debt-based startup funding sources that need 3 to 5 times payback. The ugly part is what could happen if you aren't able to pay back your debt holders; namely, they could, like a bank, seize your assets or entire company. Despite these drawbacks, it's definitely in my consideration set. The risk is offset by the chance to run the company exactly as I want, without outside interference or exit requirements.

4. Crowdfunding is a truly interesting option, especially given some of the advantages I have as a second-time founder (a large social media audience, lots of connections and friends who've expressed interest in backing my next project, and experience earning attention and amplification). The money raised, especially in a rewards-based scenario, is essentially early revenue, and it can help expose the company to potential customers and gauge their level of interest. There's equity-based and debt-based crowdfunding, too, which

leverage some of my network-effect strengths but retain a bit of the drawbacks mentioned in number 3 (though, in an equity-funding scenario, crowdfunders may be more flexible than angel investors).

5. One hundred percent bootstrapped is the last option. It's fraught with personal financial risk, and while my wife and I have a couple hundred thousand dollars in savings (now a tiny bit more because you bought this book; thank you!), neither of us are too keen on burning through it all and leaving nothing for a rainy day. But bootstrapping is massively compelling from a freedom and flexibility perspective. It retains full ownership and control. It means we can dial back personal expenses and do some consulting, writing, speaking, or other projects to help extend the runway. And if I can get this new entity to a decent level of profitability, the sky's the limit from every perspective—additional funding, distribution of profits, future options for how to scale and run the firm, etc.

When choosing your own funding, think hard about what you want in the long run. Are you totally comfortable chasing a big exit and okay with the limitations on pay and control, and the high failure rates? If so, venture capital is exactly the model you're seeking. Are you looking for complete control, profitability, and 100 percent ownership with slower growth? Bootstrapping on nights and weekends while you're at a day job (or consulting, or living with a very supportive partner) may be the right match.

Market Validation: One of my major worries is that the Venn diagram of what I want to build and what people actually need will have too little overlap to be an exciting startup. To combat that, I plan to:

1. build a list of about one hundred people I strongly suspect will want the product I'm creating;

2. interview each of them about the problem and how they solve it now;

3. create a landing page that teases the product even before it's available, and see how many are willing to enter their email for later access; and

4. share that landing page broadly, buy some ads to it, get it ranking in search engines, and use my connections to help amplify it.

This process overlaps elegantly with crowdfunding, and I might leverage one of the existing platforms or roll my own. One of the biggest causes of early-stage business failure is lack of real buyers hungry for your solution. Validating that the problem you're trying to solve is real, the market exists, and customers are willing to take a chance on a new type of solution from a brand-new company is a huge weight lifted.

Document Core Beliefs and Biases: This time, I don't want to wait until several years in to define why the company exists, what the core values will be, and what kinds of people will and won't be a match for the culture. I know, for example, that I want to try my hand at a remote-centric work environment (versus Moz's big, central office in a major metro). I know that transparency will always be crucial to my happiness at a job. I know I don't work well with people who aren't fast, thoughtful, and empathetic over email.

Rather than trialing different approaches, or taking a "wait-and-see" attitude with these cultural elements, I'm documenting them in detail. That way, anyone who wants to join the company knows exactly what they're getting into and can decide if the organization is a match for them. If I recruit cofounders, partners, advisers, or investors, this documentation can prevent a lot of hard conversations and heartache by setting the stage from day one with expectations.

These cultural elements fall into several buckets:

1. Core Beliefs about Work—These are the theories I've come to believe about how people do their best work, and what elements deserve optimization. For example, I don't think butts in seats in an office is necessary or ideal. Thus, I want to experiment with an all-remote team. I do believe strongly in paying top-of-market-rate salaries but hiring fewer people. I'm convinced diversity in early hires is essential to building the best team for the long run. Optimizing for psychological safety, giving ICs equal paths to move up, and striving for focus all fit under this umbrella.

2. Exit Goals—Do I want to sell my next business early? Aim for a longer-term, big exit? Or run it profitably over the long term and distribute profit dividends? All are appealing, but more than anything else, I want the freedom to make decisions as I see how the market opportunity plays out. Thus, I'm specifically choosing to optimize for optionality and not to make moves that remove any of these possibilities. That means being up front with any potential investors (and, probably, not raising traditional angel or VC), potential employees (who may be seeking something else in their careers), and potential partners.

3. Purpose, Values, Mission, and Vision—It took too many years to nail these down at Moz. For my next venture, I'm starting from my personal purpose (at least, my personal, *professional* purpose): to help people do better marketing. I still like TAGFEE, the values we established at Moz, but I'll likely have some refinements. Establishing a vision for the foreseeable future and a company

mission for the long term, even if they need refinement over time, will better enable focus (one of my core beliefs about work).

4. Customer, Market, and Problem Space Hypotheses—Initially in a new business, everything is a theory. We *think* product A will solve problem B. We *think* problem B is a bigger, more-important-to-address one than problem C. But in the past, I've failed to document these theories specifically. That's a mistake I don't intend to repeat. Instead, I'm keeping track of ideas that fit this mold, engaging in work to uncover the answers, and then recording what we learn about them over time.

5. What Won't Change in Our Field over the Next Ten Years—I'm stealing this directly from Amazon's Jeff Bezos, who applied it thusly:

> In our retail business, we know that customers want low prices, and I know that's going to be true ten years from now. They want fast delivery; they want vast selection. It's impossible to imagine a future ten years from now where a customer comes up and says, "Jeff, I love Amazon; I just wish the prices were a little higher," [or] "I love Amazon; I just wish you'd deliver a little more slowly." Impossible. And so the effort we put into those things, spinning those things up, we know the energy we put into it today will still be paying off dividends for our customers ten years from now. When you have something that you know is true, even over the long term, you can afford to put a lot of energy into it.

My early research efforts in whatever field I pursue will focus on understanding the answers to this question first. If I can accurately ID these, I think it will give this venture a huge leg up.

Doing the work that I've just described can seem like it's putting the cart before the horse. But I'd counter that asking these questions is a forcing function for greater thoughtfulness about your business as a whole and boosts the odds of surviving those early, perilous years. No matter what stage of life your organization is in today, my advice is to have a written, transparent road map. Plans change. The value of a team with a shared plan doesn't.

So here I go. Into the unknown future, still lost, but far better prepared than last time. And hopefully after finishing this book, you are, too.

FOLLOW RAND'S NEXT ADVENTURE AT SPARKTORO.COM

ACKNOWLEDGMENTS

This book's purpose, as my amazing editor, Niki Papadopoulos, often reminded me, is not to tell the stories I want to tell or to exorcise my professional demons. It is to serve you—the reader. YOU have a project, a company, a career, an investment striving for success. This book's job is to give you the knowledge I wish I'd had, to mark on the startup map those strategic pitfalls and tactical traps I've now learned to avoid.

If the past few hundred pages have done their job, that's because a wide range of people contributed their time, their assistance, and their willingness to share. I'm humbled and honored to thank them all:

To the team at Portfolio and Penguin, first and foremost Niki herself, a deep thank you for your patience, perseverance, and guidance. I'm a horribly picky SOB, but even *I* am proud of this book ☺.

To the team at Moz, without whom there would be no story to tell—my deep appreciation for the sacrifices you've made and continue to make. I'm heartbroken not to be able to join you on future legs of this journey, but hope you find great success and happiness.

ACKNOWLEDGMENTS

To the Seattle startup community, whose consistent support, especially in my early years when I had no way to repay your kindnesses, nor any evidence to suggest that mine was a venture worth your time, thank you. The hours you spent upgrading my understanding of technology, of company-building, of the investment world, and of people contributed mightily to Moz's growth. I'm proud that my hometown has such a generous, thoughtful group of startup enthusiasts so willing to offer help without thought of returns.

And to the SEO world, among whose ranks I count many of my best friends, strongest allies, and kindest amplifiers—I have been honored to count myself among your ranks. Thank you for all the support, the forgiveness, and the unwavering belief in me and Moz you've shown this past decade and a half. It is thanks to you that this company became anything but a twinkle in my and Gillian's eyes.

In addition to these groups (and Niki), I'd like to call out a number of individuals as well:

- Geraldine DeRuiter—You are my gravity. My sunlight. My love. Without you, Moz wouldn't exist, and I'd be a different (almost certainly worse) person. Although these last years have been difficult, I've never wanted anyone else by my side in the face of hardship. I am so lucky to spend the rest of my life with you.
- Gillian Muessig—Mom, thank you. For your love and support, your dedication to me, Evan, and Meri, and for being my partner on the path to entrepreneurship.
- Pauline and Seymour Fishkin—Your love and unwavering support, your wisdom and kindness, and your progressive ideals have been a beacon to me. I hope to always make you proud.
- Nicci Herron and Jess Stipe—For your years of support, going above and beyond what any CEO/founder should expect from an

EA (and a friend), thank you so much. I'm honored to have you both in my professional and personal lives.

- Wil Reynolds and Nora Pillard Reynolds—I will always cherish and be thankful for the friendship we have, the help with this book, and the kindness you've shown to me, to Geraldine, and to Moz. Let's go celebrate sometime soon.

- Dawn Shepard—This book's visuals and branding make me proud to hold it in my hands and to share it with the world. Thank you for your superb work and your deep empathy for *Lost and Founder*'s audience.

- Danny Sullivan—You gave me and Moz a chance when we needed it most; I'll always be in your debt.

- Dharmesh Shah and Kirsten Waerstad—Hubspot and the two of you have been the strongest of supporters for me, for Geraldine, and for Moz. I don't know what we did in a past life to deserve so much gracious help, friendship, and extraordinary meals together, but I'm constantly thankful for you both.

- Kelly Smith, Michelle Goldberg, and Brad Feld—Your belief in me and your financial, emotional, and strategic support have made me a better entrepreneur and a wiser man. Thank you for taking a chance on an unproven kid in an unproven market.

- David Mihm, Matt Brown, Tim Resnik, and Jay Leary—Despite all the struggles, the ups and downs, I'm honored that we got to work together, and even more honored that you continue to show me and Geraldine such deep affection and support. All of you should be proud of your work at Moz; I know I am.

- Adam Tratt, Ben Huh, Liz Pearce, and Dan Shapiro—Thank you for the excellent early feedback and the many hours in restaurants and coffee shops discussing the topics that led to many of these chapters.

- Emily Grossman—Your friendship, your kindness in reviewing this book, and your superb critiques have seriously upgraded these pages. Hopefully you'll read this while enjoying a sublime meal with me and Geraldine in some far-flung locale.
- Ben Hendrickson and Chas Williams—You are two of the finest engineers and people I know. It's been an honor working with you (twice now!), and I owe you a deep debt of gratitude for the long hours and stressful work spent making Moz's tools worth using.
- Shawn Edwards, Evan Battaglia, Kenny Martin, Kiki Kuchin, Christine Ryu, Jason Younker, Tony Bye, and Russ Jones—Thank you for helping to make Keyword Explorer a reality and a great product (that's now imitated by everyone else in the field!). I know you all sacrificed and fought to make that product ship, and I, along with thousands of SEO practitioners, am deeply grateful.
- Will Critchlow and Duncan Morris—Thank you for sharing this journey through these many years with me. Our time together is always too short, but the echoes of those moments carry forward for me and I'm always looking forward to our next meeting.
- Sarah Bird—Thank you for your contributions as COO and your stewardship of Moz in 2014 to right our ship.
- Brian Halligan, Mike Cassidy, Jessica Mah, Jerry Colonna, and Nirav Tolia—An immense thank-you for sharing your stories, your emails, and your experiences with me and with this book's readers. I feel so lucky to have you all as friends and colleagues.
- Eric Ries, Kim Scott, Mark Suster, Seth Godin, and Nirav Tolia— Thank you for your contributions to this book's process, for allowing me to publish your works and quotes, and for connecting me with your networks. Moz and I are deeply thankful.

- Adam Feldstein and Rachel Burnside—Our friendship and your sacrifices to help Moz grow have meant so much to me over the years. Thank you for carrying the torch when I cannot.
- Maura Hubbell and Marc Mims—Your willingness to share your stories with the Moz team, and with the wider world through this book, are a mitzvah. Thank you for opening my mind and my heart, and for making so many people around you more empathetic, more thoughtful, and more aware.
- Jane Friedman—Thank you for the incredibly helpful call and advice about the publishing process. It's been a long journey, but your tips never missed the mark.
- Last, but most certainly not least, Sylvie Greenberg (my agent)— You've been a champion of support, of positivity in the face of my cranky pessimism, of wise advice at trying times, and a confidante when I needed it most. You have my deepest gratitude. Fingers crossed, we'll get to take this journey again together in the future.

NOTES

INTRODUCTION

5 **University of California–Berkeley economists** . . . Aimee Groth, "Entrepreneurs Don't Have a Special Gene for Risk—They Come from Families with Money," *Quartz*, July 17, 2015, https://qz.com/455109/entrepreneurs-dont-have-a-special-gene-for-risk-they-come-from-families-with-money/.

5 **More than 75 percent of early-stage technology companies** . . . Stephanie Walden, "Startup Success By the Numbers," *Mashable*, January 30, 2014, http://mashable.com/2014/01/30/startup-success-infographic/#XiiallxpsOqZ.

CHAPTER 1

21 **Tinder grew to** . . . Mary Emily O'Hara, "Tinder Co-Founder's Lawsuit Reflects Tech Industry's Rampant Sexism," *VICE News*, July 2, 2014, https://news.vice.com/article/tinder-co-founders-lawsuit-reflects-tech-industrys-rampant-sexism.

21 **Zipcar, one of the** . . . Arielle Duhaime-Ross, "Driven: How Zipcar's Founders Built and Lost a Car-Sharing Empire," *The Verge*, April 1, 2014, https://www.theverge.com/2014/4/1/5553910/driven-how-zipcars-founders-built-and-lost-a-car-sharing-empire.

CHAPTER 2

29 **"(Consulting) is dancing . . ."** "When It Comes to Startups, Products and Services Don't Mix," Giff Constable, GiffConstable.com, January 26, 2010, http://giffconstable.com/2010/01/when-it-comes-to-startups-products-and-services-dont-mix/.

41 **That's slightly higher** . . . Sammy Abdullah, CFA, "The Median Level of Founder Ownership at Exit," *Blossom Street Ventures* (blog), November 3, 2016, http://blossomstreetventures.com/blog_details.php?bcat_id=106.

42 **In 2012, Scott Shane** . . . Scott Shane, "Small Business Failure Rates by Industry: The Real Numbers," *Small Business Trends*, last modified October 1, 2013, https://smallbiztrends.com/2012/09/failure-rates-by-sector-the-real -numbers.html.

CHAPTER 3

49 **"Your work is going to . . ."** Steve Jobs, "'Find What You Love,' Steve Jobs at Stanford University," *Wall Street Journal*, last modified August 24, 2011, http:// www.wsj.com/articles/SB10001424053111903596904576520690515394766.

CHAPTER 4

61 **"Ideas are worthless . . ."** Scott Adams, "The Value of Ideas," June 4, 2010, *Scott Adams' Blog*, http://blog.dilbert.com/post/102627956681/the-value-of-ideas.

CHAPTER 5

69 **"Writing code? That's the easy part . . ."** Jeff Atwood, "Usability on the Cheap and Easy," *Coding Horror* (blog), March 31, 2010, https://blog.codinghorror.com /usability-on-the-cheap-and-easy/.

CHAPTER 6

89 **"The best entrepreneurs . . ."** https://www.goodreads.com/quotes/7452753 -the-best-entrepreneurs-are-not-the-best-visionaries-the-greatest.

93 **But if you define startup** . . . Deborah Gage, "The Venture Capital Secret: 3 Out of 4 Start-Ups Fail," *Wall Street Journal*, last modified September 20, 2012, http://www.wsj.com/articles/SB10000872396390443720204578004980476 429190.

95 **A further 10 percent** . . . "The Meeting That Showed Me the Truth about VC's and How They Don't Make Money," https://medium.com/the-mission/the -meeting-that-showed-me-the-truth-about-vcs-and-how-they-don-t-make -money-ab72b52b50cd.

99 **National Venture Capital** . . . Scott Shane, "What Slow Exits Mean to Startup Investors," *Entrepreneur*, https://www.entrepreneur.com/article/253459.

99 **When EquityZen limited** . . . Russell Lange, "But When Will They Go Public?," *Meditations* (blog), August 13, 2015, https://equityzen.com/blog/company-at -ipo/.

CHAPTER 7

108 **Statistics are on your side** . . . Rüdiger Fahlenbrach, "Founder-CEOs, Investment Decisions, and Stock Market Performance," *Journal of Financial and Quantitative Analysis* 44, no. 2 (April 2009): 439–66, https://doi .org/10.1017 /S0022109009090139; Joon Mahn Lee, Jongsoo Kim, and Joonhyung Bae, "Founder CEOs and Innovation: Evidence from S&P 500 Firms," *SSRN*, February 17, 2016, http://papers.ssrn.com/sol3/papers.cfm?abstract_id=2733456.

CHAPTER 8

111 **"Economically, you can . . ."** Paul Graham, "How to Make Wealth," May 2004, http://paulgraham.com/wealth.html.

118 **The venture capitalist and blogger Mark Suster . . .** Mark Suster, "How to Discuss Stock Options with Your Team," *Both Sides of the Table*, September 6, 2010, https://bothsidesofthetable.com/how-to-discuss-stock-options-with-your -team-d903304e4dde.

CHAPTER 9

121 **"Growth hackers are a hybrid . . ."** Andrew Chen, "Growth Hacker Is the New VP Marketing," *@andrewchen* (blog), http://andrewchen.co/how-to-be-a -growth-hacker-an-airbnbcraigslist-case-study/.

124 **That new page was almost eight times . . .** "How We Made $1 Million for Moz (Formerly SEOmoz)—Using Landing Page Optimization and Email Marketing," Conversion Rate Experts, http://www.conversion-rate-experts.com/seomoz -case-study/.

129 **When Drew Houston . . .** "New Strategy: Encourage WOM, viral," *Dropbox Startup Lessons Learned* (slides), http://www.slideshare.net/gueste94e4c/dropbox -startup-lessons-learned-3836587/30-New_strategy_encourage_WOM_viral.

CHAPTER 10

139 **"Corporate values, usually chosen . . ."** Ray Williams, "What Do Corporate Values Really Mean?," *Psychology Today*, February 7, 2010, https://www .psychologytoday.com/blog/wired-success/201002/what-do-corporate -values-really-mean.

145 **You can find the original version . . .** Rand Fishkin, "What We Believe and Why: SEOmoz's TAGFEE Tenets," *Moz Blog*, February 15, 2010, https://moz .com/blog/what-we-believe-why-seomozs-tagfee-tenets.

147 **"In describing the alignment process . . ."** Jim Collins, "Aligning Action and Values," JimCollins.com, June 2000, http://www.jimcollins.com/article_topics /articles/aligning-action.html.

153 **According to Namely's . . .** Max Nisen, "Statistically Speaking, What Does the Average Startup Look Like?," *The Atlantic*, December 31, 2014, https://www .theatlantic.com/business/archive/2014/12/statistically-speaking-what-does -the-average-startup-look-like/384019/.

157 **Research from McKinsey . . .** Vivian Hunt, Dennis Layton, and Sara Prince, "Why Diversity Matters," McKinsey, January 2015, http://www.mckinsey.com /business-functions/organization/our-insights/why-diversity-matters.

157 **PE Hub, *Venture* . . .** Sonya Mann, "How Women VCs Affect the Performance of Firms and Startups," Mattermark, October 3, 2016, https://mattermark.com /women-vcs-affect-performance-firms-startups/.

157 **When First Round Capital . . .** Tucker J. Marion, "4 Factors That Predict Startup Success, and One That Doesn't," *Harvard Business Review*, May 3, 2016, https://

hbr.org/2016/05/4-factors-that-predict-startup-success-and-one-that
-doesnt.

CHAPTER 11

163 **"A great way to build . . ."** "What's Your Problem?," *Getting Real*, 37signals, https://gettingreal.37signals.com/ch02_Whats_Your_Problem.php.

173 **Eric Meyer famously . . .** Rebecca Web, "Inadvertent Algorithmic Cruelty," Meyerweb.com, December 24, 2014, http://meyerweb.com/eric/thoughts/2014 /12/24/inadvertent-algorithmic-cruelty/.

CHAPTER 12

177 **"If you are not embarrassed . . ."** Anthony Ha, "LinkedIn Founder Reid Hoffman's 10 Rules of Entrepreneurship," *Venture Beat*, March 25, 2011, http:// venturebeat.com/2011/03/15/reid-hoffman-10-rules-of-entrepreneurship/; http:// www.businessinsider.com/the-iterate-fast-and-release-often -philosophy-of-entrepreneurship-2009-11.

181 ***"I wanted to like this tool . . ."*** Marie Haynes, comment on "Spam Score: Moz's New Metric to Measure Penalization Risk," *Moz Blog*, https://moz.com/blog /spam-score-mozs-new-metric-to-measure-penalization-risk#comment -328203.

188 **I sent out a pair . . .** Rand Fishkin, "A Look at the Keyword Research Tool Universe in 2015," *Moz Blog*, November 25, 2015, https://moz.com/rand/a-look-at -the-keyword-research-tool-universe-in-2015/.

CHAPTER 13

193 **"An anti-IPO . . ."** In Alyson Shontell, "These Startups May Have Blown It by Turning Down $100 Million," *Business In/sider*, May 2, 2013, http://www .businessinsider.com/startups-that-rejected-100-million-offers-2013-5.

203 **It could be building a business . . .** Maciej Cegłowski, "Pinboard Turns Seven," *Pinboard Blog*, July 9, 2016, https://blog.pinboard.in/2016/07/pinboard_turns _seven/.

203 **It could be the creation of a new . . .** Amy McKeever, "Inside Sun Noodle, the Secret Weapon of America's Best Ramen Shops," *Eater*, July 22, 2014, http:// www.eater.com/2014/7/22/6184305/inside-sun-noodle-the-secret -weapon-of-americas-best-ramen-shops.

CHAPTER 14

207 **"In a hierarchy . . ."** Laurence J. Peter, WikiQuote, https://en.wikiquote.org/wiki /Laurence_J._Peter; http://www.nytimes.com/1990/01/15/obituaries/laurence-j -peter-is-dead-at-70-his-principle-satirized-business.html.

211 **In their research . . .** "Learn about Google's manager search," re:Work, https:// rework.withgoogle.com/guides/managers-identify-what-makes-a-great -manager/steps/learn-about-googles-manager-research/.

CHAPTER 15

219 **"In Silicon Valley . . ."** Maren Kate, "Silicon Valley Has a Vulnerability Problem," Medium, May 4, 2016, https://medium.com/@marenkate/silicon-valley -has-a-vulnerability-problem-5c314bf5b005#.dnnwo9m9u.

224 **Project Aristotle . . .** Charles Duhigg, "What Google Learned from Its Quest to Build the Perfect Team," *New York Times Magazine*, February 25, 2016, http://www.nytimes.com/2016/02/28/magazine/what-google-learned-from -its-quest-to-build-the-perfect-team.html.

224 **A 2012 North Dakota . . .** Lisa Bender et al., "Social Sensitivity and Classroom Team Projects: An Empirical Investigation," Feb. 29–March 3, 2012, 43 ACM Technical Symposium on Computer Science Education, http://dl.acm.org/citation .cfm?id=2157258.

224 **The *New York Times* . . .** Charles Duhigg, "What Google Learned from Its Quest to Build the Perfect Team," *New York Times Magazine*, February 25, 2016, http://www.nytimes.com/2016/02/28/magazine/what-google-learned-from -its-quest-to-build-the-perfect-team.html.

225 **"The term is meant . . ."** Amy Edmondson, "Psychological Safety and Learning Behavior in Work Teams," *Administrative Science Quarterly* 44, no. 2 (June 1999): 350–83, https://www.jstor.org/stable/2666999?seq=1#page_scan_tab_contents; https://www.researchgate.net/publication/27699668_Social_and_cognitive _factors_driving_teamwork_in_collaborative_learning_environments _Team_learning_beliefs_and_behaviors.

228 **Elizabeth Schmidt, a Seattle-based . . .** E. S. Ringwald (@esringwald), Twitter, December 24, 2016, https://twitter.com/esringwald/status/812738601255436288.

CHAPTER 16

233 **"People LOVE change . . ."** Richie Norton, *The Power of Starting Something Stupid* (Salt Lake City: Shadow Mountain, 2013).

233 **"I don't waste time . . ."** Steve Hamm, "The Education of Marc Andreessen," *Bloomberg*, April 13, 1998, http://www.bloomberg.com/news/articles/1998-04 -12/the-education-of-marc-andreessen.

236 **Rachel Adelson described . . .** Rachel Adleson, "Probing the Puzzling Workings of 'Depressive Realism,'" APA Science Watch, April 2005, http://www.apa .org/monitor/apr05/realism.aspx.

236 **less than 1 percent . . .** Lydia Ramsey, "A Tiny Percentage of the Population Needs Only 4 Hours of Sleep per Night," *Business Insider*, November 11, 2015, http://www.businessinsider.com/people-who-sleep-short-hours-2015-11.

236 **most of us need . . .** "Insufficient Sleep Is a Public Health Problem," Centers for Disease Control and Prevention, updated September 3, 2015, https://www.cdc .gov/features/dssleep/.

239 **The night before the Foundry . . .** Rand Fishkin, "A Long, Ugly Year of Depression That's Finally Fading," *Moz Blog*, September 19, 2014, https://moz.com /rand/long-ugly-year-depression-thats-finally-fading/.

241 **I like how Dr. Jonathan . . .** Jonathan G. Koomey, "What Is Intellectual Honesty and Why Is It Important?," June 18, 2012, http://www.koomey.com/post/25385125958.

245 **Rewarding weight loss . . .** This *New York Times* piece about the TV show *The Biggest Loser* does a great job explaining this complex irony: http://www.nytimes.com/2016/05/02/health/biggest-loser-weight-loss.html.

CHAPTER 17

247 **"I knew that if I failed . . ."** Ben Carlson, "The Jeff Bezos Regret Minimization Framework," *A Wealth of Common Sense*, October 11, 2016, http://awealthof commonsense.com/2016/10/the-jeff-bezos-regret-minimization-framework/.

271 **Human beings are wired . . .** Alina Tugend, "Praise Is Fleeting, but Brickbats We Recall," *New York Times*, March 23, 2012, http://www.nytimes.com/2012/03/24/your-money/why-people-remember-negative-events-more-than-positive-ones.html.

273 **David Strayer, professor . . .** David M. Sanbonmatsu et al., "Who Multi-Tasks and Why? Multi-Tasking Ability, Perceived Multi-Tasking Ability, Impulsivity, and Sensation Seeking," *PLOS ONE*, January 23, 2013, https://doi.org/10.1371/journal.pone.0054402; https://www.ncbi.nlm.nih.gov/pmc/articles/PMC3553130/.

AFTERWORD

281 **"Silicon Valley has become . . ."** Quote for Chong Moon Lee et al., *The Silicon Valley Edge: A Habitat for Innovation and Entrepreneurship* (Stanford: Stanford University Press, 2000).

283 **There's even research . . .** Mark Peplow, "Simple Sounds Make for Sound Investments," *Nature*, May 30, 2006, http://www.nature.com/news/2006/060529/full/news060529-2.html.

289 **"In our retail business . . ."** Jeff Bezos quoted in Bill Gurly, "Uber's New BHAG: UberPool," Above the Crowd, January 30, 2015, http://abovethecrowd.com/2015/01/30/ubers-new-bhag-uberpool/.

INDEX